CW00919627

VAMP
UNTIL
READY

VAMP
UNTIL
READY

A LIFE LAID BARE

KATE O'MARA

ROBSON BOOKS

First published in 2003 by Robson Books, The Chrysalis Building, Bramley Road, London, W10 6SP

A member of **Chrysalis** Books plc

Copyright © 2003 Kate O'Mara

The right of Kate O'Mara to be identified as the author of this work has been asserted by her in accordance with the Copyright, Designs and Patents Act 1988.

The author has made every reasonable effort to contact all copyright holders. Any errors that may have occurred are inadvertent and anyone who for any reason has not been contacted is invited to write to the publishers so that a full acknowledgement may be made in subsequent editions of this work.

British Library Cataloguing in Publication Data
A catalogue record for this title is available from the British Library.

ISBN 1 86105 700 8

All rights reserved. No part of this publication may be reproduced, stored in a retrieval system, or transmitted in any form or by any means, electronic, mechanical, photocopying, recording or otherwise, without the prior permission in writing of the publishers.

Typeset by SX Composing DTP, Rayleigh, Essex
Printed by Creative Print & Design (Wales), Ebbw Vale

To Dickon, the joy of my life.

ACKNOWLEDGEMENT

My gratitude to Bill Kenwright for the faith he has shown in my ability and for keeping theatres open all over the country and countless actors in work.

VAMP UNTIL READY

'Vamp until ready' was an old music hall term, which was an instruction to the pianist or orchestra in the 'pit' to keep 'playing' until the next act was 'ready' to come on stage. It took the form of a series of descending chords with a bouncy optimistic accompaniment. It was repeated ad lib to keep the audience happy and in anticipation of more and better to follow!

There is an old theatrical joke which describes in brief, and with a jaundiced eye, the six stages in the perilous career of any actor. I'll use myself to illustrate it.

Contents

1

'Who is Kate O'Mara?'

Beginners Please

In 1941, at the age of eighteen months, I was attending a cocktail party given by my parents. By midday, a considerable crowd had assembled with their drinks by the side of the pool in the garden of our house in Trinidad in the West Indies. My father was stationed there during the Second World War. However, being only knee-high to a cicada, I found I was being overlooked and largely ignored. My efforts to help things go with a swing by engaging the guests in small talk on a variety of topics, were falling on deaf ears. Plainly, my subject matter did not grip.

Even as a toddler, my preferred position was in the limelight, centre stage. Having been born the fifth generation of a theatrical family and possessed of a low threshold of boredom, I sought to create a dramatic diversion. A minor aquatic display might please perhaps – the fact that I had not yet learnt to swim did not deter me – I had seen how it was done. Child's play, I thought.

Carelessly brushing aside the overhanging branch of an avocado tree, I strolled nonchalantly into the deep end of the pool. In a matter of seconds, I was in it, up to my neck! According to contemporaneous accounts, before anyone was aware, I was in the middle of the pool, having instinctively adopted a doggy-paddle in order to keep my head above water.

Watched in mute disbelief by my now transfixed, appalled and frankly pissed audience – their horrified silence relieved only by the occasional stifled sob from the more sensitive among their number – I completed a length and emerged triumphant from the water, like a diminutive Aphrodite rising from the sea.

I received my first standing ovation.

This is a highly coloured version of the incident as told to me by my mother, embellished to entertain as only an actress knows how! That it was true, there is no doubt. It was how I learnt to swim. By plunging in at the deep end! Sadly, I remember nothing of the event or of my life in the West Indies, which is a pity, but hardly surprising as we left when I was two. However, I have had a lifelong addiction to avocados, pineapple and coconut drinks, and various tropical fruits, so I suppose it left its mark.

Even in those days, I had the reputation of being an autocrat. It was rumoured that when I was in my highchair, I was known as Queen Victoria and people would exit backwards out of my presence! We lived in a tea planter's house and had black servants – everybody did in the colonies in those days. It was called Paradise House and from photographs, it appears to have been like something out of a Somerset Maugham novel. I understand that we shared the premises with a family of tarantulas, which I always claim is the reason for my acute arachnophobia.

I fear I was petted and adored because the only other anecdote that has come down to me through the mists of time is of me, as an infant, being introduced to an equestrian who had just ridden up the drive, with the cooing words, 'look, darling, it's a gee-gee!'. I have it on good authority that I drew myself up in my pram and declared scornfully, 'It's not a gee-gee, it's a horse!' I was a pedant even at that early age.

My father, a flying instructor in the RAF was then transferred to Canada, so from the humid heat of the tropics, we found ourselves in the snow-bound streets of Montreal, with its large French population. This forced me to learn a sort of pigeon-French, so that I could play with children of my own age. I vividly recall tobogganing, skiing and ice-skating. None of these activities holds any attraction for me now, so I have conveniently forgotten how to do any of them.

We also spent some time in New York and I was taken to the top of the Empire State Building. As a three-year-old, I had no perception of perspective and thought the cars I could see hundreds of feet below me were toys and refused to accept any other explanation. I was taken to see Santa Claus in Macy's famous department store, an unforgettable experience. I was in a wonderland, undreamed of by children in England, who were in the throes of war. By this time, I had already seen my first production of Shakespeare, *A Midsummer Night's Dream* (I was terrified of the ass's head and declined forcefully to stroke it afterwards backstage) and had made my stage debut in public in the local theatre in Montreal, Canada.

Why my mother decided to return to England in 1943 during the most perilous days of the war, I shall never know and it's probably as well that I had no idea of the terrible danger we were in. We travelled by train down through the United States. The journey seemed to take forever, and I dare say it did. We somehow made it to Venezuela. There were only two ships leaving for Europe and we were on one of them. We later discovered that the first had been hit by a U-boat and sunk with no survivors. We were more fortunate but we did have a bad scare. As we were approaching the coast of Spain, German planes were spotted in the area. Terrified Portuguese sailors rushed around shouting and pointing to the skies. My mother, being made of sterner stuff, admonished them roundly and told them to pull themselves together. She and I then retired to our cabin where she held me tightly in her arms, until the danger had passed. One of the few moments of tactile affection I ever received from her. She then gave me an apple which I promptly threw up, so perhaps the tension of the peril had affected me after all.

We reached Lisbon where it was extremely hot. Being an intractable child, I adamantly refused to wear a sun-hat. My mother got very cross and I got very sunburnt. A few days later we boarded a plane bound for Britain. It was night-time, but I wanted to look out of the window. I tried to prise a corner of the black-out away. There was immediate uproar in the cabin. I was admonished and smacked and told to behave. I was amazed at what I considered to be an awful lot of fuss over nothing. I could not know that I had very nearly put everyone's lives in jeopardy. Having nothing to do, I soon fell asleep.

We landed at RAF Brize Norton in the early hours of the morning. My mother never tired of telling me that the most wonderful words she ever heard in the whole of her life, were the cultured tones of the officer who helped us down the steps from the aircraft, saying, 'Welcome to England, madam.' Later, sitting in the officer's mess, my mother created a sensation by producing a banana from her bag for my breakfast. No-one had seen a banana in England since war began.

*   *   *

I don't recall seeing my mother again on a regular basis for most of my childhood. She was a remote glamorous figure, who was never present at any Parent's Day or Sports Day. I would get taken backstage from time to time or plonked in the front row of the stalls to see a production she was either in or had directed. I saw her play the Fairy Godmother in *Cinderella* at the Leeds Empire: I watched from the wings, as her face suddenly materialised through the gauze of the clock-face at the ball, as the chimes of midnight started to strike. I heard her voice calling eerily to Cinderella to warn her that she must leave the ball before her beautiful dress changed back to rags. I was mesmerised as Cinders ran frantically up the huge, curved, glittering staircase, then disappeared in her ball-gown behind the clock, only to emerge seconds later on the other side in her pathetic rags, her blonde curls flying. Although, from my vantage point, I could see how the trick was done, I still thought it the most marvellous magic.

Then the lights on the stage dimmed almost to black-out, a spotlight picked out the tall dashing figure of Prince Charming as she strode forward to the audience. Very softly, the orchestra started playing 'Rose of England'. The Prince, clad in black velvet and silver and with the longest legs I've ever seen on any

4

principal boy, looked straight out to the packed house and in a low thrilling voice, spoke the famous lines from John of Gaunt's speech in *Richard II*: 'This royal throne of Kings, this scepter'd isle, this earth of majesty, this seat of Mars, this other Eden, demi-paradise, this fortress built by nature for herself against infection and the hand of war' – to that audience in the grim times of the war in the winter of 1943/4, this was the rallying cry, the spur they needed to help them through the dark days that lay ahead – 'This happy breed of men, this little world' – the Prince and the orchestra started to build to a crescendo – the audience was hanging on her every word – 'this blessed plot, this earth, this realm, this – England!' – she almost shouted the last line. The spotlight snapped out and the huge velvet curtains swung together.

There was a moment's silence, then the audience was on its feet clapping and cheering itself hoarse. Peeping through the black gauze at the side of the stage, I could see that many of them were clutching their handkerchiefs to their faces and weeping openly. It was a moment of pure theatre I will remember all my life. It is the sort of theatre I try to recreate whenever I direct a play, even when I'm on stage myself. I try to engage an audience's mind, imagination and emotions, to inspire them to make them believe that all is for the best in this best of all possible worlds. I believe that this is what theatre is all about and why I prefer working in the theatre to any other medium. It is, after all, my heritage. In the dark days of my life and there have been many, there has always been one place where I could find sanctuary. In the darkened auditorium or the subdued lighting of an empty stage, there is a solace and a comfort that is almost tangible.

* * *

My mother had joined ENSA (Entertainments National Service Association) and disappeared from my life again. My father was still in Canada. My grandparents, with whom I was left, solved the vexing question of child-minding – in those days hardly a social or moral issue – by taking me with them to whatever theatre they happened to be running: the New Theatre, Oxford, the Theatre Royal, Brighton, and for me, most memorably, the King's Theatre, Southsea. This was the glorious Edwardian Variety Theatre which had been built by my great-grandfather in 1907. Happily, it still stands today, a marvel of Italian Renaissance opulence, designed by arguably the greatest theatre architect of all time, Frank Matcham.

During the day, I was given the run of the place and left to my own devices. I made the most of it. I would tear up and down its many staircases, all thickly carpeted in red. I would visit all the boxes in turn, trying them out for the best view of the stage. The safety curtain would, of course, be in place, but even that was covered with elaborately painted advertisements. I would gaze up in admiration at the partially clad decorative nymphs which flanked the boxes, holding up the tier above with their raised plaster arms. I thought them immensely beautiful. I would then climb up to the 'gods' with their vertigo-inducing, dizzying height (closed these days due to being considered too dangerous) and find myself on the same level as the chandeliers that hung from the ceiling where yet more classical maidens disported themselves in permanent, painted, Olympian bliss.

If it was a matinee day, I would be put into one of the boxes, sometimes the Royal Box, where I would sit in a solitary state, observing the audience coming in. It was always full, even the upper tiers – I had seen the occupants of the 'gods' earlier, queuing up patiently all around the theatre. The usherettes were clad in black dresses with white frilled aprons and little white starched caps. They not only sold programmes, but brought trays of tea around during the interval to those patrons who could afford to indulge in this little luxury. This practice continued into the fifties and sixties. I greatly miss the sound of the tinkle of teacups amid the murmur of expectant chatter.

The most evocative sound of all though, is that of the orchestra tuning up. I would watch eagerly for the appearance of its various members, as they emerged from beneath the stage into the 'pit' which was partitioned off from the audience by a large gleaming brass rail, from which hung a rose-red curtain that echoed the red and gold plush of the auditorium. After five minutes of muted cacophony, as each orchestra member tuned his or her instrument to their satisfaction, there would be a minor disturbance in the pit and the conductor would make his entrance to a smattering of applause from those among the audience who had been concentrating.

Excitement would mount as he exchanged a few words with the first violin, then he would suddenly open the sheets of music on his stand, pull himself together, look expectantly first one way, then the other at his team and then raise his baton. This must have been the visual cue for the house-lights to dim, as the two events always seemed to coincide. The theatre would now be in darkness, except for the muted lights above each of the musicians' stands and the glow of the footlights on the curtains – 'tab-warmers' as they're known. There followed a short overture which was always received with expectant enthusiasm by the audience. Finally the curtain would rise on a world of glowing colour, elaborate sets and painted backcloths and, of course, front-cloths to allow for the changing of the scene behind.

I saw the show every day and on matinees. I saw everything. In the early days it was romantic old-fashioned musicals: *The Maid of the Mountains*, *Chu Chin Chow*, *Flora Dora*, *The Arcadians*, *The Bohemian Girl*, *The Desert Song* and much Gilbert and Sullivan. I loved them all. Later on, though, the big American musicals were all the rage and started to tour the provinces. They were not to my taste, I thought them brash and vulgar and this exposure to a surfeit of musicals left me with a lifelong dislike of the genre. In 1991 I found myself cast in *Kiss Me Kate*, which I had first seen in 1951, forty years previously! I quite enjoyed it, but I still prefer *The Taming of the Shrew* on which it is based, to Cole Porter's tacky parody.

Music hall was still popular then, but this form of entertainment did not appeal to me. I found its crudeness embarrassing. I saw many famous comedians, including Max Miller, whom I heard my grandmother describe as 'being very blue'. I had no idea what she meant, but I knew it wasn't complimentary.

My grandmother was a tall, big-boned Yorkshire woman with a wonderful sense of humour. She wore her long hair carelessly fastened into a bun in the nape of her neck. She was a chain-smoker. I used to help her in the kitchen and watch, fascinated, as ash from the fag-end in the corner of her mouth got longer and longer, waiting for it to drop into the food, which it frequently did.

I would accompany her to the shops, where she would argue amiably with the girls behind the counter at the Home and Colonial. I loved watching them cut through the butter, cheese and lard with a thin wire and then lift the small segments with wooden butter pats onto the marble scales, finally wrapping the portions up in muslin. We all had ration books which showed how much we were allowed. There was a row of shops in Southsea which ended suddenly in broken masonry and jagged brickwork, where a bomb had fallen and demolished the rest of the street. To my childish eyes, there seemed to be grey rubble everywhere, in sharp contrast to the sumptuousness of the baroque interior of the theatre.

I was always on the move. Most of the time I was with my grandparents although, occasionally, I was farmed out to my great-aunts, who also lived in Southsea. They had never married and knew nothing about children. I had to be on my very best behaviour and was only allowed to play with the playing cards and the chess-pieces on the green baize card table. The elder of the two aunts dressed exactly like Queen Victoria, in long dresses with a lace 'modesty vest' in the deep 'v' at the front. Her long, white hair was pinned up with tortoise-shell combs. The younger sister, who had decided to stay in the twenties, wore short skirts, silk stockings, pointed strap and button shoes with a Louis heel, and a coat with a huge fur collar that stood up around her face. Her hair, which was shingled and marcel-waved, was squashed down with a cloche hat. Gloves, of course, were de rigueur. My great-aunts were strict but kind and the days I spent in their company were not unpleasant. One certainly learned good behaviour, which makes life so much more bearable.

When my grandfather was manager of the New Theatre, Oxford (latterly the Apollo), we lived on the outskirts of the city.

He was possessed of a fierce manner and I was very much in awe of him. I would listen attentively as he and my grandmother discussed the box-office takings from the night before. He was a fitness fanatic who slept outside in all weathers in a camp bed covered with a tarpaulin. There was a sort of half-tester above his head, also waterproofed. I found him alarming.

There had been no sign of my father for years, but my mother made a sudden dramatic reappearance. She was not alone. It transpired that I had a new baby sister, Belinda. At last, the mystery of 'the pram in the hall' was cleared up. It has never failed to amaze me how no-one ever told one anything in those days. I was taken to the nursing home to meet the new arrival, but before setting off, my grandmother asked me if I would like to take my new baby sister a present. I decided magnanimously to give her my very best pink satin ribbon, which was about two inches wide and which I wore for 'best' and parties.

My mother was sitting up in bed; in a bassinet beside her was a tiny creature with a tuft of golden brown hair. I shyly put my gift into the cot beside the baby. 'What on earth is it?' demanded my mother peremptorily. I handed it over for approval: my mother gave a snort of derisive laughter. 'She can't wear that!' she exclaimed scornfully, 'she's hardly got any hair at all!'. I was mortified. My present was worthless. I felt humiliated and inadequate.

I tried not to cry, but it was a cruel rejection and I never forgave my mother for her insensitivity. I don't suppose she meant to upset me. She just wasn't cut out to be a mother, at least not to her own children. Her many homosexual friends adored her and she certainly 'mothered' the younger actors and actresses with whom she worked. But then the theatre was her life. She lived for the theatre. From her, I learned the true meaning of the well-known dictum that 'the show must go on' whatever the cost. It has proved to be a useful maxim, and has got me through many a trauma. She was as tough as old boots and had a grip of iron. She had to have.

* * *

My father, a charming gentleman when sober, became, like a lot of alcoholics, unbearable after a few drinks. My sister claimed that he was devastated when he lost his adored sister to cancer when she was only nineteen. This was followed shortly by the death of his mother, a double blow from which he never recovered. My father's family came from old Irish stock, descended, so he claimed, from the Kings of Ireland! There were both Catholic and Protestant branches, the original name of which is both unspellable and unpronounceable but translates as O'Carroll. Rostrevor, County Down, which is on the border, was the family home. I visit the Old Country at least once a year and always meet up with my cousin Marguerite who lives in Bangor. I also have a cousin living in Ireland who is a priest. My Celtic origins, plus my mother's Bavarian forebears, probably account for my somewhat unusual looks!

I have never been a party girl. Parties are my idea of hell, mainly because people have a tendency to get drunk. I loathe drunkenness in any degree – being the daughter of an alcoholic may explain my abhorrence and intolerance. My father's drinking ruined my mother's life and certainly impinged on mine. On my sixteenth birthday, my mother had arranged a party for me in Worthing, where she was playing in the theatre. I had been making a film in London and my father also had to be in London on that day to see someone about a possible job. He was due to pick me up at the flat in Barnes and drive me down to the coast in time for the party. My mother had organised it all, but what she had omitted from her plans was closing time in the pubs.

Much time passed. I waited and waited, thinking he was held up in traffic. By 3.30, I was convinced he'd had an accident. I didn't know what to do. At four o'clock I went out to the pavement to watch for his arrival. To my intense surprise, I saw his car parked in the driveway. I looked more closely and realised that it was not empty. My father was slumped over the steering wheel. I opened the door and tried to rouse him. He was dead drunk. I felt that I couldn't leave him there and tried to get him out of the car. I pulled and pushed and managed to get him on to the drive.

A neighbour saw what was happening and came to the rescue. Between us we succeeded in getting him indoors, where he was unceremoniously doused with cold water to rouse him. I then gave him a strong cup of coffee to try to get some sense into him. All in vain, for as soon as he had consumed the coffee, he fell into a deep sleep from which there was no waking him. I gave up and went to phone my mother. On hearing my news, she became virtually hysterical, but I told her to cancel everything or have the party without me as my father was incapable of driving and I was not yet old enough even to learn to drive.

When we finally got to the coast the next day, our arrival provoked one of the biggest rows between them that I had ever witnessed, and I'd already seen many. Between fury at having married someone weak and selfish (a view I thoroughly endorsed) and disappointment at spoiling her daughter's day, my mother's rage continued for some time. My father seemed quite unrepentant and chuckled at what he considered to be a huge over-reaction to a very minor offence.

I despised him and wished with all my heart and soul that my parents would get divorced. At least the rows would stop. But, in those days one married for life, so I suppose that's why my mother never left him. She could have done so easily. She was, after all, the breadwinner. She provided everything, even managing to give my sister and me a very superior private education. He was thoughtless to us all throughout his life, in one instance due to major religious bigotry. Of course, he came round eventually, but not before having inflicted deep wounds which have never healed.

On one occasion, we all sat down in front of the television to watch my mother play a very large part in *Play for Today*. It had been prerecorded and was in black and white. It was in the days before colour. In high anticipation we arranged ourselves so that we all had a good view of the screen. It started. As my mother's name came up on the screen in the pre-show credits, my father suddenly got up and said, 'I don't want to watch this rubbish' and left the room. We heard the front door slam and his footsteps walking away in the direction of the pub.

I stole a sidelong glance at my mother. She was staring at the TV screen, tears streaming down her face. I put out my hand and clasped hers tightly. She gave a marvellous performance in the piece, but, of course, that was the trouble. She made him feel inadequate. Her triumph would have been yet another reminder of his failure.

* * *

At the age of seven, I was sent away to boarding-school in Sussex. I was quite alone. I was put in the care of the guard. I had a label around my neck proclaiming my identity and destination and a packet of paste sandwiches wrapped in greaseproof paper in my lap. I was happy at that boarding-school. It exactly measured up to all the school stories I had read by Elsie J Oxenham and Elinor M Brent Dyer. The latter was a close friend of my mother, so I was very familiar with her work. The war was over, but we were still very much at the mercy of wartime strictures. I have always felt that I benefited from the postwar diet. I remember brown bread, very rough with no butter, but we had marmalade. Scrambled egg made from powdered egg was truly delicious. There didn't seem to be any sweets, but there was malt, which had to be taken by the dessertspoonful, concentrated orange juice and the horrible cod-liver oil. There was Fennings Fever Cure, made, I believe, from quinine and ammonia, quite revolting, but known to cure all ills.

I was not at all phased when I found I had to spend the holidays at school. Again, no explanation was forthcoming. I can only suppose that there was no-one available to care for me at home. Not that we had a home. Sadly, I had to leave that school after only a year. Thereafter followed several others, about which I can remember virtually nothing as they were so short-lived. Without a doubt the happiest time in my childhood occurred when we went to live on a farm in Nottinghamshire. My mother had joined the company at the Nottingham Playhouse and my father had miraculously reappeared. He was still in the RAF Reserve, but didn't seem to have any other job. His return meant

I had to go to a convent school. My father, being a staunch Roman Catholic, insisted on it.

So, against all my mother's wishes and in spite of her copious tears, I was uprooted from my hitherto Protestant upbringing and forced to become a Roman Catholic. The nearest convent that could take me was in the next county, which was Lincolnshire.

To get there, I was obliged to embark on nothing short of a personal odyssey! On my first day at my new school in September 1949, aged ten, I left home at dawn on my bicycle. In those days children were allowed to roam freely, but of course it was much safer to do so. I had to ride across, what seemed to me, an enormous field. I could see the grey shapes of the huge carthorses looming out of the mist. I was terrified lest they should charge me as I wobbled uncertainly over the turf. Then I came to the railway line; to cross this, I had to push open the two large gates, no mean feat, encumbered as I was with the bicycle, my music-case and my school satchel. I prayed fervently that no train would come hurtling towards me while I was in the midst of this manoeuvre and listened apprehensively for the bell that would warn of its approach. But all was well and I pushed the gates back as I had found them. I re-mounted my bicycle and rode along the track that led to the village, Sutton-on-Trent, where I was to leave my bike in the care of the local garage. I could see no-one around, so I propped my bike against the wall and hoped for the best.

I walked the rest of the way to the bus stop and waited patiently for what seemed an eternity for the bus to Newark. I began to be afraid that I had missed it, but it rumbled up eventually and I boarded it, sitting near the conductor, so as not to miss the stop. I needn't have worried. It was only going as far as Newark and the conductor called out 'everybody change!'. I was to be met there by one of the senior girls from the convent whose name was Claire. We had never met before and I hoped she hadn't forgotten me, a mere junior. But she turned up and claimed me, although I got the distinct impression that she was not particularly thrilled by this extra burden of responsibility. We caught another bus which took us into Lincoln itself.

13

I recall trudging up the last bit of Lincoln hill, which is notoriously steep and on the top of which sits the magnificent Cathedral. We finally arrived at the convent gates. I was met by the sight of 400 schoolgirls all rushing in different directions, some chattering, some yelling, shouting, laughing, all of whom seemed to know each other. I stood helplessly on the edge of the playground, wondering what on earth to do next. Claire had disappeared and left me to fend for myself, obviously feeling she had fulfilled her duty. I gazed around me, bewildered. Suddenly, a girl of my own age, seeing my plight, disengaged herself from a group and came towards me, saying in a friendly north country accent, ''allo luv, are yer new? Doan't yer know where to go? That's all right, luv, doan't you wurry, I'll show you where to go, coom with me!' And so saying, she took my hand and led me across the huge playground, into the cloakrooms, where she found my peg and locker and then escorted me to the Hall for Assembly. All I can remember about her is that her name was Maureen and I shall bless her until the day I die.

Being a bright child and of a studious disposition and not the least bit shy, lessons themselves held no terrors for me and the rest of the day passed quickly and easily. However, after school was over, I had to tackle the long and arduous journey in reverse.

It was dark and the stars were out before I wearily pushed my bike up to the farmhouse we were renting. My mother had been watching anxiously for me. Ever the drama queen, she took one look at me and exclaimed, 'Oh, you poor darling! Oh No! No! No! This will never do, will it? It's too much for you! It's nearly nine o'clock!'

She led me up the narrow twisting wooden staircase which, characteristically, she had already given a theatrical name. It was called 'The Admiral Benbow', after the inn in one of her favourite productions, *Treasure Island*, in which she had played 'Jim Hawkins' when *she* was ten. In the small room at the top of the house, which was all my own, there was a paraffin heater burning – there was, of course, no other form of heating in those days. The light from the top of the stove cast a huge pattern on the ceiling and the smell was not unpleasant. She had put a hot-water bottle in the camp bed in which I slept and my flannelette pyjamas were warming at the foot of the bed. I got undressed and snuggled under the covers while she went off to fetch my supper. She reappeared shortly with warmed-up macaroni cheese. I don't think I've ever tasted anything more delicious. It was washed down with a mug of hot, sweet cocoa and before I knew it I had collapsed, exhausted, into a dreamless sleep.

Thankfully, the ghastly journey was soon abandoned and alternative arrangements were made. Lodgings were found for me in the city. I had to share a bed with the daughter of the family, but the only other obstacle was the long walk up the very steep Lincoln hill. I repaid this consideration for my welfare, by coming top of the class for the whole year. I was never congratulated on this achievement, nor did it merit any comment. It seems to have been taken for granted. As soon as I had settled in there and started to make friends, I was dragged away again and sent to yet another new school – I think it was in Hertfordshire.

* * *

However, that summer holiday on the farm was the happiest of my childhood. My sister and I were allowed to run free. In those halcyon days, everyone left their houses and cars unlocked and so long as we kept away from the main roads, no-one worried about us. My father and I would rise at dawn and go out into the early morning mist to look for mushrooms in the wet grass. We would come back laden and my mother would cook them for breakfast on the kitchen range.

I would go down to the dairy to watch the cows being milked and return with jugs of warm frothing milk. We kept chickens which I would feed from huge sacks of corn. From time to time, I would venture into the hen-house to collect the eggs, much to their owners' indignation. The hens would cluck and squawk as I sneaked my hand under their warm feathers and retrieved the beautiful, brown eggs with little bits of fluff on them. We climbed the bales of hay in the barn and went on explorations across the fields with our cocker-spaniel. It was idyllic and so, of course, couldn't last.

We led a typically middle-class farming existence. I was obliged to join the Pony Club and learn to ride, which I loathed. I continued my piano lessons which I loved and went to ballet class, which came in useful later on in life when I was cast as a Russian ballerina in a movie. We socialised with the local farming community, going to gymkhanas and point-to-point meetings, neither of which interested me. My mother would make my sister and me do scenes from Shakespeare. This was much more fun. We loved the dressing-up and my mother provided suitable background music from a wind-up gramophone. This custom turned into something of an ordeal, when, as we grew older, she insisted that we perform for her actor friends. Not only scenes from Shakespeare, but from Victorian melodramas, song and dance numbers and soliloquies from the classics.

I would accompany myself on the piano as well as showing off my ability on the keyboard, by dashing off some Bach or Chopin, all of which was guaranteed to dispel any tendency to nerves, self-consciousness or worst of all, stage-fright. 'As an imperfect actor on the stage, who with fear is put beside his part . . .', the opening lines from one of Shakespeare's sonnets, always strikes a chord of recognition and dread in any actor and Shakespeare, himself being an actor, knew only too well the terror of 'drying' or forgetting one's lines. This early training certainly eradicated all such doubts and gave me confidence and as a result, I found myself in all the leading parts in school productions.

To Surrey and yet another school and another convent. But this one was a hell-hole. Admittedly, the educational standard was high, but bullying was rife. I was spared the worst of it because I was clever, always being among the first three in the class, thereby earning a grudging respect from the bullies, or maybe they didn't see me as an easy victim.

There was one girl who was not so fortunate. Highly strung and of a sensitive and nervous disposition, she was an easy target for the intimidators, who tormented her beyond endurance. They subjected her to a debilitating and humiliating form of mental torture, nothing short of the destruction of a personality.

It continued day after day, the perpetrators laughing mercilessly when they reduced her to uncontrollable sobbing. We were all appalled, but had no idea how to bring about an end to this reign of terror. The nuns, practised as they were in the precepts of Christian charity and compassion, chose to ignore it.

Then, one ghastly night, the poor girl could stand no more and her mind gave way. The long dormitories housed about 30 girls. The room was divided up into cubicles, fifteen on each side. At each end of the row of curtained enclosures was a larger area where a nun slept. It was in the early hours of the morning when we first heard the sounds. A low muttering, punctuated by whimpering, high-pitched hysterical laughter, followed by a heart-rendering moaning. Then snatches of gibberish, inter-spersed with cries of anguish; more meaningless chatter, agitated exclamations, then uncontrollable weeping. I don't know when I've heard anything more distressing.

Gradually, some of the girls began to stir. I, who am the lightest of sleepers, had awoken at the first moment. We none of us dared to move or do anything, but lay in our beds, hardly able to breathe. Suddenly we heard the tramp of footsteps on bare floor-boards approaching. Then the clink of rosary beads, the swishing of long skirts and the crackle of starched wimples, as two nuns advanced on the girl (who someone said later was clad only in her night-gown) as she made her way down the full length of the dormitory. I heard firm hands roughly clasp hold of naked arms, small gasps as they attempted to subdue the demented creature then, still babbling incoherently, she was removed swiftly and silently from our midst.

They must have taken her away that night, for we never saw her again. The next day, her absence went unremarked by the nuns. Nothing was said. No mention was made of the incident, no explanation was forthcoming. One daring soul plucked up courage to ask if the girl had been taken ill and enquired after her welfare. She was given short shrift and more or less told to mind her own business. It was as though the girl had never existed. I, personally, was thankful that her ordeal was over at long last. She had suffered enough and I was mortified that I had been

17

unable to help her in her plight, although I had done my best to be kind and smile and make encouraging remarks to her.

Years later, when I came to play Lady Macbeth, I found I was haunted by the event and decided to use it and reproduce it faithfully for the sleep-walking scene. It was unbearably distressing to perform, but was, at least, based in reality. News came to me a while later that the girl had spent the intervening years in a lunatic asylum, but that she had made a recovery – eventually. I was allowed to leave that hateful school and was sent to France to stay with a French family to complete my education. It seemed to me that I was always being sent away. I longed just to go home, but it was not to be and I hated every second of it. I think this is why my home is so precious to me now.

The Paris of 1953 was still the romantic city of post-revolutionary France: the embodiment of the *fin de siècle*. The Côte d'Azur was still just a scattering of fishing villages. I have a potent memory of sitting in the darkened auditorium of L'Opéra, Nice, a gorgeous little nineteenth-century theatre, listening to the students from the Conservatoire perform Beethoven's fourth piano concerto one after the other. I stayed there the whole day not wanting it to end. Afterwards, I went straight out to buy the sheet music, so that I could play it for myself on the piano. By this time I had passed all of my piano grades. Sir Edward Downes was one of my adjudicators and I smile now when I hear him conducting on the radio and wonder if he remembers the small girl, nervously playing her scales for him.

At one point in my diverse educational pursuits I went to art school in Tunbridge Wells, where I studied stage design and set-painting. My academic career may have been unorthodox, but it was certainly all-embracing. I had also taken to writing. My efforts had been spotted and I was given film parts as a result! Hardly the conventional route to an acting career. But then, I was not a conventional girl.

By the time I was sixteen, I had posed for my first pin-up pictures – in a pale cyclamen satin corset – and had been seen by Otto Preminger for the part of St Joan! I was mildly surprised by the former as I didn't see myself as glamorous. I liked to think of myself as an intellectual, an aesthete even! I was precocious to say the least. In my spare time, I wrote poetry in the style of Alexander Pope and tried to emulate the 'sprung rhythm' of Gerard Manley Hopkins! (At the read-through of a play, recently, the director introduced me to the rest of the cast as 'Miss O'Mara, the well-known pedant'!) When I was a girl though, my mother was very impatient of my academic pretensions. I don't think she knew what to make of me.

Act I. Sc. II

I suppose it was because I had been shunted around from pillar to post all my life and had never had a close friend, that I was ignorant of the facts of life. In those days, no-one ever mentioned sex. Certainly no-one had ever mentioned it to me. I had no idea what went on. Even though I had had a boyfriend, it had all been very innocent and romantic. There was no question of sleeping together or of any physical contact, other than holding hands and kissing. He was witty and charming and extremely clever and I adored him. We had, I thought, a wonderful relationship which lasted for over a year and then without any warning he ditched me, refusing to give me any reason, adamantly denying the existence of any other girl and indeed, I could find no evidence of one.

Our parents had been lifelong friends and I had first met him in infancy, then again in our early teens and both families had been delighted when we fell for each other. I had fondly imagined we would spend the rest of our lives together, childhood sweethearts and all that. I was devastated and heartbroken when he threw me over. It had been so sudden and shocking. From loving, laughing intimacy to absolute cold silence. He is now a very high-profile Q.C. Maybe he was trying out his technique on me! I was eighteen when this all took place and obviously a virgin, as I was totally ignorant of anything to do with sex, including the anatomical details.

Heart-sore and grieving for my lost love, I had taken to going for rides on my bicycle in and around Barnes, which truly was a village in those days and where my mother had rented a flat while she was committed to a long run in the musical *Salad Days*. My father, meanwhile, was happily drinking the proceeds of her labours. I was going up for various plays and TV interviews and getting quite a few. Nothing startling, but the odd small part which kept me going, and gave me some financial independence. I did not want to be an extra drain on my mother's slender resources. She had been as upset as I, over the unaccountably sudden breaking off of relations between myself and Tim, my first love. He was, after all, the middle son of one of her oldest and dearest friends and she had been exceedingly fond of him.

I went out for an afternoon ride in Barnes and dismounted in the High Street to look in the shop windows. I was approached by an attractive young man, who asked me to go to the local coffee bar with him. Flattered, I readily agreed. We got on very well and for the first time for weeks I felt immeasurably cheered. We went on to the Odeon Cinema to see a war film which I found tedious, but was happy just to be in male company again. Afterwards, he said he would walk me home and suggested a short cut across Barnes Common. We were chattering away, when he suddenly wrenched the bicycle out of my hands and slung it to one side. He grabbed hold of me and forced me back onto the grass. Then he put his hand up my skirt and started to pull down my pants.

Some instinct told me that this was all wrong and I tried to stop him. A struggle ensued as he began to undo his denims. I started to protest, so he glued his mouth on mine to keep me quiet. I realised he was trying to force himself in between my legs. I desperately tried to push him away but he was tall and much stronger than I. 'What on earth do you think you're doing?', I managed to gasp out. 'Shut up!' he replied. He started to pump away. I fought like a tiger and began to scream for help. He tried to put his hand across my mouth, so I sank my teeth into his finger. It can't have hurt much as I only managed to nip him, but I think he was surprised and annoyed at my resistance. He struck me. I screamed, then he said, 'Oh, for Christ's sake, shut up and let me finish!' This he did very quickly. He then got up and walked away without a backward glance, doing himself up as he went.

Dazed and shaken and profoundly shocked, I got to my feet and tried to pull myself together. I was wearing my favourite skirt, a pretty blue denim dirndl which had several large white daisies appliquéd on it. It now had grass stains as well. My little white cotton top with its fashionable 'boat neck' was torn under one arm. My hair, which was waist-length, was tousled and tangled and had bits of twig and dried grass sticking in it. As I stood up, I became aware of an unpleasant stickiness between my thighs and I felt a trickling down my leg. I tore at a clump of grass and tried to wipe it away. The smell was abhorrent to me. I cleaned myself up as covertly and as best as I could, then rescued my bicycle from where it had been unceremoniously flung and slowly pushed it back across the Common, feeling bewildered and ashamed. Deeply ashamed and humiliated.

I had been made a fool of, a total fool. I had stupidly imagined that the young man had sought my company because he liked me, because he found me intelligent, interesting and attractive. Instead he had abused me physically, had subjected me to violence and treated me with utter contempt. I felt worthless and degraded. I never told anyone what had happened. I didn't mention it to a soul. But it destroyed my self-esteem and self-confidence. Coming so soon after my broken romance, it confirmed in my mind that I was useless.

* * *

As an actor or actress has only one thing to sell, and that is him or herself, self-belief is a prerequisite for the job. One has to be convinced that one has something to offer an audience, which it is prepared to pay to see. After the events described above, I decided I had nothing to offer anyone, least of all an audience and my self-belief disintegrated overnight. I had no confidence either in myself, my looks or my ability. I was convinced that I was plain and untalented. I became desperately shy, introverted and even more of a loner. This state of affairs went on for four years. Not until I was in my early twenties did I have the courage to get up on stage or face a camera again.

Instead I went to work backstage. I worked in virtually every department. I learned a hell of a lot, not least that those behind the scenes are every bit as important as those in the limelight. I worked backstage at the Royal Opera House and Glyndebourne, where I was surrounded by my beloved music. Classical music has been my constant companion in life and made up for the lack of close friendships. I do have four very dear girlfriends whom I seldom see, but speak with frequently on the telephone. Fortunately they are all passionate about classical music as well. For an obsessive like me to be working at one of the world's great opera houses was a considerable thrill. There I met Rudolph Nureyev and was amused a few years later, when, cast as a Russian ballerina in a movie *The Limbo Line*, I had to perform the 'Dance of the Little Swans' with members of the Royal Festival Ballet. It was the production of *Swan Lake* that starred Nureyev and Margot Fonteyn! In scenes from the film these illustrious dancers can be seen performing in the background!

At the Garden, when going about my business backstage, I suddenly stopped in my tracks, electrified, the hair on the nape of my neck quivered. I heard the voice of an angel. It was Joan Sutherland on stage rehearsing 'The Queen of the Night' aria from *Die Zauberflote*. I was transfixed, and overwhelmed. In later years I was to see many productions at the Royal Opera House, including the glorious *Don Giovanni*, directed by Franco Zefferelli, a production which, in my view, has never been surpassed. I met Zefferelli at Glyndebourne where, one night, he flung me on a table and pretended to seduce me. Admittedly, I was wearing a very fetching turquoise green, wild silk shift dress – all the rage in 1961!

While at Glyndebourne, the premier of 'Elegy for Young Lovers' took place. This was my first experience of 'modern music' – a-tonal and extraordinary. It was by Hans Werner Henze, the German 'enfant terrible', with lyrics by W H Auden,

22

aided and abetted by his lover Chester Kallman. They seemed to spend all their time indulging in very public screaming matches which one was hard put to avoid. Chester seemed to bring out the worst in Auden, for when one encountered W H on his own, he seemed very charming and cordial. Being an ardent fan of his work, I was very awe-struck in his presence. I attended the first night of this appalling offering and I'm happy to say the audience left in droves. They then spent the rest of the evening getting pissed on champagne in the lovely grounds.

Working in this beautiful little opera house in Sussex was a wonderful experience. It was a glorious summer on the whole, although I think it was Luigi Alva, the famous Italian tenor, who was heard to complain about the wet English weather, 'it a break-a-da-balls!' For the most part the music was glorious as well, Henze providing the only jarring notes!

I have a particularly fond memory of a charity garden party at a local manor house, where part of the entertainment was provided by the Royal Philharmonic Orchestra, the incumbent band for the season at Glyndebourne. The entire orchestra – or at least as many as could be squeezed in – were crammed into a summer-house in the grounds, attempting to play Percy Grainger's 'Country Gardens' without inflicting severe damage on each other, while small children dressed variously as rabbits, fairies, mushrooms, hedgehogs and assorted other flora and fauna, cavorted under a mulberry tree. That afternoon, for me, summed up all that is uniquely English and irresistible.

At Glyndebourne there were many wonderful pianos, where I could practise covertly. I was caught one day by Geoffrey Parsons, the renowned accompanist, who thereafter insisted on playing duets with me. That season was probably the most carefree and fulfilling time I have ever had and the last time I was ever to know such freedom, for the following year my life changed dramatically and for ever.

* * *

The failure of my first romance was exacerbated by the rape on Barnes Common. I felt I was no earthly use to anyone. This, plus my total isolation as a child and teenager, and my continually being sent away from home by my parents, resulted in my flinging myself into the first arms that embraced me. I was working backstage at Stratford, having completely lost my confidence as an actress. One of the young men in the company took me to bed after a first night party. In my naiveté I thought it was the beginning of a new romance, but after an idyllic morning spent lying in the April sunshine, listening to Vivaldi's 'Four Seasons', while I heard his lines for his forthcoming understudy rehearsal, he took no further notice of me. I was again heart-broken. I couldn't believe it when I found I was pregnant.

I don't know which I think worse, the gross preoccupation with sex that is prevalent today or the ignorance and shame with which it was imbued in those far-off innocent days. Ignorance of the facts of life gave me my beloved son, Dickon, but at what cost to both him and me, I cannot hazard a guess. The stigma which was attached then to childbirth out of wedlock cannot be understated. It is probably difficult for anyone to comprehend now, when it is so commonplace, but in those days it was a heinous offence, one which had to be either obliterated or covered up.

The lengths I had to go to in subterfuge and deception were unimaginable. I hated telling lies. I loathed pretending my husband was 'away working'. I despised myself for wearing a wedding ring to which I was not entitled. But to gain admission to a hospital, a health clinic, to receive pre- and post-natal care, it was *de rigueur*. My parents insisted on it. Initially, I went home for comfort and advice. Both were in very short supply. My father stated unequivocally that if I didn't leave at once, he would divorce my mother. She, of course, insisted I stay. He refused to speak to me and would have nothing to do with my son in the early days. He came round when I left home, soon afterwards. On hearing the news of the birth of my son, my grandfather cut me out of his Will. But that was 1963.

The day my son Dickon was born was without doubt the happiest of my life. Every mother thinks her baby is the most beautiful she has ever seen and I was no exception, but he truly was exquisitely beautiful, with ears that lay flat against his head and a dear little thatch of pale honey-coloured hair. I lay for hours gazing at him in wonder as he slept in the bassinet by my side in the hospital. When they had taken him away to weigh him and clean him up after he had been born, I sang like a bird for sheer joy as I lay recovering in the labour ward. It was January 1963, and the snow lay thick upon the ground. There were power cuts, so when we got home, I had to go to bed and hold him against me under the covers to keep him warm as it was bitterly cold. In those days we knew nothing about 'bonding' but I suspect that this initial physical closeness was exactly that. We have been close ever since and can communicate telepathically. The number of times I have been in distress and have received a phone call from him to ask me what was troubling me are countless. And vice versa. I have had nightmares when he has been unhappy and sobbed inexplicably when he has been in despair. I love him more than anything else in the world.

Although Dickon's father initially took an interest in him, I soon realised that this would not continue. My son's birth was the spur I needed to resume my acting career. With the arrival of the most beautiful baby I have ever seen, my old confidence returned. Actually I think it was more like bloody-mindedness. Rejection from my father and my son's father hurt deeply. I was determined to succeed in spite of them. I was soon back on stage again and was working in Rep. up in Newcastle. Naturally Dickon had to come with me, I could not bear to be parted from him.

A couple of days before Christmas, I received a note at the Stage Door from Dickon's father, telling us that he was taking us to his parents for Christmas Day. I was thrilled. I told my landlady and she let us sit in her front parlour so that we could watch for his arrival through the window. We sat there all day. He never showed up. Nor did he ever send any note of apology or explanation. I realised then that I was on my own and would have to work like a Trojan to support my son. I was kept on at the Rep. for a while, but then summarily dismissed. This was a bitter blow, as I had nowhere to live and no income. It was notably cold that January and my son suddenly developed bronchitis. The doctor was called and he told me that my baby might not make it through the night. I kept a vigil by the cot and he pulled through.

One of the actors in the company very sweetly said that we might rent a room from him in London for a while, until his flat-mate returned. It was a life-saver. We somehow struggled through the spring on what I had managed to save from my earnings. But they didn't last long.

* * *

I was on the point of desperation when I heard that auditions were being held for a group called the Shakespeare for Schools Company. They were doing two plays, *The Merchant of Venice* and *Macbeth*. I had already been in other productions of both plays, so knew them well. There were three phases to get through. To start with, about thirty actors assembled in the auditorium of the Comedy Theatre in London. We had to get up on the stage and audition in front of each other. Quite a few lost their nerve. The director, a sadist of the first water, would yell out 'Thank you' sometimes before the actor had managed to utter three lines, and that was the dismissal. If one passed muster, he would shout 'stay behind'. Fortunately, I fell into the latter category. Sitting in the wings was an assistant who took one's details as one came off-stage.

A few days later I was called for the second phase, which took place at a rehearsal room at the back of Drury Lane. This time we were asked to perform in groups. We did scenes, mainly from *Macbeth*. On each occasion the director chose me to start the proceedings. I auditioned all day and staggered home eventually, picking up my son from the crèche in Queensway where I had to leave him each day when I was working.

I was called a third and final time to do yet more scenes and to my great relief and joy was given one of three female parts: 'Jessica' in *The Merchant of Venice* and 'Lady Macduff' doubling with 'The Gentle-woman' in *Macbeth*. I couldn't believe it when my then agent, a deeply stupid man, said he felt the money they were offering was not enough. I screamed down the phone at him, that *any* money was enough, didn't he understand I had a small child to feed and clothe? Reluctantly he agreed to accept the offer, which was £15 a week. I had only been earning £11 in Rep. so it seemed like a fortune to me.

About this time, I had to move 'digs' as the flat's occupant had returned. I found dubious accommodation in Soho. It was in Chinatown above a Chinese restaurant opposite a first-floor brothel. Not ideal, as the entrance was overrun with cockroaches, but convenient, as we were doing matinees only at the Shaftesbury Theatre. After the season in London, we had to go for two weeks to Plymouth. I had to leave my son behind with a carer from the Social Services, as I was unable to find digs that would take him and look after him in Plymouth. I don't know how I survived that fortnight. I swear they were the longest of my life, but finally they were over and we were reunited.

*   *   *

Back in London, I managed to get some television work, very small parts in *The Saint* and *Court Martial*, much better ones in *Danger Man* and *No Hiding Place*. Unfortunately on the latter programme I met a man who used me. Throughout my life I seem to have had very poor judgement when it comes to human nature. I have always thought the best of everyone and so have invariably been let down. I was in dire straits financially when I met him, as there were long periods out of work. He took me up and became my regular 'boyfriend'. He seemed fond of my son and at least we began to eat regularly and well. Then the worst thing happened. I became pregnant.

When the child was born, the father came to pick me up from the hospital, bringing his new girlfriend with him to make sure that I didn't harbour any false hopes. She then disappeared and he took me and the baby to an address somewhere near Croydon to a foster mother whom he said would look after the baby until I was able to cope. I handed the baby over, not realising that I would never see him or the father again. A week or so later, I rang the foster mother to ask if I could see the child. She sounded dubious, but agreed. I had to use a public telephone as

I couldn't afford to have one installed in the basement flat I was sharing with two other girls and my son, Dickon.

I went by bus to Croydon as obviously I didn't have a car. When I arrived, I could see from her face that all was not well. She had not been paid for her services and argued persuasively that the most selfless act I could perform would be to give the child up for adoption. It was a body blow, but I had no money and no means of getting any. I could see no way out. Very reluctantly, I agreed. She asked me if I would like to see the child for the last time, but I couldnt bear to. I glanced over her shoulder, where there was a crib in the sunshine of the bay window. All I could see was a golden glow and I could hear the baby noises of chuckling and gurgling, sounds that haunted me for the next nineteen years.

I took the bus home too stunned even to cry. I sat in mute black despair for three days before plucking up courage to ring the father. His mother answered the phone and seemed surprised to hear from me. Didn't I know that he had emigrated to America she enquired? I was shocked to the core and I knew that there was no hope. I then telephoned the foster mother and told her. She seemed overjoyed, as she informed me there was a couple who couldn't have children and who had seen my baby and wanted him desperately. She said I would be giving them great happiness and they would be giving him the best start in life as they were very wealthy. (It was later revealed that this was not the case.) To follow any other course would be an act of supreme selfishness.

I agreed that I was being selfish and went to sign the adoption papers. I was told by the authorities that I must never try to see my baby again, that I had relinquished all rights absolutely, that the baby was no longer mine and at no point in the future must I try to trace him, that I was doing the best thing possible for him. He was going to a wealthy family who could give him the sort of life I never could. I seemed to have no option. I had been out of work for ages. I had absolutely no money. I was sharing a damp basement flat with two other actresses as well as Dickon, and we were behind with the rent.

*   *   *

I grieved endlessly for the loss of the baby and gave all my love to my son. Then, mercifully, work started to come in. I was in the BBC Classic series *Hereward the Wake* and a television comedy written by and starring Donald Churchill called *It's Not Me, It's Them*. I did a musical version of a Victorian melodrama called *The Drunkard*(!), when I acted with my sister Belinda for the first time, which was directed by Sir Alec Clunes (father of Martin, whom I dandled on my knee when he was a baby!). It starred Denis Quilley, Warren Mitchell and, at that time, a relatively unknown character actor called Ronnie Barker. A season of Rep. followed, then another, then I joined the Welsh Theatre Company to play Lydia Languish in *The Rivals*. I took Dickon with me everywhere. In this instance, he toured Wales with me.

There were times when we were living on peanut butter sandwiches – it always cost me twice as much to get accommodation, as I had to pay someone to look after him whom I hoped to God I could trust while I went to work at night and on matinees. But however lonely I was in real life, for three hours a night on stage I was 'love-breathing seventeen', and I knew I was going to be wooed and won by the time the curtain came down. I think it is one of the main attractions of the theatre. You know how the story ends. It's a certainty, and more often than not it's a story that ends happily.

One night on tour with *The Rivals*, I was standing in the wings waiting for my entrance, when I suddenly noticed to my horror that a 'flat' or piece of scenery, six feet wide and sixteen feet high, had come loose from its moorings and was quietly descending inexorably on the two actors below who were in the middle of a scene. I reacted instantly and grabbed the steel and wooden brace which should have been anchored to the stage weight, a huge lump of solid iron which stood at the stage end of the 'flat'. I held it as best I could, but it was terribly heavy and I was only able to retain the status quo. Not only that, my cue was getting nearer and nearer and I was on the wrong side of the stage! What on earth could I do? I suddenly saw a burly stage-hand. I gesticulated wildly to him. He took in the situation and came to my

29

rescue. I thankfully ran like a hare behind the scenery to make my entrance – too late! My cue by now, had come and gone.

I was greeted on stage by two or three furious actors, two of whom had no idea that I'd just saved their lives. The dreadful thing is, that they refused to accept my explanation, so that instead of being the heroine of the hour, I was the villainess. Not only that, but years later, when I recounted this story when asked what amusing incidents had happened on stage during my career, I received a vituperative letter from one of the actresses concerned, denying the whole thing and accusing me more or less of lying! I was deeply shocked and upset, firstly, to receive such an unpleasant letter and secondly, to think that anyone would suppose me capable of making up such a preposterous tale if it weren't true. Anyway, she wasn't backstage. I was! Because I always think the best of everyone, I am invariably stunned when they don't return the compliment.

After my return from an extensive tour of Wales – I swear we played every venue possible from huge theatre to village hall – I managed to get another episode of *No Hiding Place*. I should have known that it was to prove as fateful as the previous one. In the cast was the actor Jeremy Young, who was to become my husband.

Our wedding took place at The Morden Registry Office, hardly the most glamorous of locations and we celebrated afterwards at the Good Earth, a popular Chinese restaurant in the King's Road. There were just us, our two witnesses and Dickon.

2

'Well, I suppose we could always try Kate O'Mara'

Jeremy, like me, was a Leo. True to our star sign we were both arrogant, determined, dominating and indomitable, but generous to a fault. The trouble with having two people of the same temperament, is that they don't complement each other – they are too alike.

I was in a desperate way when I met Jeremy. I think I was having some sort of breakdown after losing my baby. That Jerry had to pick up the pieces, there was no doubt. At the time when we met, he was still married to the actress Coral Atkins, but they had been separated for some time. She was the most wonderful woman. A considerable star after the major TV series, *Family at War*, she gave up her thriving career to start a home for autistic children, an undertaking that would daunt the bravest of individuals, but Coral rose to the challenge and triumphed. A truly remarkable achievement. I liked her enormously when I met her and, of course, I admired her more than I can say.

Jeremy's best friend at that time was the brilliant actor, Tom Bell, who had all but ruined his promising film career by getting drunk at an awards ceremony and making a few ill-chosen remarks in a loud voice when the Duke of Edinburgh was in the middle of making a speech. Tom's talent was a blazing one which

31

had been recognised by the film industry, then in the process of a postwar resurgence, but as a direct result of this debacle, he was dropped by the powers that be. Happily, Tom's career has since re-burgeoned and in the last twenty years or so he has given many fine performances. At the time when I originally met him, however, he was in the first throes of the effects of the cold-shouldering he was receiving from the film industry. I remember being told by one film director that my own career would be in jeopardy if I continued to associate with Jeremy and more particularly Tom.

*　*　*

It was around this time I had the first of my many close encounters with 'the casting couch'. Again, nobody had warned me or prepared me for this phenomenon. Fortunately my distrust of men was such that I was unlikely to fall prey to this very unpleasant and humiliating procedure. It seemed to be peculiar to the movie business. I have never encountered it in the theatre, nor in television with one notable exception.

One of my first agents, who was a fool and unscrupulous to boot, had been asked by a well-known television casting director to supply a young actress to accompany him to a first night in a theatre on the outskirts of London. My ghastly agent looked upon this venture as an opportunity for me to engage the man's interest and thereby obtain work. I, being a green girl, knew nothing of this plot. I thought I was filling in for the man's wife and using a spare ticket. Luckily, as I was sharing a flat with two other actresses, there was in-house baby-sitting. The casting director duly picked me up early in the evening and we saw the show, which was very entertaining, and I was able to con-gratulate the leading man afterwards, who was excellent. I was then put into the car and thought I was going to be driven home, a mere mile-and-a-half away. Instead I found myself taken to local open parkland.

I feared the worst, and I was right. He stopped the car and immediately started to make a violent pass at me. I was absolutely furious and told him in no uncertain terms that I

32

would not tolerate such behaviour and tried to get out of the car. He called me a fool and became quite angry and told me that if I didn't comply, he would not cast me in anything, ever. I said I didn't care, nothing would persuade me to give in to him. Fortunately, I was near enough to my flat to be able to escape and run home. He was as good as his word.

Nearly 40 years have elapsed since that evening and he has never cast me in anything; indeed years later, he actually lied to a director about my availability. They were making a series at Elstree Studios entitled *The Return of the Saint*, starring Ian Ogilvy. They had already shot an episode with a French actress, whom I was given to understand couldn't act. They wanted to re-shoot all of her stuff with me playing her part. This casting director assured them that I was not available. In fact I had just returned from filming in Morocco and was kicking my heels. Time elapsed, then the director rang my agent himself to ask if I couldn't somehow manage to do it. 'Do what?' was the immediate response from my agent, who had no idea what he was talking about. So, of course, I played the part in spite of that awful man. I suppose the studios must have thought it an oversight or misunderstanding. I knew better.

* * *

However, all this was in the future and my feelings after that outing convinced me that if this was the only way one could get on in television, then I'd better stick to the theatre. My agent seemed to be in the habit of getting me involved with all sorts of publicity 'dos'. Very early on in my career, I was sent off to an event at the Battersea Fun Fair, in aid, I believe, of the Variety Club of Great Britain, a charity which has always done so much for deprived or disabled children. I found myself with a group of other actors. We all had to wear badges with our names on, so that the public knew who we were and we didn't have to suffer the indignity of youngsters coming up to us, shoving their faces at us and demanding 'Who are yer? Famous are yer?'

I found myself standing next to a tall, fair-haired, handsome young man who regarded me with some interest. As nobody had introduced us, he looked at my badge and said, 'Hello, Kate O'Mara'. He was unknown to me, but not to be outdone, I glanced at his badge and replied, 'Hello, Michael Caine'. We chatted for a bit, then we were shepherded off to mingle with the hoi polloi, sign autographs, have our pictures taken, participate in a donkey derby, be bumped about on the dodgems and generally have a thoroughly ghastly time.

It is odd having brushes with people who are just about to become terribly famous. Fame so often happens for people overnight. I remember Malcolm McDowell sitting with me on the foyer stairs at the Aldwych Theatre. He was mildly pissed and quietly sobbing on to my shoulder. I was doing my best to comfort him and find out what the trouble was. He was fairly incoherent, but I gathered he was being given the push from the Royal Shakespeare Company for being disruptive during rehearsals – something to do with chairs, I think. He needn't have worried. A few weeks later he had got his first big break in Lindsay Anderson's *If*, a contract with Twentieth Century Fox and then went on to do Stanley Kubrick's *A Clockwork Orange*, which was a ground-breaking film if ever there was one.

* * *

I was getting quite a bit of work in television at that time in the late sixties, in series' like *Z Cars*, *The Trouble Shooters* and *Honey Lane*. The latter was a forerunner of *EastEnders* and was immensely popular. It was filmed at the ATV Studios up at Elstree, where I had worked years before when it was still British Lion. One evening I found myself stuck at the studios through bad weather. It had snowed all day and as usual in England, this meant that all public transport was at a standstill. However, rescue was at hand. The then boss of the studios kindly offered me a lift in his chauffeur-driven limousine. I was very impressed and, of course, very grateful. But not grateful enough it seems.

Almost as soon as we were settled in the back of the car, he slipped his hand up my skirt. Politely, but firmly, I removed his hand, telling him that I was 'not that sort of girl'. He wouldn't take no for an answer and persisted, getting higher up my leg with each attempt. I could see the chauffeur's ears on stalks as he listened to the struggle behind him. I eventually said that I would rather get out of the car and take my chances in the snow than put up with this onslaught any longer. Beaten, he finally gave up and said, 'You're a very silly little girl, you'll never get anywhere in this business with that sort of attitude and I shall make sure you never work for ATV again.' And I never have.

However, I was seen for lots of movies, none of which I got: *Dr Zhivago, The Taming of the Shrew, Women in Love, Far From the Madding Crowd* to name but a few. I am happy to say none of the above involved the horror of the casting couch. Then, early in 1966, I was seen for a TV series for Anglia all about rural vets, a sort of early *Emmerdale*. It was called *Weavers Green* and was set in and around Norfolk and Suffolk. I was called in to meet the producer, John Jacobs, who was also the boss of the studio. We chatted a while about what I'd been doing and he told me about the series and the part.

'She's just come down from University,' he explained, 'she's the sort of girl who's very familiar with Latin, of course.' '*Discordia demens viperium, crinem vittis innexa cruentis*', I replied. 'What!?' he exclaimed. 'It's Virgil,' I said. 'I was just demonstrating that I too was familiar with Latin.' 'Good God!' he mopped his brow, 'Well, that's amazing!' The interview really had nowhere else to go after that, so he sent me home saying he would be in touch with my agent.

The next day I was sent to meet Albert Finney, who was seeing actresses for his film *Charlie Bubbles*, which was being made by the company he had started with fellow actor Michael Medwin. Finney was charming and we were getting on famously, when the phone suddenly rang on his desk. He picked it up and said, 'Oh, yes, she's here – it's for you,' handing me the phone. I was mortified and apologised profusely. 'It's all right,' said Finney grinning, 'it's your agent, you'd better see what he wants.' He seemed highly amused at the interruption.

Embarrassed, I spoke to my agent as briefly and tersely as I could, with Finney watching me, chuckling all the while. I apologised again as I handed the phone back to him. 'It was just to say I've been offered a TV series, that's all,' I said trying to make it sound unimportant. 'I think you'd better take it, don't you?' said Finney in his charming flat north-country accent. 'Well, you know just in case you don't get this,' he added kindly, and I realised he was letting me down gently as he didn't think I was right for the part in his movie. 'All right, thank you, I will,' I replied breathlessly.

I had seen Finney in *Tom Jones* and thought him devastatingly attractive. He eventually cast Liza Minnelli in the film, so it was quite obvious he thought I was completely wrong for the part. I remembered he had described the character as 'Kookie' – I'm a lot of things but 'Kookie' is not one of them! So I took his advice and accepted the part of 'Mick Armstrong' in *Weavers Green*, a gentle everyday story of country-folk in East Anglia. I spent the summer filming. Megs Jenkins played my mother and Eric Flynn – father of Jerome – was my love interest; years later I played opposite Jerome and it amused me to think I'd played opposite both father and son! Dennis Waterman and Susan George were both in the series playing teenagers! It was a very happy easy time, although I had to do a lot of horse-riding, which I have already mentioned I don't enjoy!

Someone had the bright idea of bringing a cheetah into the series and I was designated to do the scenes with the animal. We were filming at a stately home somewhere in East Anglia. It was a pleasant afternoon with birds singing merrily. The keeper opened the back of a van which was caged inside and out leapt a very large cheetah on the end of a chain. 'Don't let her know you're frightened,' said the keeper encouragingly, 'they can smell fear.' The scene required me to lead this creature down a very long flight of stone steps, at the bottom of which was the camera crew filming the whole sequence. The keeper tried it with the cheetah for the camera rehearsal, then it was my turn.

I took the chain carefully and on 'action' started to lead the cheetah, whose name was Cleo, down the steps. We had descended about three of them, when she suddenly snarled at me and pulled violently away. I remember thinking, 'Well it's better than leaping at me,' but I forgot the keeper's instructions about not showing my fear. I was frightened witless and Cleo must have known. The keeper was hiding in the rhododendron bushes by the side of the steps murmuring soothing noises to try to reassure her. Nobody thought of reassuring me! We continued our perilous descent, with me saying (rather unconvincingly, I thought), 'Good girl, Cleo, good girl.' She suddenly charged ahead, dragging me behind her, then stopped abruptly and started to prowl around in a circle, her tail waving ominously. Eventually, after she'd sat down for a few minutes, sniffing the air, I managed to persuade her to follow me to the foot of the steps.

It was only when we got there that I realised, on looking up, that there was no sign of the camera crew. They had disappeared! They'd all run off like frightened rabbits, leaving me to my fate! We did manage to shoot the scene finally, but when we came to do the studio scenes, Cleo took great exception to the heat under the lights and became very agitated as Eric and I pretended to give her an examination. She began to snarl and bare her teeth in a most alarming manner. Her keeper came in to try to calm her down. As soon as he was near enough, she took a swipe at him, badly mauling his forehead. He was taken off to hospital to have stitches in his head and Eric and I flatly refused to have anything further to do with the scene unless the cheetah was not among those present. After that we all had our own close-ups, but not at the same time!

The series was taken off after 56 episodes, as the Network kept on altering the time it was to be shown and it was not able to retain a regular audience. I went back into the theatre to do a season of Rep., to keep my hand in. Then, in 1966, I got the first of my many breaks.

* * *

I was asked to go along to the old ABPC Studios at Elstree, where they made, among other things, *The Saint*, *The Baron*, *The Avengers*, *The Champions* and countless other programmes in the same vein. I was to meet the producer and director of *The Saint* series. Accordingly, I 'glammed' myself up as best as I could. The producer, Bob Baker, was a charmer, who looked a bit like an old-fashioned movie star and had a Ronald Colman moustache. Leslie Norman (father of Barry Norman) was the director, an absolute darling, one of the nicest men I've ever met.

There was absolutely no fear of the casting couch in their office. They sat and chatted to me quite happily, but I could tell, from their reactions and readiness to bring the meeting to an end, that they didn't think me quite right for the part, that of an Italian racing driver. 'Well, thank you, Miss O'Mara, for coming to . . .' I snatched up a script that was lying on the coffee table between them and me. 'Is this the episode?' I asked, and without waiting for an answer started to flick through the pages. Bob said, 'Er, yes, er . . .' I found some lines of dialogue allotted to the character, Gina or Lisa, or some such name. 'May I read it for you?' I asked eagerly. 'Well, er . . . yes . . . yes, of course,' and before they had time to change their minds, I plunged straight into an over-the-top Italian accent and gave it all I'd got. When I'd finished, they both looked at each other smiling. 'Shall I read another scene?' I asked breathlessly. 'No, it won't be necessary,' said Bob chuckling to himself. 'You've got the part!'

And what a part! I was playing Roger Moore's love interest for the week. She was a flamboyant, volatile, raunchy, racing driver and I had to drive a Lotus around Brands Hatch! Not *actually*, you understand. It was all faked in the studio against BP (back projection). I *did* have some exterior shots in the Lotus, but they were filmed on the back lot at Elstree. Jan Holden played my blonde rival; she was a darling. I found myself being poured into an evening dress of pink sequins that had been worn by Diana Dors!

In one scene with Roger, he had to suddenly grab me and kiss me, then as we came out of the clinch, I had to slap him around the face in a fury. We rehearsed it without the slap, then went for a 'take'. He grabbed me by the shoulders, kissed me passionately, released me. Thwack! I slapped him good and hard. I saw Roger reel back. I heard a scream as Luisa, Roger's wife at the time, who had been on set watching the filming, jumped to her feet and ran over to him to see if any damage had been inflicted on his excessively handsome face. I was mortified and very apologetic, but the studio were all laughing at the sight of this tiny actress (I am only 5ft 4in) nearly laying out the urbane Roger Moore, who is 6ft 4in! There was much hilarity after that and Roger would pretend to flinch whenever he saw me.

I worked with him on several occasions subsequently and I found him to be the most charming, professional and hard-working of actors. The atmosphere on the set was always relaxed and happy and playing opposite him, truly a delight. I was such a success in the episode that I was asked back again a few weeks later to play a dual role in another episode of *The Saint*. I was thrilled. It is always nice to be asked back!

* * *

It was while I was filming *The Saint*, that a call came through to my agent's office from Maude Spector, one of the most famous and respected of all casting directors. She had seen me in *The Rivals* and thought I might be suitable for one of the two juvenile parts in *Great Catherine*, a film adaptation of Bernard Shaw's one-act play. It was to star none other than Peter O'Toole and was being made by his own company, Keep Films.

In 1965 I was still sharing a basement flat in Wimbledon with my son and two actress girl-friends. When any of us left the premises to go out shopping or for a walk on the common, we would say airily, 'If MGM calls while I'm out, say I won't be long!' or 'If Hollywood needs me, say I'll think about it!' And because of his recent enormous success in *Lawrence of Arabia*, 'Should Peter O'Toole ring, say, yes, I'm available as from now!' The point here is that for my two actress friends this was all a huge joke, for in their hearts they knew that none of these unlikely events would take place. For me, it was different. In my heart of hearts, I believed that it *would* happen. I believed it absolutely. I regarded it as my birthright. It was funny, yes, but it was no joke. So, of course, when I was called to audition for Peter O'Toole, I was excited, but not surprised.

My first meeting with O'Toole took place in Maude Spector's office. He seemed to like me, asked me what I'd done on the stage and was pleased about *The Rivals* and the classical work I'd been in. He asked me how old I was. I replied apprehensively, 'I'm afraid I'm 26,' thinking he would regard me as too old for the part. 'Faugh!' he exclaimed, 'that's nothing, I'm 32!' Then he said he'd like me to meet his producer and read for them both. I was delighted to have got over the first hurdle. As I got up to go, I told him that I had adored *Lawrence of Arabia* and hadn't wanted it to end. He shot me a candid look but I assured him that it was true, I hadn't wanted to leave the cinema.

I was tremendously excited about the interview because I knew I was in with a really good chance. I had heard that many film starlets had been considered for the role, but I thought to myself, 'What do they know about Bernard Shaw?' In those days, there were quite a few models breaking into movies. We actresses were pretty cross about it as, of course, they were taking work from us. I was to go the following night to audition.

Naturally, I broke the news to Roger Moore the next day. 'I have to audition for Peter O'Toole tonight,' I said excitedly, 'after we've finished filming – they're sending a car for me!' Roger raised a quizzical eyebrow. '*Really*,' he drawled. 'I see. What's the matter, aren't I tall enough for you? Oh, no, of course, we only work with classical actors now!' He made these remarks loud enough for the studio to hear and they all had a chuckle at my expense.

Full of anticipation and not a little nervous, I set off in the limousine they had sent and was whisked off to Eaton Place. Peter greeted me warmly and introduced me to Jules Buck, a charming if somewhat retiring American. They were already drinking champagne and invited me to join them. I hesitated. I had never had a head for alcohol and have now been teetotal for many, many years. But at the time I thought it ungracious to decline as they were obviously trying to put me at ease. As I had eaten nothing since lunch, I decided first to sip at my glass as infrequently as I dared. I mentioned timidly that I had to be at the studios at six o'clock the next morning, as they appeared to be just happy to sit and drink and chat. Thus galvanised, Peter arose and announced, 'Right, I'm going to play all the other parts, Kate, you just do Varinka.'

We started. Fortunately, I am a good sight-reader and all my mother's early training now helped immeasurably. I gave it all I'd got, but Peter was stupendous, in the part that Zero Mostel was going to play. When I laughed appreciatively, Peter said, 'I played Patiomkin at RADA, and I wish I was going to do it now, but I've got to play the silly-arse English Officer!' And jolly well he played it too. We went through all my scenes several times, both Peter and Jules nodding at each other from time to time which I took to mean approval.

At one point Peter left the room, then came bursting in explosively, yelling the place down. 'I want you to top me vocally', he said when he'd finished. 'Right,' I replied uncertainly. O'Toole has always been renowned for having a huge voice, so it was quite a challenge. However, I did my best and bellowed as loudly as I could. He seemed pleased. When I thought we could do no more, Peter suddenly said 'Now, I'd like you to do the big scene with Catherine and Edstaston, decide which speech is addressed to whom, and then reverse it.'

I was desperately tired by this time – I'd been up since dawn and had been working all day. It was many hours since I'd eaten and the champagne was starting to make me light-headed. I looked at my script, the typewritten words seemed to dance in front of my eyes. I took a deep breath, plunged in and hoped for the best. When we got to the end of the scene, Peter clapped and said approvingly, 'Good girl, you got it the right way round!'. More luck than judgement, I thought privately. At last the session was at an end. Peter showed me out to the hall. He took me by the shoulders and kissed me on the forehead. 'I think you can do it,' he said quietly, 'I think you can do it.' I hardly dare breathe. 'I'm so glad, thank you,' I replied, quite subdued by now, as I was exhausted.

The original director for the movie had been sacked and a replacement had been found. He now put in an appearance. I discovered he'd witnessed the last part of the audition. Peter introduced us and then sent us both off in a car together, as the director lived somewhere near me. We exchanged remarks in a desultory fashion, as by now I was nearly asleep and knew I had to be up at five. To my horror, I realised suddenly what he was saying. He was implying that if I were 'nice' to him, he would make sure I got the part. I couldn't believe my ears. I was suddenly awake and told him, in that case, then I didn't want the part! He shrugged his shoulders as if to say 'so be it'. He dropped me off at my flat and, deeply dejected and disappointed, I fell into bed.

The next morning, I somehow got to the studio on time, but whether through shouting or tiredness or the drink, I found I had hardly any voice left. I was croaking like Joan Greenwood. Roger, while admiring it for its unusual quality, remarked that this was what came of working with 'classical actors'. At lunchtime, there was a call from my agent to tell me that I'd got the part. I realised the director had just been 'trying it on' and actually had no say in the matter. There was general jubilation on the set. Everyone seemed genuinely pleased at my success, only Roger jokingly remarking that 'obviously he wasn't good enough for me!'

* * *

A few weeks later, after a whirlwind round of costume and wig fittings, I found myself at Shepperton Studios at the court of Catherine, Empress of Russia. I was clad in a most beautiful, eighteenth-century dress made of silk taffeta in the subtlest shade of slate turquoise. It is absolutely my favourite colour and, if I'd chosen it myself, I couldn't have done better. My hair was piled on top of my head and luxuriant hair pieces had been added to it for the opening sequences. Yes, I had been convinced that I would work with Peter O'Toole and therefore was not surprised when the job came along, but here I was standing on this magnificent set and it was snowing. Just pretend snow, you understand, for we were inside in a film studio.

The snow was falling steadily to make it look like Russia and there were various farmyard animals wandering about. Anyway, there I was and I distinctly remember pinching myself just to be sure it was all really happening. I had two blissful weeks of filming alone with the supremely talented American comedian, Zero Mostel. He was a joy to work with, immensely generous and had me in stitches off-camera with his sharp, witty, New York Jewish humour and yet at the same time, he had tremendous vulnerability. At one point we were joined by Akim Tamiroff, the wonderful Russian actor. I considered myself a very fortunate girl indeed. The leading lady of the film was to be the gamine French actress Jeanne Moreau, whom I had admired ever since seeing her in *Jules et Jim*. She had not turned up yet, as she did not appear until about fifteen minutes into the film.

One day, Zero and I were rehearsing a scene and I became aware of a figure sitting in the shadows, immediately outside the intense pool of light where we were shooting. Because of the brightness of the lights I could not see her face, but I was convinced it was Jeanne. I tried not to stare, but I noticed she was wearing a cream trench mackintosh with the collar turned up. I thought her very chic. We continued to film the sequence. Then came a break. I glanced over in the direction of the woman, she was beginning to feel the heat of the studio and was undoing her mackintosh. She slipped it off still sitting and I gasped, as I saw it was lined entirely with mink. We were then introduced and I bade her welcome in French. She seemed delighted and laughed, although I was not sure if she was laughing with pleasure or at my accent! Each morning when we came on set, I would greet her with *'Bonjour*, Jeanne!' and she would reply with 'allo Ket!'

Filming continued unabated for three months and for the most part it was highly enjoyable, if at times a little nerve-racking. There was always an air of tension on the set, due, I think, to the fact that a great deal of money was at stake, that we were all in unyielding corsets, which were very restricting and uncomfortable and also that we were doing a 'classic'. There were many visitors to the set; Tommy Steele turned up one time and of course Siân Phillips, Peter's then wife, appeared with their two small girls. One could have cut the atmosphere with a knife on that occasion; however it was not until many years later that I was to get to know her and discover her enchanting personality and generous soul.

Two incidents stand out in my memory. There was a scene where I had to help carry Peter to meet the Empress Catherine. It was a long sequence and we were trying to get the shot in before the end of the day's filming. It was vital as, if they went 'over', the whole studio staff went into overtime payment, which for a crew of at least ninety, was a lot of money. The alternative was to fall behind schedule, which was also disastrously expensive and added thousands to the budget. We duly rehearsed the scene with one eye on the clock. Then Peter was taken off-set to have his wig adjusted. It was a race against time. The duplicitous director, doubtless feeling redundant on a film which was actually becoming directed by Peter and the lighting cameraman, the award-winning Ossie Morris, gave me a note on how to play the scene, in the brief hiatus while we waited for Peter to return.

It was not how we had rehearsed it and I felt his interpretation was wrong, but being a good little girl and not wishing to waste studio time, on Peter's return I did as I was told. The cameras rolled, and the ghastly director said, 'action'. I played the scene with the amended inflection. 'Cut!' bellowed O'Toole. He wriggled free from our collective carrying posture, grabbed me fiercely by the wrist and swung me round, yelling, 'What the hell do you think you're doing?' There was an immediate deathly silence. You could have heard a pin drop. White with fear, I met O'Toole's headlamp like eyes, which were blazing with fury. The director never said a word. I said something like, 'I'm sorry, I made a mistake.' I could hardly utter the words from terror. 'Right, let's go again,' said the first assistant director, 'first positions everybody!' Peter released me, and we rearranged ourselves, with me holding up one of Peter's legs, he being in a semi-recumbent position. I pulled myself together, determined not to let him down again. We shot the sequence. I went back to my original inflection, which I had done previously by instinct. It was successful, it was a good 'take', and we 'wrapped' just in time. Peter turned to me and said gently, 'Well done, Kate, well done'. To this day I have not forgiven the director for not owning up to his pathetic attempt at directing me. He would never have dared give O'Toole a note, so tried to take it out on a supporting actress.

There was a huge ballroom scene which involved hundreds of extras and had several cameras trained on the action at once. Some were very high up on 'cherry pickers', and some were at ground level. The enormous ballroom set was filled with hundreds of dancers who were executing a complicated gavotte in pairs. There were several columns of dancers. This scene took several days to shoot, the gavotte at one point being interrupted by Cossacks leaping over everyone's heads and causing mayhem. I had a little scene with Jack Hawkins, a dear man, who by that time had succumbed to cancer of the throat and was somehow managing with a microphone in his trachea. Playing Peter's fiancée in the film was the delightful comedic actress Angela Scoular. She and I were sharing a dressing room and got on like a house on fire. O'Toole was being partnered by Angela and they were due for close-ups at eleven o'clock. But up in our shared dressing-room, Angela was lying on her bed, prostrate with food poisoning.

There was a knock at the door. 'Miss Scoular to the set, please'. I opened the door. It was the third assistant looking expectant. 'Angela is sick,' I explained briefly, 'I think the unit nurse ought to see her.' The third assistant vanished without another word, looking frightened. A few moments later there was another knock at the door. This time it was the second assistant. He asked tersely, 'What's the matter with Angela?'. 'She's dreadfully ill,' I said gesturing towards the bed where Angie was moaning and writhing in agony. He peered around the door, then shot off like a rabbit. A few moments later, the door opened and without bothering to knock, the first assistant strode in, and went straight to the bed. 'Angela, what's all this?' She was unable to answer save for groaning loudly. 'I'll see if we can get a doctor to her,' he said to me. 'Are you ready?' 'Yes,' I replied quickly. He left the room. I tried to comfort her, but she was beyond comfort.

Suddenly the door burst open, one of the producers came in, went straight to the bed, grabbed Angela by the wrist, yanked her off and dragged her out of the room. Appalled, I followed, trying to hold her up as she was barely able to walk. He got her to the set which was packed and silent. She was put in her

45

position next to Peter; I hurriedly found mine. 'Cameras! music, play-back! And ACTION!' The music started, the huge array of dancers with Jeanne and Zero leading the central column, swung into action. I shall never know how Angela got through it, but she did. As soon as the shot was over, she was violently sick and they were able to shoot around her for the next couple of hours, so she had time to recover. The whole episode taught me a lesson I'd never forget. In this profession, one must *never ever* be ill! The show must go on, whatever the cost.

The very worst thing that happened during filming, however, was a visit from a journalist from a rag called *The Daily Sketch*. He came to interview me and asked me what I thought about O'Toole. I was fulsome in my praise of him both as a performer and as a person. But this was not what this scumbag wanted to hear. He proceeded to write the most appalling rubbish with snide comments on O'Toole's drinking, none of which I had said nor would I ever have mentioned even had it been true. I adored Peter and said so. I was weeping openly as I tried to explain to Peter that it was all untrue. Peter shrugged his shoulders philosophically and said, 'You know what they're like, they're all the same.' I hadn't known what they were like up till then. I learnt the hard way. Another valuable lesson.

Great Catherine opened all sorts of doors for me. In 1967 I was immediately booked for another movie and then another. I started to do a lot of television as well; in fact I never seemed to stop working. I was still living in Wimbledon just around the corner from Oliver Reed and his first wife Kate. They had a dear little boy called Mark with a mop of blonde curls. He and my son Dickon used to play endlessly together in a battered old toy jeep that they loved.

Meeting Ollie in the local pub was always something of an ordeal. I remember once he did a handstand in front of me and showed off, walking on his hands in a circle. Another time, he suddenly picked me up and carried me out of the door shoulder-high. I was sober; he, needless to say, was paralytic. I had actually been in a film with him when we were both a lot younger and he was still beautiful. There was a sort of pub culture around in the late sixties and it was considered socially desirable to drop in of a Sunday morning, but the bellow 'O'MARA!' that greeted me from Ollie always unnerved me.

* * *

On completion of *Great Catherine* I was put forward for another film, an adaptation of a novel by Victor Canning, *The Limbo Line*. It was the story of a Russian ballerina who defects to the West, falls in love with the American hero and is hotly pursued across England and Europe by KGB agents.

By now, we were able to move into larger rented accommodation and I could afford a new car. I drove off to London in it for my interview with the producers and director of the film. As I was driving my little white bubble car up Park Lane, there was a sudden cloudburst, the first for some time, making the streets very greasy. I turned into Orchard Street. A white van, which was in the next lane, braked suddenly to avoid the vehicle in front and skidded right across in front of me. I took evasive action and ended up on the pavement, my bonnet crumpled up like a concertina into the wall of the very offices of the film company where I was due for my interview.

I emerged without a scratch and strode nonchalantly up to meet the producers. I was clad in highwayman garb, as was fashionable in 1967 – black velvet suit, white ruffled shirt and thigh-high black PVC boots. 'I've parked my car in Reception,' I announced airily as I shook hands with them all. They were very concerned and solicitous and immediately organised a secretary to call the Police and arrange to get my car removed.

I read for them in my newly acquired Russian accent – I had already secured the services of a Russian student to ensure that my accent was authentic – and was passed as competent by the choreographer who was in charge of the dance sequences. I secretly blessed the tortuous hours I had spent in ballet class. I was to perform the 'Dance of the Little Swans' from *Swan Lake* with members of the Royal Festival Ballet and had to be seen in the final moments of Stravinsky's *Firebird*. There was also a horse-riding sequence, and I realised that the much hated sessions in the Pony Club and during filming for *Weavers Green* would pay off.

I got my car fixed; it looked as good as new. I loved it. It was of course tiny, but then so was I, and so then, was Dickon. He was very happy in our new home, as there was a large garden to play in and he was going to nursery school which he adored. I had taken my girlfriends with me when I moved as it helped with the rent and in any case they needed somewhere to live. We were a jolly crowd. Although Jeremy was around, we were not living together. One didn't so much in those days. It may have been 'The Swinging Sixties', but I suppose I was still a bit old-fashioned, in spite of my many unfortunate adventures, or perhaps even because of them.

My leading man in the movie, Craig Stevens, was an American who had been very popular on American television in a series called *Peter Gunn*. He was married to the actress Alexis Smith, for whom Cole Porter had written 'Night and Day'. Filming was to take place at Pinewood Studios with locations at Littlehampton, Marlow and Burnham Beeches, the last named being a favourite location spot for countless films. Craig Stevens turned out to be the most charming and urbane of men. I couldn't have wished for better. Also in the film was Robert Urquhart, Vladek Sheybal and Moira Redmond. Moira and I immediately chummed up and had great fun.

We were filming a sequence at Marlow Brewery, where Vladek, playing the villain, had to meet a sticky end in one of the huge vats of fermenting malt and hops. Moira had heard that the scum of the mixture was supposed to be terribly good for the complexion. We were given a conducted tour around the brewery, which was fascinating and she begged to be given some samples of this 'scum'. She obtained jars for both of us with screw-on lids. It resembled, if anything, horseradish sauce. She went home, while I was whisked down to Littlehampton to film the final scenes for the movie in the harbour. I was given a caravan in which I could change and keep warm and dry and learn my lines, while waiting for my next scene. I put the little jar containing the fermenting hops and malt on the ledge by the window, oblivious to the fact that the sun would gradually make its way around to that very spot. I forgot all about it.

Two days later, I was taken by car to the next location. I snatched up the jar at the last moment and put it in my bag. My leading man was sitting in the back with me. I told him all about this magical stuff with its reputed curative properties. He was curious to see what it was like, so I produced the jar. He took it, decided he wanted to smell it and, with some difficulty, unscrewed the metal cap. There was a huge report as though someone had been shot and I swear I do not exaggerate when I say that the entire interior of the car was covered with what appeared to be vomit. Craig was covered, so was the chauffeur. I escaped relatively unharmed and became apoplectic with laughter. Craig was definitely *not* amused. Both he and the chauffeur had to change and have their suits cleaned. I tried to tell Moira about it later, but found myself unable to speak from laughing. She was sorry to have missed the fun.

I enjoyed making the film, but the producers made the mistake of giving it an unhappy ending, contrary to the author's intentions. So, instead of wandering off into the sunset with the hero, the last shots of me were of being bundled down into the hold of a Russian boat and taken back to the Soviet Union. The audience didn't like the unconventional ending one bit and it was booed wherever it was shown. I have to say I agreed with them. I love happy endings. I think it gives one hope for the future and it's partly why people go to the cinema, most particularly if it is a romantic adventure story. I suppose the audience felt cheated and I don't blame them. On that movie set I first encountered Jean Marsh, who was a delight and was playing a secretary. Our paths have continued to cross ever since, in unexpected ways.

It was while I was filming at Pinewood that I first set eyes on Joan Collins. It was lunchtime and we were sitting at adjoining tables, partaking of a light luncheon. In those days it was 'de rigueur' to eat in the commissary – to be 'seen'. It was an almost foolproof way of getting more work. I've got any number of jobs in the canteen or restaurant over lunch. Joan was sitting at the next table and I couldn't take my eyes off her. I thought her the most beautiful creature I'd ever seen and said so to my companion. 'So would you be if you wore that much make-up', he observed tartly. I was faintly shocked by the remark and defended her stoutly. 'Well, I still think she's lovely.' I replied, and I still do. I've seen her at 5.30 in the morning without a scrap of make-up on and I actually think she looks even better.

*　*　*

I think it was around this time that I started working on a regular basis at Elstree. I went literally from one series to another as the 'foreign interest' for the week, such as *The Avengers*, when I sustained a huge lump on my chin (being on the receiving end of a right upper cut from Linda Thoresen!) and *The Troubleshooters*, when the wonderful actor Bernard Lee (the original 'M' in the James Bond movies) played my father. I have never smoked – ever, but the director requested that I do so in one scene with Bernard. It was an intimate father/daughter scene and they thought it would be nice if we were seen sharing a quiet cigarette.

Come the take, they lit me up and someone said 'action' and off we went. It was quite a long scene (they were in those days), and it was going frightfully well. Then I became aware of a searing pain in my left wrist. I couldn't imagine what it could be. I soldiered on in agony. Finally the scene was over and I discovered a ghastly, raw, red mark where the cigarette had burnt into my wrist! I have always flatly refused to smoke either on TV or film or, indeed, stage, since I do it very badly! I have managed to get away with holding a cigarette without actually taking a puff in *Who's Afraid of Virginia Woolf* and *Noel & Gertie*, both on stage. I cheated in the latter with a long cigarette holder. I tried to smoke herbal cigarettes in *Arms and the Man* and stank the theatre out. I pretended to smoke in *Absolutely Fabulous* and let Joanna Lumley do it all.

It was while I was filming up at the ABPC Studios in Elstree – I think it was an episode of *The Champions*, that I was asked to test for the lead female role in *Department S*, a new series starring

Peter Wyngarde. I duly learnt the scene and gave it my best shot. After I'd finished filming, I got called up to Monty Berman's office. He virtually ran the studios and I gathered was in charge of production. He offered me the part on the spot and asked if I could cope with the tough schedule it required. I assured him that it would not be a problem. He said the part was mine and he would call my agent. I didn't get the job. The American 'money boys', who were major backers in the studios then, decided that I was too 'exotic'. I was very upset, but philosophical. At least I got one episode out of it.

*   *   *

This profession is beset with disappointments. One such was my determination to get into the Open Air Theatre in Regent's Park. More than anything else I wanted to be part of the company – mainly because I was passionate about Shakespeare. I was a true 'Bardolater', a phrase I believe coined by John Barton, the resident Professor Emeritus at Stratford. I auditioned three years running for Regent's Park and was rejected thrice. My disappointment was intense. In desperation I remember begging if I couldn't at least play a fairy, but David Conville said 'I don't think so, do you?'

I was heartbroken and I sobbed for hours after I heard that I hadn't got in again. It took me nineteen years to get there and when I did, I got rave reviews for my 'Beatrice' in *Much Ado About Nothing* in 1981 and mentioned in the same breath as Peggy Ashcroft! But all that was to come and for the present, I had to content myself with TV appearances. I was in *Adam Adamant* with Gerald Harper, who was to be my leading man on two occasions in the West End. I did two episodes of *Z Cars* and appeared in *The Dick Emery Show*. I was getting a reputation for being professional and reliable. I appeared in *Lord Peter Whimsey* with Ian Carmichael who was one of the most delightful men I have ever worked with. In my 'story', *Cloud of Witness*, my father was played by Harry Lockwood West, father of Timothy West (who later played my lover) and grandfather to Samuel West, who eventually played my son!

51

In the spring of 1968, I was told that I had been cast in a spaghetti western called *The Desperados*, being made by Columbia with Jack Palance, Vince Edwards, Sylvia Syms and George Maharis. I was to play George's girlfriend, quite a thrill really, as I had thought him divine in *Route 66* when I was a teenager. I didn't have to meet anyone or read or anything. I was sent the script and that was it. I took my son with me to Madrid where the unit was based. Filming was entirely on location in the mountains outside Madrid, but initially we were all put up in the Hilton. I was congratulating myself that I had now managed to make three movies without having to be chased around the casting couch and had proved to myself that one could get by on talent and looks alone.

The phone rang in my apartment at the Hilton. 'Hi, Katy,' said a friendly American male voice. 'Hello,' I said thinking it was my make-up call for the morrow. 'Vince Edwards here, say, listen, Katy, why not come on down to my suite for a drink, so we can get to know each other, how about it, huh?' 'That's very kind of you, Mr Edwards, but I have my small son with me here and I have to attend to him,' I replied in a world-weary manner. But Vince turned out to be the most charming of men and very affable and easy to work with. He had starred in an American TV series called *Ben Casey*, in which he played a doctor. In fact, it may have been called 'Dr Ben *Casey*', I'm not sure. It's all so long ago now. I decided that while I was in the hotel, I was a sitting duck and asked the production manager if I could move to an apartment nearby. He was delighted, as it would save the company money.

The movie also starred a wonderful actor called Neville Brand, who was playing the sheriff and had been one of the stars in *Laramie*. He was the most congenial of men, an absolute darling. However, to maintain this perennial affability, it seemed it was necessary for him to consume at least one large bottle of vodka before lunch and another afterwards, to get himself through the afternoon. I never saw him in the evening after shooting. Nor did I ever see him in any clothes other than the sheriff's outfit. Everyone else went to the location in their own gear and then got changed and made up in specially appointed caravans. Not so Neville! He lived in his costume. It seemed adhered to him and looked as though it had been to the Wild West and back!

I recall one day's interminable shooting, when he had spent most of the time bellowing abuse at the camera crew and director, who were miles off in the distance up a mountain and had no idea what he was saying. He was in fact complaining, between swigs of vodka, that he'd been waiting all day to shoot and was getting extremely fed up. They took absolutely no notice of him whatsoever and the last I saw of him, he was out for the count and being carried shoulder high into the Hilton reception area. I adored him, but then I didn't have to live with him.

The worst torture on that film was a long sequence when I was supposed to be being raped by Jack Palance. Jack was a gentle giant, a charming man off-set, politeness itself. But he had been a prize-fighter before becoming an actor and was obviously under the impression that young actresses could not be relied upon to convey pain, unless they were actually in pain! I had three days of unmitigated hell, filming that sequence with him. I was bruised black and blue all up and down my arms and my ribs. At the end of the sequence, he lifted me bodily above his head – he was 6ft 6in – and then dropped me without any warning onto the earthen floor of the adobe in which we were filming. There was a horrified silence, then I started crying from shock and pain. The film crew were all appalled and thank God that was the end of the sequence. On a more pleasant note, I had love scenes to do with George Maharis, another charming man whom I had been mad about when I was a teenager.

* * *

On my return to England, I had to audition for two different managements. There were two female parts going in a West End play which was to star Dudley Moore. Three hundred girls were up for it. I auditioned no less than six times. It finally got down to two of us. By this time I was past caring. I had to improvise with Dud on stage which was fun, but I noticed he had to hide behind his 'Pete & Dud' voice to do it. As it transpired they gave the part to an actress who'd only turned up that day and had missed all the other auditions. That's showbiz, kid!!

The other audition was for the director Val May, which later bore fruit. Sylvia Syms (who had been the leading lady in the Western) and I had become friendly. She got in touch soon after our return and invited me to a party at her place. I had a lovely time, as there were lots of actors there whom I knew. At one point I found myself sitting on the floor chatting with a charming woman. I had no idea who she was and was demonstrating some limbering-up exercises to her. She decided to 'have a go' at them.

The next day, my agent received a call from the production office of *The Adventurers*, a best-seller by Harold Robbins which was being adapted for the screen. Paramount were to fly me to Rome to test for the female lead! I was to be put up at a beautiful hotel on the Via Veneto for a week, at Paramount's expense. Needless to say, I was astounded and thrilled but baffled. It transpired that the charming lady with whom I'd been exercising was none other than the wife of the director Lewis Gilbert, who was to direct the movie and was later famed for directing several Bond movies.

I gathered up my son, determined that he too should experience the delights of Italy. We had quite a few glorious days exploring Rome before I was called to test at Cinecitta. There I met Rossano Brazzi, who was playing one of the leads. I did my test. I thought I'd done well, but a few minutes after I'd finished, Lewis Gilbert came into my dressing-room and told me that he didn't think I was right for the leading female role, but that he would like me to play the part of the Italian opera singer in the movie instead.

I spoke to my agent in London and I told him the news. 'You've been offered two jobs in the theatre this end,' he said, sounding smug. 'You can play Polly Garter in *Under Milk Wood* at the Bristol Old Vic, or take over from an actress who's being given the push from *The Italian Girl* by Iris Murdoch, at Wyndam's. I thought it over, then asked, 'Why are they getting rid of her? What's she done?' sensing trouble. 'Put twenty minutes on the show, by being drunk and disorderly or possibly drugs,' he added meaningfully. Having never taken a drug in my life and being virtually teetotal even in those days, I was puzzled and thought her very foolish.

'I'll do the Iris Murdoch play,' I said without hesitation, knowing that my Welsh accent was not up to Dylan Thomas. Also, I'll confess, I was peeved at not getting the film part I'd been tested for and did not want to be downgraded to a small part in the movie. Such is the arrogance of youth. In hindsight, I should have taken the part. It would probably have led to another movie, perhaps even a Bond movie. But my decision took me in the direction of the theatre and I think I missed the chance of consolidating my career in films.

That evening, which was my last in Rome, I decided we should go for a final look around the city with my son and another actor, who had tested with me. We did the tourist thing and hired a pony and trap. I shall never forget it. Then we wandered down the Via Veneto, vaguely thinking about supper. We were suddenly hailed by two familiar voices. 'Hello, well, I say hello, what-ho and all that rot!' The unmistakable tones of Peter Cooke and Dudley Moore doing their Leighton and Johnston act. '*Do* join us for a bite, won't you? Oh do, do, *do!*'. Laughing, we sat down under the stars and had an absolutely hilarious and delightful supper. I laughed ceaselessly throughout and soon forgot my disappointment over the movie.

* * *

I was then invited to the 1968 Cannes Film Festival, where my film *The Limbo Line* was due to be shown. I flew out there almost immediately for just a couple of days before starting rehearsals for *The Italian Girl*. I was put up at the Majestic Hotel in Cannes, but was very disillusioned by everyone parading themselves around, intent on being 'seen'. Except, of course, Geraldine Chaplin, Orson Welles and Monica Vitti, who didn't need to be seen because everyone knew who they were.

I was about to return to London, when we learned of the strike that had paralysed France. I had to get back to start work, so with no planes, no trains, and no buses, there were only two choices: as a 'guest' on Sam Spiegel's yacht, or hiring a car and travelling up the Napoleonic route to Switzerland. I chose the latter. If it was good enough for Napoleon, it was good enough for me. I arrived in Geneva and managed to get a Swissair flight out to Heathrow.

I was playing another Russian in the Iris Murdoch play. Also in the cast were Timothy West, Richard Pascoe, Jane Wenham, Elizabeth Sellars and, sharing a dressing-room with me, the glorious Deborah Grant, who became a chum at once. We have shared dressing-rooms since over the years and we recently toured together in *A Woman of No Importance*. I had the great delight not long ago of casting her daughter, Miranda, as Lydia Languish in our production of *The Rivals*, where she demonstrated most forcibly that she had inherited her mother's beauty and talent.

The Italian Girl ran at Wyndham's Theatre in London for over six months. During that period, several things happened. I got myself a new agent. I met Iris Murdoch when she turned up for the party to celebrate however many performances we'd done. I endeavoured to engage her in conversation in an animated way. I told her how much I admired her writing – how I loved doing the play and how I had enjoyed *A Severed Head*, all of which was true. She seemed vague and mildly interested but baffled and I suspect she was wondering who I was and why she'd been landed with me. Our conversation could, at best, be described as desultory. John Gielgud came to see the play one matinee and terrified us all to death.

John Osborne's play, *Hotel in Amsterdam*, opened next door at the New Theatre (now the Albery). The two theatres are linked by a covered bridge running between the two fly floors. In our play, Timothy West and I had a fairly long 'wait' while a big scene was being played on stage. On the first night of 'Hotel', Tim suddenly appeared and said, 'Come on, let's get a sneak preview.' Quiet as mice, we hurried over the bridge into the Albery. The fly floor, from where the scenery is 'flown', is just below the lighting grid, so one has to be very careful of ropes, wires and cables. We were now thirty odd feet above the stage and looking down on the actors on stage: Judy Parfitt, Joss Ackland and Paul Scofield. Their nervous tension and the terror of the first night was almost palpable, even to us in our eyrie. We had a wonderful aerial view of the whole proceedings and I was just getting immersed in the action when Tim gesticulated and mimed that it was time for us to return. We crept away as silently as we'd come. This facility prompted a rather more notorious incident which happened a few weeks later.

At one point in *Hotel in Amsterdam*, Paul Scofield had to glance off into the wings on Stage Right, where his wife was supposed to be packing in their bedroom off-stage. At each performance there would be a member of the cast pulling a face or making a rude gesture at him, in a vain effort to try to get a reaction. Various people had tried assorted tactics and the cast was now getting short of ideas. Somebody (and I strongly suspect that it was Joss Ackland, aided and abetted by Tim West) hit on the brilliant idea of putting me in the wings – topless! I was wearing a rather fetching, torn nightdress, which left very little to the imagination. In *The Italian Girl*, I was supposed to expose myself to Richard Pascoe in an attempt to seduce him – he was playing a rather uptight, repressed character – so the top of the very décolleté nightdress was elasticated.

It just so happened that this moment in the Osborne play coincided nicely with the scene that Tim and I had 'off'. So at the appointed hour, Tim came to fetch me and we sped across the covered bridge and then crept down the ladder (which was only supposed to be used by the technical staff – we'd have been shot if the management had known) to stage level. There, in silence, I was conducted to the appropriate position in the up-stage wing. Isobel Dean, Judy Parfitt and Joss Ackland were already there, all stuffing handkerchiefs into their mouths to stop themselves laughing. On stage were Paul Scofield and David Burke, the former totally ignorant of the joke about to be played on him, the latter only too aware of what was about to happen off-stage and doubtless wondering how he was going to get through the scene without laughing. I was instructed in mime, by the men, I noticed, to pull my top down.

I have to say, I had misgivings about the whole thing and wondered whether I wasn't being just a touch unprofessional.

Too late now. I was then given a placard to hold up with some lines from the play on it, writ large. I have no idea what they were, nor for that matter did Scofield when a moment later he came to the wings and waved a lugubrious hand in my direction. He wandered back down-stage, then two seconds later was back for a second look as though hardly able to believe his eyes. By now Isobel, Judy, Joss and Tim were crying with silent mirth. Scofield walked down-stage and then there was absolute silence for what seemed to be an eternity. He'd 'dried' totally and he was quite unable to speak. We heard David try to help him out in a voice shaking with barely suppressed laughter. Another interminable pause.

By now, I was trembling with terror, as I realised my unscripted appearance had brought the play to a grinding halt. Then we all heard an extraordinary noise, not unlike an ostrich trying to swallow a golf-ball. It was followed by another. I could hear David audibly trying to suppress his giggles. A third time Scofield attempted to speak a line and failed. Unfortunately I knew no more, for at that moment, Tim yanked me up and we had to tear across into our theatre, so as not to miss our entrance. I was beside myself with fright and fairly appalled at what I'd done. To my surprise, I was accounted a heroine, as Tim gleefully recounted the events to our cast between the matinee and evening performances.

After a while I began to relax, as the whole adventure was regarded by all as a huge success. I was still seeing Jeremy at this time and he was horrified when I told him. He said he'd never heard of anything so unprofessional, that I was a disgrace and ought to be ashamed of myself. I cried myself to sleep that night, as I had a sneaking suspicion that he was right. But the next day I received a charming note from Scofield himself, thanking me for my contribution to the afternoon's performance, which he said would make it memorable! I hope he's forgiven me.

* * *

While I was playing a supporting role at Wyndham's Theatre, my sister Belinda was starring in *There's a Girl in my Soup* at the

Globe Theatre on Shaftesbury Avenue. She had her name in
lights and in true 'showbiz' tradition, had been the understudy
for the leading lady and had been given the chance to take over
and star in the show. My father, I think, unwittingly, had hurt
me deeply by taking all his cronies to see her show and had
never once come to see me in mine. I was greatly upset by this,
what seemed to me, deliberate snub, so much so, that Jeremy
rang my father up and told him, in no uncertain terms, that I
was distressed. My father seemed completely unaware and did
not seem to understand. Over the years I found myself
excluded from my family, but I started life as a loner, so it was
a situation with which I was familiar. I just shrugged my
shoulders, philosophically, and got on with life. I suspect they
haven't found me easy. I'm inclined to speak my mind very
freely and often make cutting remarks which are intended to
raise a laugh, but hurt and humiliate instead. A habit I have
never managed to curb.

*   *   *

I was being seen for countless movie parts and not getting them.
I tested twice for Cathy in *Wuthering Heights*; two different
companies were producing it. I had already been for four
interviews and still I didn't get the part. I suppose I wanted it too
much. I thought I was perfect casting for the wild, tempera-
mental heroine of Emily Brontë's novel, which I had adored
reading as a teenager. But it was not to be.

There were some strange films being made in the late sixties. I
was in one such called *Promenade*. It was shot entirely on location
in Brighton during Festival time. It was half in black and white
and half in colour and there were psychedelic sequences all
trying to emulate the Nouvelle Vague of the French cinema,
which was all the rage at the time. I have no idea what this film
was about, but I remember that I and my fellow actors Robert
Morris, Michael Coles and Richard Leech all reassured each
other by saying that it would not see the light of day. No-one
could possibly be so foolish as to release it! Thus comforted, now
shooting had finished, I forgot all about it. Imagine my horror

when I discovered it was doing the rounds as the second feature to *Planet of the Apes*! So not only did it get seen, but just about everybody I knew had seen at least some of it!

Then in the spring of 1969, I went to see Yorkshire Television about a big new TV series they were doing, *The Main Chance*, starring John Stride, whom I had seen being brilliant as Romeo in Zefferelli's ground-breaking production at the Old Vic. Judi Dench had played Juliet. I met the director of the series. I read a couple of scenes and the part was mine. I was cast as the female lead opposite John Stride. He played David Main, a successful solicitor, and I, Julia Main his wife; their marriage on the point of breaking up. We filmed mainly in the YTV studios in Leeds, with location work in and around London. The opening scene, I recall, was shot in the Restaurant Car of the fast train from Euston to Leeds. There were several pages of dialogue of an emotionally strained nature between John and myself. The entire scene was realised as close-ups on the salt and pepper pots, the cutlery, the napkins, the glasses of wine, everything in fact, except the actors. I was disgusted and I don't think Stride was too pleased either. But the director, John Frankam, was adamant. I can't say it was the happiest of times.

The crunch came when the *TV Times* came to take stills of John and me to go on the cover for the launch of the series. They said they would also like to whisk me away to Ireland to Rostrevor, County Down, from where some of my Irish antecedents hailed. This was readily agreed to, as all publicity for the show could only help raise its profile. (We didn't use terms like that in those days, or 'exposure', but that's what everyone meant.) My visit to the land of my forefathers coincided with the renewal of hostilities in Ireland in the late spring of 1969. I remember the furore caused by a sewer pipe being blown up in Belfast. I spent a few days travelling from one location to another (my family comes from both sides of the border) modelling lovely gowns in romantic Irish settings.

Come the big launch of the series, to my horror and dismay, the front cover of the *TV Times* did not feature the picture of John and me in a bitter-sweet embrace as had been intended, but ME

ALONE, looking whimsically out at the camera. It provoked the most awful rumpus, screaming matches down the phone from various agents' offices to Yorkshire Television and back. It was no-one's fault of course, least of all mine. The *TV Times*, being an independent publication, had decided that the Irish pictures of me were prettier and the article that went with them more interesting! I had this incredible exposure for three weeks running. Needless to say, I was not in the second series of *The Main Chance*. 'Internal politics' was how my dismissal was explained to my agent. Whether my *TV Times* cover had anything to do with it or not, I shall never know, but I don't think it helped.

Act II. Sc.I

I was consoled by getting more TV work: *Don Quick*, with Ian Hendry, a space-age version of the Don Quixote story, with Ronald Lacey playing the Sancho Panza character. Dickon was involved in an accident in the school playground while we were rehearsing. Ian was wonderfully sympathetic and insisted I leave rehearsals to go to see my son in Moorfields Hospital where he had been taken. Dickon was all right, but he had almost lost an eye. All was well, however and he has always had perfect vision thanks to the excellent emergency treatment he received there.

I went back to Anglia TV to do a play with Richard Johnson and the American actor Al Hedison. (For some reason, in Britain he was known as David Hedison.) In among these rather good jobs I was seen for an Elvis Presley movie and had another horror brush with the casting couch! It was a boiling hot day in high summer and mini-skirts were in vogue – 'pussy pelmets' they used to be called. I was dressed entirely in pink, I recall. I trotted along to the Hilton in Park Lane and asked to see the director. I was sent to the penthouse suite, where a stocky American greeted me effusively. He remarked on the extreme heat, offered me some water, handed me a script and disappeared. I thought he was just leaving me in peace so that I could get acquainted with the lines, which is what I did.

I was faintly alarmed when he reappeared clad only in a white towelling robe. He came and sat next to me on the sofa. I nervously made some comments on the script and asked him which of the two parts he was considering me for. He didn't seem to think it mattered. We read the script together with him doing a passable impersonation of Presley. He seemed very pleased with my reading and asked me to do another scene. This I did to his satisfaction. He then asked me to stand up so he could see my figure. This cattle market approach was the norm in those awful days before women's liberation, sexual equality and the sexual harassment law had been put into effect. I stood up, trying to look as though I didn't care, when in fact I found the whole thing deeply humiliating.

He asked me to turn around, with my back to him. I obliged. With one swift grab, before I knew it, he had put his hand up my skirt and wrenched my pants down. I screamed out loud, out of shock and fury at the insult. I yelled abuse at him. I slung the script, which I still held in my hands, at him with considerable force. I tried to get to the door of the suite with my pants still around my ankles. I got out and slammed the door. As I paused briefly to pull up my pants, I heard him calling after me, 'Katy, Katy, come back.' I hurried down the corridor to the lift. He opened his door and peered out. 'Katy, what did I do? What did I do?' I didn't wait for the lift. I raced for the stairs and, half sobbing, tore down them. It was only when I reached the lobby that I felt safe enough to phone my agent and tell him of the debacle. His comment was 'Well, I don't think you handled it very well!'

My photo on the cover of the *TV Times* may have lost me a TV series, but it had persuaded my bank manager that I was a good risk and I was able to borrow £1,000 as the deposit for the purchase of my first house. It was a three-storey Victorian villa in Merton Park and cost £6,000! Jeremy, Dickon and I moved in. In spite of my increasing workload, money was tight. I did an episode of *Jason King*, again with Peter Wyngarde. I had always admired him as an actor and I thought he enjoyed playing opposite me. At one point during shooting, we were told to repair to our dressing-rooms as the lighting for the next set-up would take some time. To my immense surprise, Peter suddenly picked me up in his arms and carried me off to his dressing-room. Disappointingly, nothing happened!

But at home, we were struggling financially. Jeremy, who had been by far the more successful of the two of us, was now finding that work was drying up for him. Knowing him to be a brilliant director, I suggested he pursued that avenue. He did so and had enormous artistic success at the King's Head, Islington, with its opening production *The Collector*.

I was offered a horror film for Hammer, *The Vampire Lovers*. I was not keen to do it, but we desperately needed the money, so against my better judgement, I accepted. The film starred Ingrid Pitt as a Countess Dracula figure. The storyline had strong lesbian overtones, which I found slightly distasteful. I have never been able to stomach a combination of sex and violence. Fortunately, I was the only one of the array of female glamour in the movie who didn't have to do a nude scene. Thank God! We girls were automatically expected to discard our clothes at that time – it was always pointed out to us that 'Glenda had done it, so had Vanessa, even Judi! So if they would do it, why shouldn't lesser mortals such as we!' Pointless to argue that they had already established their reputations, whereas we were still struggling and nude scenes could do us nothing but harm.

Around this time came another disappointment. I had been to meet the eccentric and talented director Ken Russell, some time before, for *Women in Love*. On entering his office he looked up at me and exclaimed. 'At last, some pulchritude!' I smiled at the compliment. He turned to an acolyte sitting by his side. 'You don't know what that means, do you?' he demanded aggressively. His assistant, somewhat abashed, grinned foolishly and admitted his ignorance. Ken Russell turned to me, 'You know what it means, don't you?' 'Yes.' I replied promptly, 'beauty'. 'There, you see?' said Ken to his assistant as though the matter was settled. In spite of this display of superior knowledge on my part, he did not give me the part in his movie. That went to Jennie Linden. However, he did remember me and later offered me a part in one of his films for television on great composers. He wanted me for the one on Delius – I was devastated at not being available, Delius being one of my favourite composers and I longed to work for Ken Russell. But, I was doing a horror movie, a genre I despised.

However, George Cole and Peter Cushing were also in *The Vampire Lovers*. I was to work with both actors again, to my great delight. On the second occasion with Cushing, it was a rather bizarre movie called 'Corruption', which also featured the ebullient actor Anthony Booth, later to become the father-in-law of Tony Blair, the Prime Minister. To say that he was a character would be understating the case, but it was an enjoyable experience for all that!

It was soon after we completed filming that Peter Cushing invited me to the pictures and supper. He took me to see *Bonnie and Clyde* and then to an expensive supper afterwards. I was collected by chauffeur-driven car and delivered safely home afterwards. He behaved, as always, with the utmost charm and courtesy and as a true gentleman, kissing my hand on parting. He merely wished to share my company for an evening and show his appreciation for my being an affable and professional leading lady to him on the movie. One of the few men I was able to trust absolutely in the whole of my career.

While I was still working on *The Vampire Lovers*, I was approached by the director and script-writer Jimmy Sangster to do another 'Hammer', *The Horror of Frankenstein*, which was to star Ralph Bates as the Doctor and Dave Prowse as the monster. The latter was later to gain fame as Darth Vader in *Star Wars*. In both movies was John Finch, an extremely talented and good-looking young actor, whom I had met in Rep. years before and who, immediately after 'Frankenstein', was discovered by Roman Polanski to play the Scottish King in his film of *Macbeth*. I had the great pleasure of working with the wonderful Dennis Price in 'Frankenstein'; he was a joy. Mentioning Polanski reminds me that he invited me to tea with him at MGM Studios.

Why, I cannot fathom and unfortunately I have never worked for him. While I was up at Elstree filming, the director Douglas Camfield asked me to do *Dr Who* for him, but sadly I was unavailable. I made up for it later though by playing a Time Lord in the series.

* * *

I was back in the theatre again. The play was *The Spoils of Poynton*, an adaptation of the novel by Henry James. There were only three main characters in it: Martin Jarvis, myself and Josephine Wilson. She was the wife of Sir Bernard Miles and together, they had the remarkable achievement of getting the funding to build the marvellous Mermaid Theatre in Puddle Dock in the City of London. The American adapter of the play was, we were led to believe, a great friend of Princess Anne and indeed the furniture for the production had been loaned by Buckingham Palace. The 'author' was away in New York during rehearsals so was unaware of the somewhat drastic changes being made to the text in his absence. The director thought the piece very 'under-written' and far too short, so took the liberty of inserting great swathes of dialogue from James's novel. By this method, he added at least three quarters of an hour to the running time of the show.

I had *reams* to learn, huge, huge speeches, pages long. So did Josephine and so, indeed, did Martin, although I think Lady Miles and I came off worst. 'I'll never learn all this!' I cried to Jeremy, aghast. 'Yes you will, because I'll make sure you do,' he replied with alacrity. And to his eternal credit, he heard me perform that script, until I knew it frontwards, backwards, inside out and upside down, which was just as well, in view of what was to happen.

We were to perform for a short season at the Mayfair Theatre, which is just off Piccadilly. We arrived on the day of the dress rehearsal and duly admired the set and Princess Anne's furniture and indeed her taste, which was excellent, if a trifle baroque. As the 'spoils' of the title referred to the contents of the house, it was appropriate that the trappings should be antique and virtually priceless. We rehearsed all day, before doing a proper dress run in the evening. We broke for supper and congratulated each other on how we'd managed, all three of us, to get on top of the immense amount of dialogue that had been thrust upon us. We heard that the American adapter had arrived and was happily ensconced in the back of the stalls, in eager anticipation of seeing his 'baby' come to life on stage.

The opening music, which was 'Brigg Fair' by Delius, was, to my mind, not entirely appropriate and in any case far too well known. Anyway, it played us in and we went to it with a will. During the interval, we thought we could hear a muffled commotion over the tannoy, coming from the stalls. We took no notice and carried on with the second half. In the action of the play there had to be a huge conflagration off-stage with flickering red lights against the back-cloth, while the stage was plunged into darkness apart from a deep red glow. The music the director had chosen for this sequence was 'Mars', from Holst's 'Planet Suite'. I thought this a big mistake. We got through to the end and repaired to our dressing rooms to await the director's notes and verdict.

We then heard a noise which could only be described as cataclysmic. From the auditorium, shrieks, screams and banshee-like prolonged wails rent the air. We sat wide-eyed and silent. Plainly, a scuffle had broken out in the theatre. There were shouts, angry threats, bellows, the sound of theatre seats rising and falling abruptly. It became obvious that a chase was in progress around the auditorium. There were crashes, bangs, thumps and wallops followed by loud sobbing. Finally, there was a huge explosion and a crashing of doors. Then silence. We waited, hardly daring to breathe.

A few moments later the stage manager appeared, looking white to the gills. 'Er, ladies and gentlemen,' he said shakily, 'er, I'm afraid the show has, er well, there is a possibility there may not be a performance tomorrow night. Will you all please go home and await further instructions. Your agents will be informed as soon as a decision has been made.' He then wished us goodnight and feeling decidedly dejected and unnecessary, we made our way to our various homes in a subdued frame of mind. I got a call from Martin the next morning. 'Heard the news, dear heart?' he asked blithely. 'No, what?' I shot the words out. 'We're not doing it!' he said happily. 'Thank God!' I replied with fervour. I relaxed mentally, emotionally and physically. It was a hell of a relief, for although we knew we had got on top of the text, we weren't at all sure whether we had a play that was playable.

At teatime, I got a call from the stage-manager, asking if I could be at the Mermaid Theatre by five o'clock for a company meeting? My nerves, which had been lying dormant, suddenly leapt back into life and went into overdrive. A grim-faced little group had assembled at the Mermaid. The theatre management for our play were there, looking strained and as though they hadn't been to bed. And I daresay they hadn't. There had been, they explained, a difference of opinion which had resulted in the author's resignation. We felt this hardly adequately described the sounds of mayhem and bedlam we had heard over the tannoy the previous night, but we let it pass.

The author, they went on, had refused to have anything further to do with the production and was already on his way back to the States. They had, therefore, decided to remove his name from all the posters and go on with the show anyway. The programmes would be 'slipped'. That is to say, a sliver of paper would be inserted into each programme announcing that 'the author would like it to be known, that this is not his play in any respect and wishes to dissociate himself entirely from the production' – or words to that effect.

We arrived at the Mayfair Theatre that evening, jittery to say the least. The trouble was we had 'wound-down' and now had to 'wind-up' again. With trembling hands I started to get ready for the show. A knock at the door – and I was informed that the 'News at Ten' camera crew were in attendance outside and desirous of an interview. They asked me bluntly, live on camera, what had gone wrong. I gave as diplomatic an answer as possible, omitting to mention the display of advanced hysterics we had heard taking place. They asked me how I felt. 'Terrified' was my curt reply. No place here for false heroics, I thought.

Josephine and I were sharing a dressing-room. We went through the lines of our first interminably long scene together before curtain-up. We'd barely finished when 'beginners' was called and we went on stage to do our worst. I remember her gripping my hands tightly to reassure me – and herself! She was a darling, very beautiful and even more frightened than I was.

We were all right to start with and the first scene chugged along nicely. Then she cut two pages of dialogue. Fortunately, I knew what she'd done and joined her. Then *she* realised what she'd done and went back again. I mentally blessed Jeremy for forcing me to know this appalling script so well. She then jumped to the end of the scene. I was having none of this, and very firmly took her back to where we'd left the text. She recognised it, but dried stone dead. I tried to help her out but she'd gone. I then cut to my next huge speech where I knew I'd be on terra firma and she'd have time to get herself together. It worked. We arrived at Martin's entrance and I don't think I've ever been more relieved to see an actor wander tentatively through a French window in my life.

Things improved after that and we got through to the interval. Josephine and I were just recovering in our dressing-room, perspiring freely, when the door was flung open and Bernard Miles burst into our midst. 'What the FUCK have you done to your EYEBROWS?' he demanded explosively of his wife. Josephine, who had just survived the torments of the damned, looked bewildered and peered anxiously at the offending articles in the mirror. 'Take them off! Get rid of them!' he demanded in an overwrought way. 'Bernard,' I remonstrated, 'this is not a good moment.' 'You look ridiculous, woman!' he continued, unabashed. Josephine started dabbing at her face in desperation with some cotton wool. 'Show's going well,' he added airily and so saying, slammed out of the room. We both collapsed with relief. 'Take no notice,' I advised her. 'Your eyebrows look fine to me.' The second half passed off quite well, although the audience laughed at 'Mars' from 'The Planets' as I knew they would.

When we thankfully took our curtain calls, we looked into the auditorium which, at first glance, appeared to be half empty. The first two rows were certainly deserted; they had all been reserved for the 'author', Princess Anne and the Royal party. Naturally they'd stayed away out of loyalty and indeed gradually, during the run, items of furniture were stealthily removed and spirited back to Buck House. In spite of all these set-backs, we received some quite decent reviews. One of mine said, 'Miss O'Mara showed she possessed a rare theatrical magic.' The second night, as I was about to go on stage, Martin popped his head around our dressing-room door. 'Going to give us some of your rare theatrical magic, ducky?'. 'Piss off,' I replied.

* * *

Speaking of the Mermaid, I had seen the incomparable Eartha Kitt in a production there prior to this and now I had the opportunity to work with her. I played her assistant in an episode of *The Protectors*. She played a fading singer, as if she could ever fade! We hit it off immediately, to the extent that she wanted me to share a flat with her. In fact this never happened, but we had a great time filming together. This was the first time I worked with dear Tony Anholt, sadly now dead. We subsequently worked together again in *Triangle* and *Howard's Way*.

I went to work with Roger Moore again on *The Persuaders*, only this time I was playing opposite Tony Curtis, his co-star in the series. Tony, who was still remarkably handsome, looked at me with a mischievous twinkle in his eye. But when we came to do our big two-handed scene, he arrived on set, glanced briefly at his script, then threw it across the room, saying he wasn't going to say 'any of that crap!'. I had learnt my lines very thoroughly, so was somewhat dismayed at this dismissive statement. Thereupon, we proceeded to improvise the scene, which, as I was playing with a Swiss accent, was not that easy. It also meant that we had no close-ups, but everything had to be shot in close two-shot. This was quite tricky and afterwards, the director, a lovely man of the old school, murmured to me in an undertone, 'Now you know why I asked for you!'

I was sent to meet the legendary musical comedy genius Gene Kelly, for a movie he was doing in London. He seemed quite small, half-hidden behind an enormous desk in a large office. I was disappointed to see he was not wearing his toupee and consequently was quite bald. He greeted me with the words, 'So you're O'Mara?' pronouncing the name the American way. I corrected him. 'O'Mara,' I said. 'Is that so? You've got naughty eyes, O'Mara!' We chatted happily for a while exchanging banter, but I didn't get the part. Then I met Betty Box and Ralph Thomas for a movie about Lord Byron. Peter Finch was cast as Byron with Michael York as Shelley. I was offered the part of Byron's half-sister, Augusta Leigh. I accepted immediately, but the film never got made.

* * *

So back I went to the theatre: a stage version of *The Avengers* with Simon Oates playing John Steed and Sue Lloyd as Hannah Wilde, the Emma Peel of the piece. I played the villainess Gerda Von Metz, a German/Swede! Jeremy Lloyd played an assortment of chinless wonders – brilliantly. It was a very witty, clever show, but too ambitious by half. We opened at The New Theatre in Birmingham, variously re-named as the Hippodrome and I believe now the Birmingham Theatre. The play was directed by Leslie Phillips, famous for his most wonderful comedic performances in British movies, always playing the charming cad. It was a rambling production, lurching from one special effect to the next, which was a pity as the concept and script were brilliant.

In my first big scene, Gerda had somehow managed to get into Steed's apartment. On stage, in the order named, were a Trick Sofa, a Large Egyptian Mummy Case with a Secret door at the back, an Umbrella (which when opened, produced a Sword) and an Elasticated Wall! When left alone on stage, I had to play around with the umbrella, opening and shutting it. I then had to sit on the sofa, tucking my legs underneath me, open the umbrella and with one hand release the safety catch down the side of the sofa. The seat of the sofa would then tip inwards and I would disappear into its inners, leaving the umbrella behind rolling around on its own. At least that's what was *supposed* to happen.

Unfortunately, the safety catch or spring or whatever it was, would often be released accidentally by other actors in the scene prior to this and, one by one, they would disappear from view only to emerge from behind the sofa, thus giving the game away. Sometimes, they wouldn't manage to disappear completely, but would be stuck halfway and be forced to play the scene with their knees under their chin, as they were half-way through the sofa so to speak. Sometimes the umbrella would jam. Improvise your way out of that one!

At one performance, I had hidden myself in the mummy case and was supposed to make a get-away through the secret door. Meanwhile, Steed was advancing on the case with a drawn sword, which he would plunge into the closed case. This particular night, some bright stage-hand had decided to lock the door from the outside. There was no way I could escape and the sword was coming nearer and nearer! Fortunately, Simon realised what was happening, due possibly to the agitated rocking of the mummy case and cheated the plunging of the sword.

As for the elasticated wall! Steed was supposed to back me up against it, then I had to push myself forcibly through the incredibly taut sections of extremely strong elastic, which were each about a foot wide. They were so tough that as I tried to get through, they would push me out again and I would rebound into his arms! We had back-projection in one scene which occasionally was just that! It ran backwards – more tortured improvisation!

My final exit from the play was by helicopter ladder. It was made of some sort of plastic and was flown from a bar, thirty feet up above the stage. I had to climb up it, wave to the assembly below and then be hoisted up out of sight by a counter-weight system. On the first night in Birmingham, I had just disappeared into the 'flies' when the ladder broke and dumped me centre stage. It was a fall of thirty feet and I was badly bruised, though otherwise unharmed. After that, I refused to go up without a safety harness attached to me! When we came to London to the Prince of Wales Theatre, I used to hang up there for what seemed like hours, right up in the flies, not daring to look down, swaying gently backwards and forwards. Thankfully, the show only ran for three months.

*   *   *

Jeremy, by now, was directing full-time and although we tried to make things work for Dickon's sake, I know he didn't take kindly to my being more successful and earning more money than him. I think most men find it difficult. Anyway, he cast me in a 'fringe' production of *Funeral Games* by Joe Orton in 1971. I was thrilled, but then I was asked to do an episode of *Jason King*. Jeremy insisted that I did it as we needed the money. I was desperately disappointed. One of our closest friends, Sarah Atkinson, did the Orton instead. So off I went to Elstree.

I was cast as a South American beauty who was a guerrilla!

We were filming in the underground car-park at Elstree Studios, pretending we were in Buenos Aires and it was June. In fact, it was January and we were freezing. There were three of us crouching down, one behind the other, guns at the ready. I was in front, behind me was the actor Maurice Roeves, and behind him was Peter. We were waiting for the director to call 'action', but things kept getting delayed. To alleviate the tedium, Peter suddenly said conversationally, 'Maurice Reeves, I'd like to fuck the arse off you.' 'It's Roeves,' replied Maurice blandly.

I finished the episode and to my great delight, Sarah was cast in the following week's episode of *Jason King*, so I was able to take over from her in the Orton at The Basement Theatre, in Greek Street! I next found myself at Sadlers Wells doing an adaptation of a story by Oscar Wilde, *Lord Arthur Seville's Crime*' a hybrid piece which, although entertaining as an amusing tale, doesn't really work as a play, largely because it doesn't have Oscar's brilliant dialogue. I was cast as the juvenile in this piece, even though I was over thirty, simply because everyone else in the cast was so old, with the exception of Peter Green who was playing opposite me and Bill Kerr, of *Hancock's Half Hour* fame, who was cast as the incendiary anarchist. Jack Hulbert, who was playing my uncle, was in fact old enough to be my great-grandfather. Mervyn Johns, father of Glynis, was also in the cast and, best of all, wonderfully energetic Elsie Randolph, who had been Jack Buchanan's leading lady in the twenties. She was a joy and although well into her eighties, kept on breaking into a tap routine at odd moments during rehearsals!

At any given time during the day while Peter or Bill and I were rehearsing a scene, we would glance around to see who was coming on next and in every corner of the room, there would be an antique person, sound asleep! When it was Jack Hulbert's turn to come on, he would start up suddenly saying, 'Oh dear, is it me?' searching around for a missing prop, such as an umbrella or shooting-stick, 'Terribly sorry everyone, dear me, so sorry,' and would continue to mumble, throughout the scene pretending he didn't know his lines. This bumbling continued right up to the first night and Peter Green and I were getting seriously worried about him. We needn't have been. Jack was totally on top of the situation, no nerves, on cue and word perfect! After the show I went along to Jack's dressing-room with a little gift. He opened the door to me. 'Hello, Jack', I said, 'I've brought you something.' 'Who are you?' he demanded peremptorily. 'I'm Kate, I play your niece, Sybil, in the show,' I explained. 'Oh, do you? Oh, yes, so you do – you sure?' I gave up after that. His wife and stage partner of many years, Cicely Courtneidge arrived to see a matinee; she was charming but terrifying.

Around that time I was called to meet Steve McQueen for a part in a movie he was doing about racing drivers. It was in the late afternoon, so I had to pick my son up from school on the way there and take him with me to the interview. We sat in an outer office for some time, then a secretary emerged, took one look at Dickon and asked, 'Is this yours?' 'Yes,' I replied. 'This is my son.' She cut me short. 'Oh, no sorry, Mr McQueen won't be seeing you,' and showed us both out. No comment! I went on to do an episode of *Never a Cross Word*, a husband and wife comedy series starring Paul Daneman and Barbara Murray. I played his secretary and although we got on well, there was no hint of the turmoil he was to cause later in my life.

I went to meet Anthony Quayle who was directing *Harvey*, starring James Stewart, the Hollywood legend, but although

Tony said my cheek-bones reminded him of a South American woman he'd once been in love with, I didn't get that part either. Too 'exotic' again, but Tony remembered me and gave me a job seventeen years later!

Then followed a nine-month stint in the West End in *Suddenly At Home*, at the Fortune Theatre. This was a piece by Francis Durbridge which we rather uncharitably re-named *Gradually On Stage*. It was one of those thrillers where the audience has to work out not only who dunnit, but why they dunnit. I thought that I'd dunnit for some time, until somebody pointed out to me that I'd only partly dunnit.

I was in another Durbridge some years later and was equally baffled. It was during the run of this play that the first amazing pictures of the earth, as seen from space, were sent back and published on the front page of every newspaper. We gazed in awe and amazement and wondered how it was possible that somewhere in the middle of this lustrous silver globe, every night, we were standing in the wings waiting to go on and wow an ever-expectant audience. It somehow put it all into perspective. I shared a dressing-room with the actress Patricia Shakesby, who has become my lifelong chum and without whom, I seriously wonder whether I would be here to tell this tale.

* * *

By now my marriage was in tatters. I don't think I'm cut out for long-term relationships. I am not naturally an affectionate or tactile person and most particularly, I don't like being told what to do. I like to be boss. Nor do I do the housewifely things women are traditionally supposed to do. I don't mind cooking or housework, but I expect the male members of the household to do their share and the man has not been born for whom I will iron a shirt. None of this has gone down at all well with the men in my life. The trouble is they don't think I'm serious and hope that eventually I'll settle down and knuckle under. Quite the reverse. I become more and more mutinous. I insist on being independent, living my own life. I don't like to have to ask a man for anything, least of all money. I hate being bought a meal. I'd rather go Dutch, or pay for us both.

I think I was one of the first truly liberated women, but my husband did not want me to be so. Things were getting really bad between us. He had taken my cheque book and hidden my car. I had to ask him for money for everything. I felt helpless. I knew that my son was suffering too. I thought Jeremy too harsh and severe a father. I remember thinking that the bars at the windows in our house were like prison bars, or a cage.

It was at this point that I suddenly got the part of an Italian Contessa in *Spytrap*, the BBC's all-male series set in the cold war, with a lot of stiff upper-lip and repressed emotion, when Russia was still the enemy. It starred Paul Daneman as Commander Ryan (something in MI5) and I was cast as his love-interest. Although we had met previously in *Never a Cross Word*, when I had played his secretary, he behaved quite differently towards me this time. During rehearsals he pursued me relentlessly. I had a failing marriage and enough trouble at home; I was desperately unhappy, worried that my son was unhappy too and I simply did not want to become involved. I rebuffed all Paul's advances. I suppose in hindsight, this only made the chase more attractive to him. The series was rehearsed in London at the 'Acton Hilton', as we all affectionately called the BBC Rehearsal Rooms, but was recorded in Birmingham at Pebble Mill.

The night before the studio day, Paul insisted on taking me out to supper. He inferred it was his duty as leading-man in the series. I succumbed and over dinner he voiced his intentions towards me. I told him, frankly, that it was a very bad idea, as my marriage was falling apart and I didn't think an imbroglio could possibly help. He countered by telling me that he and his wife had an 'understanding', as their relationship was non-physical and had been for some time. I later discovered that this was a total untruth. I suppose I was gullible and should have known that men always say that their wives 'don't understand them', but of course I was flattered and he was undeniably attractive and charming and after the appalling treatment I was getting at home, it was a brief moment of sanctuary and escape. Little did I know that it would be four years before we were free of each other, that it would almost break up his marriage. The truth of the matter is that, overnight, I fell head over heels in love with him and if his letters are anything to go by, so did he with me.

Spytrap continued for some time. I was not in every episode, but they were spread out and we continued our affair in secret. In 1964 we went to the Bristol Old Vic together to do Noel Coward's *Blithe Spirit*. Naturally Paul's wife came to see it and I had to keep out of the way. Not at all pleasant. Then Cameron Mackintosh, who at that time shared my agent's office and was trying to get his then fledgling company off the ground, had a brilliant idea. Being appraised of the situation between Paul and me, he suggested we tour together in *Private Lives*, which was playing triumphantly on Shaftesbury Avenue, with Robert Stephens and Maggie Smith. It was all set up, dates were booked and then it was decided that the West End production should transfer to Broadway, scenery and all.

Another play had therefore to be found and fast. A simply frightful piece called *Bell, Book and Candle* was chosen and a load of tosh it was too. This was the play on which the TV series *Bewitched* was based. I hate performing in inferior plays. I always feel the audience is being cheated and after *Private Lives* it was a terrible anti-climax. Anyway, Cameron seemed pleased and it's nice to know that I helped him get started. Mind you, he has not offered me a job since!

I think it was after the tour finished that Paul's wife found out. It was all terrible. He ditched me immediately and tried to rescue his marriage. She very cleverly departed for Australia and he, of course, at once followed.

* * *

Then I was cast as another Russian in *The Tamarind Seed*, starring Julie Andrews and Omar Sharif and to be directed by Julie's husband, Blake Edwards. My old mate Sylvia Syms was also in the movie, as was George Mikell and Oscar Homolka. I was playing Omar Sharif's secretary and we had quite a few laughs on set. Blake Edwards, as is to be expected from the man who directed all the Inspector Clouseau movies, had the most wonderful sense of humour, so the atmosphere on the set was always most enjoyable.

The entire unit was put up at the Hilton (yet again!) in Paris, which had a fantastic view of the Eiffel Tower. However, the film company only paid for bed and breakfast, as lunch was provided on set and in any case, we were given per diems (daily expenses) to enable us to eat! In spite of this, we discovered that eating out was so expensive that it was really beyond our slender means. I remember one of the stunt boys on the movie saying nonchalantly, as we were sitting on the terrace of the Hilton sipping citron pressé, 'Well, I fink I'll just go and flog the car, then we can all go and get some nosh!'

We were shooting in a beautiful old Embassy building in the heart of Paris, with a sweeping staircase, marble pillars and tiled floors. I had been there about a week. I was only playing a small part and was due to finish the next day, when I received an invitation, via the production office, to accompany Mr Sharif at supper that evening after filming. Actually, it wasn't so much an invitation, more a royal command. Although I found him courteous and charming, I didn't want to find myself in another compromising situation. I said so unequivocally. I was instantly reassured that I would be a member of a party, but Mr Sharif's personal guest. So far so good. Thanking my lucky stars that I'd brought my Ossie Clark outfit with me, I got myself ready after shooting had finished for the day.

A huge chauffeur-driven limousine picked me up and whisked me off to Neuilly, a rich and fashionable district of Paris. Inside Omar's flat the rest of the party were admiring his many bridge trophies. We were given cocktails and after being shown round the apartment (the walls of which were all covered in carpet!), we set off for Maxims, the world famous Paris restaurant. I should mention at this juncture that Omar was suffering from flu and was taking medication. Feeling pretty rough, he ordered numerous drinks and wine for the party. This mixture cannot have done him any good at all and by the time we left Maxims, he was not at all well. Unwisely, he then took us all

77

off to a famous Paris night club, where I met up again with Roman Polanski and had the extreme pleasure of meeting Catherine Deneuve, a most beautiful and charming woman, and Romy Schneider, who was delightful.

Omar wanted to dance, although frankly he was not well enough to even attempt it. He asked me most politely if I would do him the honour. I pointed to several extremely attractive blondes who were hanging around expectantly, but he would have none of them and insisted on dragging me onto the dance floor. There I found myself the centre of attention, simply because I was dancing with him. On our return to our table, I saw to my dismay that our 'party' had disappeared. We left the night club soon after and were besieged by the paparazzi. Omar immediately put his arm around me for their benefit, so that my chum, Alexandra Bastedo, was astonished to find, on opening a magazine on a beach in Spain a few days later, a huge photo of Omar Sharif and Kate O'Mara with the headline – 'Is this the new woman in Omar's life?' Well, I wasn't!

*   *   *

In 1978 I had the opportunity of working with Leonard Rossiter, a wonderfully eccentric actor who, for all his playing of off-the-wall wimps, was one of the most physically fit of men and much sought after by the ladies. He was incredibly serious on set, almost morose. I found George Cole the same. It's odd that both men, who created such wonderfully entertaining characters as 'Rigsby' and 'Arthur Daley' and whose ability to make us laugh is inexhaustible, should be men full of angst. It was a play for television filmed entirely on location in and around Bristol called *Machine Gunner*. I had another nude bed scene in it, with Colin Welland! This was before his enormous triumph with *Chariots of Fire*.

Needless to say, I had heard regularly from Daneman, even while he was in Australia. He seemed completely unable to make up his mind which of us he wanted to be with. My divorce proceedings had got under way, but because they were contested, it was going to be a long drawn-out battle. As with any parting, there was much emotional trauma.

I had auditioned for the American director Charles Marowitz, who had first come to prominence as Peter Brook's assistant. He made me do 'Katerina's' last speech from 'The Shrew', but with variations, first as a schoolgirl who'd been caught playing truant, then as a whore touting for trade, then as a cook giving a demonstration on television of how to make a sponge cake! Then I had to swap 'characters' every time he clicked his fingers. It was an horrendously difficult exercise and I wasn't at all sure that I'd pulled it off. But I can't have done too badly since he cast me in a play at the Open Space Theatre, a very high-profile and well-thought of fringe theatre just off the Tottenham Court Road. It was a very bizarre piece called *Sherlock's Last Case*, based on Conan Doyle's characters and I'm not at all sure that the villain didn't turn out to be Dr Watson! He was played by Peter Bayliss in his own eccentric, brilliant way and Julian Glover was a splendid Holmes. I played Moriarty's daughter, who had returned to avenge her father's death! There was only one dressing-room at the Open Space, so men and women had to share. I remember Peter being furious and insisting on hanging an article of clothing on a line to partition we women off!

About this time I made a strange film called *Whose Child am I?'* about artificial insemination. Also in it with me were Paul Freeman, Edward Judd and Bob Sherman. I had a lot of nude love scenes to do, not very enjoyable. It's odd having to do simulated sex scenes at eight o'clock in the morning, piling into bed with someone you've just been introduced to. The director says 'Action' and off you go, making it up as you go and hoping for the best! Daneman visited the set, which didn't help!

It was while I was in this play that my agent had a telegram which threw his office into turmoil for a few days. It read: 'Send photos O'Mara re Burton picture – urgent.' We felt that I didn't have anything in my portfolio that was up to Elizabeth Taylor standard, so I had some excessively glamorous photos taken. They were sent off and went down a storm. I was invited over to Los Angeles to test. Being in *Sherlock's Last Case*, I couldn't go. Thus I missed my first chance to go to Hollywood!

* * *

By the time I left home, I was anxious and losing weight. Dickon was all that was keeping me going. My agent told me they were looking for two new girls for *The Brothers*, which in 1974 was the most popular TV series. 'They want a tall blonde to play a woman who runs an air-freight firm and an ordinary brunette to play a secretary, so you fall between two stools,' he informed me. 'Oh, so why are you ringing me?' I said rather sourly. 'Well, actually they want to see you so you might as well go along,' he replied nonchalantly, obviously having given up on me. I duly turned up at the BBC only to see Patricia Haines, Michael Caine's first wife, just leaving. 'Bugger,' I thought, 'she's tall and blonde. Oh, well, what the hell.'

I strode into the producer's office aggressively, for I was past caring about anything. 'Would you like to see a script?' Ken Riddington asked amiably. 'If you like, yes, I may as well,' I replied carelessly. He passed the character's first episode across to me. I flicked through it – it was perfect. I could play it standing on my head. 'Yep, I can play that,' I said tossing it down on the desk and then realising what I was doing, I picked it up again. 'Oh, sorry, would you like me to read it for you?' I asked without much enthusiasm. 'Oh no, no, that won't be necessary, er, just a minute, I want to fetch someone,' and he loped out of the room and I heard him running down the corridor. Out of curiosity, I picked the script up again and liked what I saw.

Ken returned in minutes with another tall man, Bill Slater, the overall series producer, who was looking expectant. I rose to my feet. I had put on high heels and had my hair piled on top of my head in an effort to make myself look taller. 'How tall are you?' asked Ken, suddenly worried. Ah, I thought, I've come prepared for that. I delved into my bag and produced some stills. 'Not as tall as you'd like, I daresay, but these are pictures of me with tall actors, see?' I held out photos of me with Peter O'Toole, Roger Moore and Richard Johnson. 'And I could wear heels all the time,' I added helpfully. They were both gazing at me, riveted. 'What do you think of the part?' asked Bill Slater anxiously. 'Right up my street,' I replied briefly. 'Good, good,' both said. 'We'll have to try her in a blonde wig,' said Ken to Bill. Bill agreed. 'What do you look like as a blonde?' asked Ken. 'Extraordinary,' I said tersely. Still they were not deterred. 'Right' said Ken, 'we'll sort something out.' Bill nodded his enthusiastic agreement.

I left, feeling I'd done well, but not sure why. I realised later that unwittingly, I'd been behaving exactly as the character behaved, even to the body language. In the series, the character, Jane Maxwell, was divorced from her husband, but still living with him, unhappily. They must have picked up on this, as I was making no attempt to hide it from them. I got the part. I had to go up to Birmingham (Brum again!) and have a long blonde wig put on me. Both Ken and Bill were summoned. They gazed at me in the mirror. 'She looks like a Venusian,' observed Ken firmly. 'It's Dr.Who' – no, she looks better her own colour, okay, so be it,' he said to the make-up supervisor. He turned back to me. 'You smoke, don't you?' 'No, I never have,' I said frankly. 'Would you be prepared to for the series?' he pressed. 'I'd rather not,' I replied, 'it's a bit obvious, isn't it?' They both agreed that it was indeed obvious.

At that point, various members of the cast came into the make-up room and looked curiously at me. I'd never seen a single episode, so I had no idea who anyone was. However, they were all delightfully welcoming. Margaret Ashcroft, one of the regulars with whom I'd worked on *The Main Chance*, appeared and I was glad to see a familiar face. I was more than fortunate in the costume designer. He was nothing short of brilliant. He put me into tight men's denim jeans and jacket covered in army badges. On top of this I wore an American baseball jacket and cap. My hair was tied back for my first scene, which was shot at Lydd Airfield in Kent. Thus clad, my tiny figure was seen flagging down a Dakota onto the runway, with those sort of ping-pong bats. I must say, I was fairly apprehensive as this huge aircraft lumbered nearer and nearer towards me. 'I hope to God it stops,' I thought to myself. I then realised it was up to me to make sure it did!

For my first studio scene, I wore my hair loose and my opening lines were 'What the hell are you doing here? Get out of my office or I'll call the Police!' They were great lines for a first entrance and I was lucky, because the director was the dearest of men, one of the old school, Vere Lorrimer, eternally affable and complimentary. He always entered into the spirit of a scene and pretended he was the audience and did their reactions. He gave me plenty of camera coverage. When the episode was shown on my first Sunday to a captive audience, I was an overnight success! At 36, I'd finally cracked it!

3

'We *must have* Kate O'Mara!'

The Brothers changed my life in every possible way. I was able to open my own bank account, independently of Jeremy. I sued him for divorce. Dickon and I moved into a little cottage overlooking The Green at Twickenham. We were sublimely happy there. I had no idea of the impact my appearance in the series was going to make. So far as I was concerned it was just another job, admittedly it was a humdinger of a part, but I insisted on playing it my way. Instead of a hard-drinking, feisty, smoking, tough cookie, she became a teetotal, non-smoking vegetarian! And somehow it worked. The script writers wrote for my personality and I played it to the hilt! I was tough and uncompromising, and made no attempt to play for sympathy. As Jane Maxwell I became the girl everyone loved to hate.

Her greatest redeeming feature was her sense of humour. She was witty and dry and had a great sense of fun. Because the part had orginally been written for a man, I was allowed to be articulate, powerful *but* glamorous as well. I am sure that my success in the role came from the fact that Jane represented the 'new woman', emancipated, successful in a man's world, doing a man's job and doing it well. Able to meet men on their own terms yet in no way sacrificing her femininity. Many women identified with her. It has often occurred to me that to be successful in this profession, one has to appeal equally to both men and women and to homosexuals of both sexes. I think I may have an inherent butchness about me that appeals to women, yet my 'glamour girl' image is attractive to men and I have quite consciously tried to nurture these different sides of my personality. Whatever it is, or was, it worked and I had a huge success in the series. *The Brothers* was one of the great drama series of all time. A family business saga, it had all the elements that made it irresistible to the captive audience at 7.30 on a Sunday evening – prime time for television in those days.

*   *   *

Paul Daneman returned from Australia and came back into my life. But of course, I was up to my eyes in filming and recording and it became increasingly difficult to see him. To my immense surprise and I have to say dismay, one evening, Paul turned up on my doorstep, surrounded by suitcases and announced that he'd left his wife and was moving in with me. He had brought a car-load of books with him! I was fairly alarmed, as I'd just managed to establish a nice routine of somehow getting my son off to school, turning up at rehearsals on time and finding someone to look after him, when I was up in Birmingham where the series was recorded. But it was working out very nicely and to suddenly have a live-in lover thrown into the equation was not entirely welcome. However, I made the best of it and took him in. I suspected that, rather than leaving his wife, she'd thrown him out! He, at the time, was on tour with Margaret Lockwood in a play called *Double Edge*. It was a three-handed thriller and was due to open shortly in the West End. So, he would spend the days in my little cottage and then go off at night to do the show. I was in the middle of a pre-filming block for *The Brothers*, which did not involve me everyday, so we saw something of each other.

It was exactly a fortnight to the day since Paul had moved in. I had been filming all day down at Lydd Airfield in Kent and had left Paul to give Dickon his supper and await my return. I knew that I would just make it back in time before he had to go to the theatre. I dashed home and flung myself into the cottage. My son was sitting by himself reading a book. He had not, it appeared, been given supper. I was furious at this neglect and went

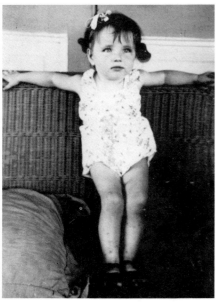

Above: My first nude scene.

Top left: T.E. Evans, the first actor in the family. A great friend of Charles Dickens.

Centre: A born poseur.

Below: Belinda and me: looking after my little sister.

(Author's private collection)

Left: Me and my Nanny, Victoria, whom you can see I worshipped.

Centre: My hairstyle seems to have changed little in the last 60 years!

Below: 'Paradise House', our home in Trinidad. My mother is standing in the porch.

(Author's private collection)

(Author's private collection)

Above: Dickon and I recreating *The Boyhood of Raleigh* for the Press!

Centre: A recent shot of Dickon.

Left: Dickon in his stage debut in *The School for Wives* by Molière at the Watermill Theatre.

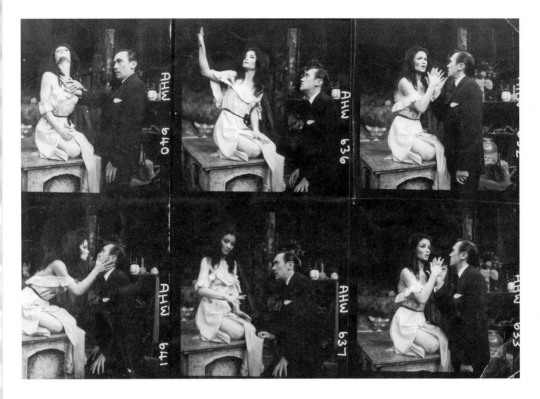

Above: Attempting to seduce Richard Pasco in *The Italian Girl* at Wyndhams Theatre, London 1968. (Anthony Crickmay)

Below left: As Lydia Languish in *The Rivals*. (North Wales Press Agency)

Below right: Harry H. Corbett reluctantly prepares for action in *Rattle of a Simple Man.* (Author's private collection)

Clockwise from top left: Titania and Oberon in *A Midsummer Night's Dream*. With Christopher Neame (Open Air Theatre, 1982) (author's private collection); Kenneth Gilbert, me and Mark Noble in *Twelfth Night* (Dennis H. Freeman); the number with 'The Boys' in *The Sleeping Beauty* (Kevin Wood Productions); taken at the dress rehearsal of *On Approval*, having just seen my son on the road to recovery after being on a life support system (John Haynes); my first panto (Kevin Wood Productions).

Clockwise from left: Ian McCulloch and me in *Macbeth* (author's private collection); a very camp fiftieth birthday shot (Joe Bangay); in rehearsal for *The Relapse* with Richard Heffer at *The Mermaid.*

(Richard Heffer)

immediately to the kitchen to remedy the situation. There was a letter propped up on the work-top for me. I snatched it up and read the contents with trembling fingers. It was from Paul explaining that he was horrified at what he was doing, and he had a wife and two children to think of whom he had to put first. So he was returning home and hoped that, in time, I would forgive him. I tore the letter into several pieces, then gave my son his supper and put him to bed. I always used to read Dickon a bedtime story every night and this was to be no exception. This routine event helped calm me and steady my nerves, which were in tatters. I regretted having torn the note up, so I stuck it back together with cellotape. I then rang my dear friend and confidante, Patricia.

'Listen to this load of old rubbish!' I snorted derisively over the phone. She was aghast and said she was coming over straight away. We both agreed over supper and cocoa, that it was good riddance to bad rubbish. She stayed with me until about 10.45 when, with many injunctions to put it down to experience and get on with life, she left me to my own tangled emotions. I had hardly closed the front door when she banged on it, demanding admittance. Thinking she'd left something behind, I opened it. She hurtled in, slamming the door behind her and leaning against it as though to keep some unwelcome spirit out.

'He's here!' she announced in dramatic tones. 'Who's here?' I demanded uncomprehending. 'Paul! He's outside on the pavement.' 'What!?' 'Yes,' she repeated in an agitated voice. 'He's here, outside. I've sent him away!' 'Good! Thank God for that.' Then, out of curiosity, I asked 'What did you say?' She said, 'I said, Paul, what are you doing here? Kate doesn't want to see you, so please go away.' 'Very good,' I said, 'and what did he say to that?' 'That there was no law that said he couldn't stand outside your house and just look.' 'Yes, there is,' I rejoined. 'It's called "loitering with intent".' We both laughed and she said she wouldn't leave until he'd gone. We crept upstairs to my bedroom, which looked out over the Green. 'Don't turn on the lights,' she urged in a conspiratorial whisper, 'or he'll see us.' We peered out of the darkness of the room. It was late October and we could see him standing by the lamp-post, eerily lit by its glow. He was gazing up at the house. 'He's gone potty,' Patricia observed succinctly. I was inclined to agree with her. He kept up his vigil for about twenty minutes before making his way to his car, which he had parked further up by the side of the Green. It was a white MG sports car, so it was easy to spot. With one last look back, he got into his car and drove off into the night.

After the excitement of the night, the next day seemed cheerless and I'll admit that I was deeply unhappy. My son was upset at Paul's disappearance, as he had, unfortunately, grown fond of him. It was hard to comfort him when I was so upset myself. After I had tucked Dickon up, I spent the evening quietly crying in the kitchen. A pointless, futile exercise. But maybe I needed to release my pent-up emotions of fury and hurt at the betrayal. Worn out, I decided to go to bed early and went to the window to open it slightly. To my amazement, I saw the white MG pull up by the side of the Green. I switched off the light and immediately phoned Patricia to report.

We both suddenly remembered that Paul was playing the Richmond Theatre that week, immediately prior to opening in the West End. He had moved, with his wife, to Barnes on their return from Australia in an attempt to start their life together afresh. Twickenham is not far from Richmond and he had taken this rather circuitous route on his way home. The same thing happened on the next two nights. Patricia and I decided to make an evening of it on each occasion. She would come round at about 10.30 and I would make cocoa for us both, then we would sit in my bedroom with the lights turned out and watch with interest this strange little nightly vigil taking place.

On the following night, however, there was a noise at the door and a letter plopped onto the mat. I read its contents with a jaundiced eye. Apparently, Paul had decided that he couldn't live without me, that he was horrified at the pain he must have caused me, that all other women seemed grey beside me and could I possibly see him the next night after the two Saturday shows at Richmond? Could I forgive him, could we at least talk about it? Would I ring the Stage Door at Richmond to let him know? I rang and said, very briefly, that yes, I would meet him. He was incoherent with gratitude. I slammed down the receiver and thought hard. Naturally, I told Patricia what had happened. 'What are you going to do, you're surely not going to see him are you?' 'Only to tell him to bugger off,' I replied shortly.

Saturday came. I was beside myself with anger at his thoughtless, juvenile behaviour. Sometime that evening I rang his home and spoke to his wife. My words, I recall, were something along the lines of, 'You don't want to talk to me, but you have to. Your husband has been pestering me, by sitting outside my house every night this week. I've agreed to meet him tonight and I want you to know that I'm going to send him straight home to you.' She said, 'But Kate, when he left me to come to you, he spent every night sitting outside *my* house looking up at it.' That took the wind out of my sails! 'Oh, for heaven's sake!' I said impatiently, 'What are we to do?' 'I don't know, do you want him?' 'I don't know, do you?' I countered. We agreed that I should proceed as I had said and then see what happened.

At 10.45 p.m. on the dot, the MG pulled up on the Green. As Paul got out and walked towards the cottage, I came out to intercept him. We met on the Green. He held out his arms towards me. 'My darling,' he began. I cut him short. 'Paul, before you say anything, I think I should tell you that I've spoken to your wife and she's expecting you home any moment.' His face was a study! So saying, I turned on my heel and went back indoors, locking the door behind me. I have to say, I was shaking. The upshot of all of this, was that his wife turned him out of the house. I had turned him out, so he was obliged to go to live in the flat his mother had owned. She had died not long before all of this had happened and the property had not been disposed of. This state of affairs lasted some six months, with him trying each of us in turn to persuade us to take him back. But we both remained adamant. He would come to see me on a regular basis, when we would meet in a local pub to talk things over, as I didn't want my son upset any further. At one of these meetings, he told me he had been asked to play 'Macbeth' and he was going to find out if I could play Lady Macbeth opposite him. Needless to say, this was just a ploy to get back with me and he reneged on this promise too. His leading lady turned out to be Dorothy Tutin.

*　*　*

In the meantime, I was going from strength to strength in *The Brothers*. I received sack-loads of fan-mail and numerous articles were written about me. I modelled for fashion shoots and was interviewed by every woman's magazine going. The series was enormously popular abroad, particularly in Scandinavia and the Netherlands. The whole cast went over *en masse* for publicity promotions to cities such as like Amsterdam, Helsinki and Stockholm. I could not believe my first visit to Amsterdam. The crowds that greeted our arrival were in the size usually reserved for pop stars. I have to say I was over-awed and a little dazed by it all.

Very sadly, the actor playing my ex-husband in the series, Mike Pratt, a hell-raiser of the old school and a lovely man, had died of cancer a few weeks before this. He was only 45 and we all missed his reassuring presence enormously. He had always told me, 'Kate, don't fight life so hard. Accept, just accept.' I used to say, 'But Mike, I *have* to fight, I have to survive somehow.' But he would shake his head and smile and repeat 'You have to learn to accept.' It's taken me nearly 30 years, but I think I now finally understand what he was going on about. God rest his soul.

*　*　*

My second series of *The Brothers* in 1976 proved to be an even bigger triumph than the previous one. We had become a cult! Now I was getting demands for public appearances on my own, both in Britain and abroad. I was asked to go to Finland for Midsummer's Eve, when the sun never sets. They would pay all my expenses and a huge fee just for me to make an appearance at some festival in Tampe. First I had to go to Enskede, which was on the German border. I arrived on a huge, new truck, which had been specially ordered for the occasion. I was sitting high up in the cab and there were hundreds and hundreds of people below me. I felt like Cleopatra entering Rome! I was taken into outlying villages and paraded along the streets, which were thronged with hundreds of people kept back by barricades. They all waved and cheered. Young men yelled out to me that they wanted to marry me. The whole royal progress (for that's what it felt like) was filmed and seemed quite surreal.

On another visit, I was taken by an amphibious 'plane and we landed on one of the many lakes with which Finland is peppered. It was a medieval castle on the shores of the Baltic Sea and I didn't get there until 3 a.m. in the morning. I had had nothing to eat for ages and was delighted to find a breakfast waiting for me in my turreted room, of a cold soft-boiled egg and crisp bread and cheese. Delicious! On this occasion I had the unnerving experience of being mobbed. I had no protection against the hundreds of people who had turned out to greet me. They thronged around me and started to pull at my clothes and my hair. My top got ripped. I thrust my way through them and tried to make a break for it. They continued to pursue me. I started to run, they ran too, I put on a burst of speed and managed to gain the pavilion (where I was due to speak to them all) before they did! It was quite frightening.

On my way back by car to the hotel where I was to spend the night before returning to England, I was amazed to see small children lying by the side of the road and, in some cases, in it, all apparently asleep. What on earth had happened? I demanded of my Finnish escort. He explained that they were drunk. I couldn't believe my ears, but apparently it was true. Needless to say, I was horrified, and highly critical of a society that allowed such things. He merely shrugged his shoulders and said that it was the norm for this remote rural area of Finland. I arrived at my destination in a very subdued frame of mind.

One of the most fascinating aspects of my job, is getting to see and meet people in their own countries in ways not available to an ordinary tourist. I have thus met and worked with people in Yugoslavia, Morocco, Spain, Jordan, France, Italy, Sweden, Malta, Israel, Lithuania, Cyprus and the Netherlands, as well as Finland, and I count myself very fortunate in this respect. Sadly, I have come across distressing incidents, as this one of the

Finnish children, as well as evidence of the unpleasant subjugation of women in other countries.

After filming on my second series of *The Brothers*, we had no idea whether or not we would be engaged for another run. Our viewing figures were 18 million, making it the most watched series of all time but they took it off at the height of its popularity. To this day, people remember it with affection and lament its passing.

* * *

There were many spin-offs from my success in *The Brothers*, not least a movie I made in and around Helsinki, Morocco and Lapland. It was made in Finnish with me playing an American. Everyone in the film spoke their parts in Finnish except for me. I did mine in English but, of course, I had to learn Finnish so that I knew when my cues came! Likewise the Finnish actors had to learn their cues in English. My lines were dubbed into Finnish for the Finnish cinema. Their dialogue was dubbed into American English for release over here. I even recorded the title song, which became a No.1 hit! But only in Finland! We went to Morocco on location. Being able to speak French was both a help and a hindrance. Translating from Finnish into French and vice versa was not easy!

Two really marvellous things came from *The Brothers*. I received what at that time was the ultimate accolade. I was asked to be a guest on the Morecambe and Wise Christmas Show in 1976. I played Mata Hari, the Dutch spy and courtesan, and I need hardly tell you that my victim in the seduction stakes was Eric. Working with them was an eye-opener. I have never seen anyone work so hard as he and Ernie. They never stopped rehearsing. One would go into the rehearsal room at the 'Acton Hilton' and imagine the two of them were having a casual conversation, it sounded so natural. They weren't, they were rehearsing.

Also in the Mata Hari sketch were John Thaw and Dennis Waterman and, of course, Des O'Connor! Elton John was a guest on the show as were the Nolan Sisters. But all the musical numbers were prerecorded in the afternoon. It was only our stuff that was 'live', that is, in front of a 'live audience'. John, Dennis and I were terrified and could be observed pacing up and down the make-up room like caged tigers. At one point Dennis said to me, 'Don't you wish we were back doing *Weavers Green*, Kate?' Didn't I just! But we got through it somehow and it was a riot. The audience loved it!

There is one expression of Eric's I use to this day. In the summer prior to my being their guest, we were all up in the BBC Canteen, which used to be a happy, creative place, in the days when they still made programmes that meant something and drama that gave employment to hundreds of people, not just actors, but technicians, make-up artists, wardrobe supervisors, scene painters, camera-men, carpenters, electricians, set designers, prop-makers, directors, assistant directors, script writers, script editors, film editors, seamstresses, sound engineers, composers, lighting designers, researchers, secretaries, production assistants, floor managers, etc. etc. etc. A thriving industry, now decimated and depleted.

This canteen used to be full of these workers. One could see everyone there at lunch-time from John Gielgud to Pan's People, via *Dad's Army*. All gone, never to return, I fear. Anyway, Eric Morecambe and I were standing at the salad bar in this canteen of blessed memory. It was a boiling hot day and for once I had chosen to discard the jeans in which I lived and don a short skirt. Eric glanced down and observed, casually, 'You've brought the legs, I see.' I roared with laughter. To this day, whenever I put on a skirt or dress, I refer to it as 'bringing the legs'! And I think of dear Eric when I say it.

As a result of the great compliment being paid to me, as a guest on their Christmas Show, I was stopped in the canteen one day by Ronnie Barker, who gave me his usual greeting, 'Hello, Kate O'Mara, how are you both?' I sat down with my tray at his table for a chat. We had worked together ten years previously, before either of us had become successful.

'I've written a part for you in the Charley Farley series,' he said amicably. 'You wonderful man,' I replied. 'I can't wait.' And so came about the famous catch-phrase, 'It's big, it's black and it's hairy and oi be afraid of it!', which is how I had to explain away my presence up a ladder in the middle of the night at Ronnie Barker's bedroom window! 'Who are you?' he demanded on opening the window to me. 'Oi'm the queen of the gypsies,' was my conspiratorial reply. 'It's a funny toime of noight to come around selling clothes pegs, isn't it?' he observed conversationally. I then had to explain about the 'thing' I'd seen and how it was 'big and black and hairy and Oi be afraid of it!' Taxi drivers would greet me with this as an opening gambit. Truck-drivers would yell it out to me from their cabs. Workmen on sites would enquire after its well-being! Again, I felt that I'd been paid a huge compliment by being in *The Two Ronnies*.

By this time, my relationship with Paul Daneman had ended. And not a moment too soon. A lot of pain had been caused to a lot of people which I deeply regret, but he pursued me and I had to end the affair after four years. He'd not only been unfaithful to his wife, but to me as well to yet another girl! He suffered the first of his heart attacks after this and, frankly, I'm not surprised. People often ask me if he was the love of my life. The truth of the matter was, he wasn't mine to love. The moral of this sad saga is never, ever have anything to do with married men, *ever*! It can only end in tears.

Shortly after this, I took over from Margaret Lockwood in the very play she'd been in with Daneman, *Double Edge*. In it with me were Peter Byrne, whom I'd known for years and who had starred in *Dixon of Dock Green* and opposite Jean Boht in *Bread*, and Nicholas Courtney, who had a following having played 'The Brigadier' in *Dr Who*. We toured the country and played to capacity audiences wherever we went. There were queues around the theatres just about everywhere. Such was the power of television in those days.

* * *

In early 1977 I was cast in Shaw's play *Arms and the Man* with Susan Hampshire, Ian Ogilvy, Nicky Henson, Eleanor Summerfield and Nigel Stock. It was a wonderful cast and a splendid production. It opened at the Thorndike Theatre, Leatherhead, with the sole purpose of being the British contribution for the Hong Kong Festival. Thus came about my only visit to the Far East, a fascinating experience. For the first time in my life, I was tall! Apart from performing in the play, we had many social functions to attend. We were wined and dined by High Commissioners, Ambassadors and Government officials.

On one occasion, we were entertained by some high-ranking Chinese. An almond-coloured Rolls Royce came to collect us and take us to what our host described as the 'best Chinese restaurant in the world'. As a confirmed vegetarian for many years, I was used to having to cope at public functions. In those days, vegetarianism was still regarded as mildly eccentric and I found I was generally humoured and sent-up. I was doing fine in Hong Kong. There were invariably many dishes to choose from on the table, so I was able to eat rice and vegetables to my heart's content and leave the meat to others. Not so on this auspicious occasion.

Our host, who was the equivalent of Chinese Nobility, explained to me with great pride that he had chosen the menu himself and every dish would be a different Chinese delicacy. I expressed enormous gratification at this honour and hoped for the best. Alas! There were probably about fifteen dishes, one after the other. Every single one contained meat or fish. There was no rice and no vegetables. Susan Hampshire, a dear girl, known for trying to be helpful, took in the situation at a glance. 'Oh, but Kate doesn't eat mea . . . !' She got no further. I shot her a look that would have done credit to a basilisk, gently shaking my head in a negative way and pursing my lips. I was able to convey this rather complicated combination of signals, because I was seated on the left of our host and the table was round. Suzy took the hint remembering, in the nick of time, that the Chinese must not be allowed to lose face.

The evening proved interminable. I somehow struggled on, playing around with each dish with my chopsticks and giving a fairly advanced demonstration of miming eating. Of course, I just had to eat some of it. I drank vast quantities of Chinese tea to wash it all down. To no avail. When we finally got back to the Hilton, I spent the rest of the night throwing the whole lot up!

The play was very well received and an invitation came from Government House for the cast to attend a banquet there. Somehow or other, both Nicky Henson and myself had been omitted from the invitation and the British Council, under whose aegis we were travelling, was unable to rectify this in time. Instead, they arranged for Nicky and me to be taken to Run Run Shaw's film studios, where they filmed all the Kung Fu movies. We had a glorious time, watching the shooting of many action sequences and being shown over the opulent offices of Run Run Shaw himself. It was like something out of Babylon via Disneyland! We were vastly entertained, given a delicious meal and, comparing notes with the rest of the company later, it became quite apparent that they had drawn the short straw, having been subjected to an evening of stuffy and starchy protocol where conversation was almost nonexistent. We were there for Chinese New Year which was wonderfully colourful, but I was glad to get home again.

*   *   *

I was inundated with work. I appeared on TV chat shows, panel games virtually nonstop. My photo continued to adorn magazines and newspapers. Teams of cameramen arrived from Scandinavia and its neighbours to film me 'at home' and interview me endlessly. I had no man in my life – I was too busy to worry about men. Best of all, my son was made head boy of his prep school and all the hard work at last seemed worthwhile.

On my return from Finland, I had been asked to do a further tour of *Double Edge* for *more* money. At the same time, I was offered another play at the Thorndike, Leatherhead, this time to play 'Rosaline' in *Love's Labour's Lost* for very *little* money. Shakespeare being one of the loves of my life, I naturally chose to do the latter. My agent said, 'I wash my hands of you!' He couldn't understand that doing something I loved was more important than earning money. Besides, I'd done *Double Edge* and how! Apart from laying the ghost of Daneman, it had been quite an ordeal. We had rehearsed in London before going to Cardiff to the New Theatre to do a dress rehearsal on the Sunday and open on the Monday. Unfortunately, somebody had neglected to tell the management that the London Mozart Players were giving a concert on Sunday night! We contented ourselves with a 'live run' in the hotel on the Sunday and another during Monday, while they were getting the set up.

I got ready at the appointed time and went down to the stage to acquaint myself with the set, the furniture and props, which I hadn't yet seen! But they hadn't finished lighting and the stage was in total darkness. The first time I set foot on the set was at curtain up. I had to spend about fifteen minutes on stage, alone, at the beginning of the play, flicking through a series of slides which were projected onto a screen at the back of the set. I was playing a History Don at Oxford and the set was my 'rooms', with which I was intimately familiar. As I'd never seen them before in my life, this was tricky! My only hope was to play her as an absent-minded professor who couldn't remember where anything was! I think I pulled it off, but it was an uneasy quarter of an hour as the audience was riveted to my every move!

In 1978, after *Love's Labour's Lost*, I was asked to join Harry H Corbett (of *Steptoe and Son* fame) in a two-handed play called *Rattle of a Simple Man*. What a marvellous actor! It was a privilege to be on the same stage with him. Unfortunately, however, we only had four days rehearsal, as Harry was making a movie at the same time! Well, we did our best, but four days is not enough. When we opened in Lincoln, we both of us knew *some* of it, *some* of the time but at no point did either of us know *all* of it at *any* time. As we were waiting just off-stage for the curtain to go up, we wished each other luck and apologised in advance for whatever we might do to each other before the night was over!

Harry was playing the north country soccer fan who is 'up for the Cup' in London and I was playing the 'tart with the heart of gold' from the East End, who befriends him when she realises that he is not a potential client, but a 40-year-old virgin from the sticks – an innocent abroad, who is out of his depth. It is a charming, funny and moving play, but although there is a very brief appearance by the tart's brother at the end of the second act, that part is tiny and there are just the two main characters, Percy and Cyrenne, in the whole play! There is an incredible amount of dialogue for the two of them. We launched ourselves into the evening and for the first twenty minutes or so, everything was fine. Then Harry dried in his first big speech. I helped him as best as I could, but I didn't really know my own part, never mind his. We struggled on, then I came unstuck and we floundered about for a while, then we got back on text, then went wrong again, then recovered, then went again.

We never stopped talking for a moment, but our words bore no relation to the script. I could hear the Deputy Stage Manager in the prompt corner frantically turning the pages of her prompt copy, to try to locate where the hell we were. An impossible task. We were nowhere in that play. We were telling the story but entirely in our own words. Harry then came to his really big speech, where he has to tell Cyrenne, and the audience of course, the story of his life. He got going, then came to a grinding halt and asked me if he could use the bathroom again. He'd already done this at the beginning of the play and it had been accompanied by a very realistic flushing of a loo. So off he went to the 'bathroom', but, of course, what he was really doing was going to look at the script in the prompt corner! But the DSM had lost the page! However, Harry managed to locate the place. She, meanwhile, had to repeat the flushing of the loo sound cue!

Harry came back on and normal service was resumed. Not for long. He was soon asking me if he could 'go' again. 'Help yerself, Perce,' I said nonchalantly, I was past caring by now. Two seconds later he was back on again and we soldiered on. We lost it again and went round the houses. This culminated in Harry saying to me hopefully, 'Do you know what I mean, Cyrenne?' I had to let him know that I had absolutely no idea of what came next, so I replied, 'No, Percy, I haven't a clue what you're going on about.' He realised that I'd arrived at a total blank. This time, he simply gestured off-stage and exited. I turned to the audience and said, 'Oh my Gawd.' We somehow got to the end of the act and we were immensely relieved to see the curtain descend.

We fared better in the second and third acts, as the speeches were not so long. At the end of the evening, Harry turned to me and said, 'Thank you for being on stage with me tonight.' We played the show for six weeks in all and on the last night, as we were waiting to go on together, I turned to him and said, 'Harry, do you think we'll *ever* know it?' 'Nope,' he replied – and we didn't!

* * *

I had been fortunate to work with the famous comic actor, the delightful Bernard Bresslaw in *Of Mice and Men*, a moving play adapted from Steinbeck's novel. He played 'Lennie' the simple-minded giant of a man who unwittingly kills a girl – the part I played; his mate, George, was played by Russell Hunter, another very fine actor memorable for his performance as 'Lonely' in *Callan*. The production was part of a season I was doing at the New Theatre, Bromley, sadly now demolished (to be replaced by the hideously conceived and designed Churchill Theatre). The previous play had been what is now called *Ten Little Indians* – though I fear when I was in it, the title was less than politically correct. Paul Darrow, who was later to gain fame in *Blake's Seven*, was in both plays with me and Valentine Dyall was the villain in the Christie. I've always said that any actress worth her salt can play 'Ophelia' or 'Juliet'. But let her make something of 'Vera Claythorne' or any other insipid Agatha Christie juvenile heroine. That takes *real* acting! I remember Paul having to say to me on stage, 'You are young, lovely and quite, quite mad!'

The theatre was renowned for the truly gargantuan size of its spiders, who had been in residence for many years. I will always treasure the memory of a huge series of bellows and roars coming from Bernie Bresslaw's dressing-room, the door bursting open and the sight of Bernie clad only in the briefest of towels charging down the corridor. The cause of this uproar? An admittedly very large spider in Bernie's wash-basin! I didn't feel so bad about my arachnophobia after that!

Then in 1978, I was then asked to go to the Ludlow Festival to play Kate in *The Taming of the Shrew*. During rehearsals, in

London, it became obvious to me and the rest of the cast, that the director either hadn't read the play, or didn't understand it. An impasse had been reached over several of the scenes and a thoroughly unhappy company set out for the wilds of Shropshire, not entirely sure whether it had a show or not. Ludlow Castle was a dream of a place in which to stage a show. To our dismay, we found that although there were about nine possible entrances, the director seemed not to have catered for any of them. We found him implacable.

The feeling in the company became mutinous and our discontent must have filtered back to the ladies' committee who ran the festival, for I received a summons from the Chairman to a meeting. I explained the problem to her. She was very sympathetic and asked whether or not she should get rid of the director. 'The best possible solution,' I replied without a moment's hesitation. 'And would the actors be able to implement their own ideas, and make the show work?' she asked eagerly. 'Leave it to us,' I said immediately. 'We'll give you a brilliant show!' My news was greeted with huge delight by my fellow actors and we got down to work at once. The whole atmosphere in the company was now one of joy and inspiration. It was the most successful of productions and the director got rave reviews!

Ah, well, 'twas ever thus, life is not fair. But the experience planted a seed in my mind. The idea of an actor's company. Ian McKellen had started his actor's company a few years before and we were all very much in admiration of him. I nurtured a great desire to emulate him and start my own company; after all, I had just proved it was possible to get a show on without a director. Don't get me wrong. I am not anti-director; there is nothing more satisfying than working for an inspired director who knows what he is doing, has done his homework and is committed to putting on a wonderful show. Sadly, this state of affairs is often the exception rather than the rule. But I have worked with some marvellous directors and it has been a joyous experience.

* * *

I found myself in Spain again, this time in Almeria in the desert, for Twentieth Century Fox television. We were doing a Biblical mini epic entitled *The Nativity*. I was playing Herod's niece Salome, not *the* Salome – I didn't have to do the dance of the seven veils or anything like that. I was really just female set dressing. It wasn't a very big part but I was around a lot. In time-honoured Hollywood tradition we British were the baddies. Leo McKern was Herod; John Rhys-Davies Freddie Jones and Morgan Shepherd were The Three Wise Men, or soothsayers. Mary, Joseph and Elizabeth were all Americans. The script was rather confusing and full of hilarious anachronisms. 'Hi, Mary, you're not looking so good these days, are you okay?' 'Oh yeah, sure, Elizabeth, I'm fine, just fine, and my soul doth magnify the Lord and my spirit doth rejoiceth in God my Saviour!' 'Huh?'

The dialogue was truly appalling and I was glad I didn't have too much of it. The British contingent did it proud, naturally. There was one scene at Herod's court with fountains and marble pillars where peacocks wandered in and out of shot and Leo and Freddie, John and Morgan all made the extraordinary dialogue crackle into life. It's amazing what a good actor can do with crap. There was one scene where Herod (Leo) had to go more or less crazy, after he'd heard the news of the Messiah from the wise men. So while Leo was in make-up having Rice Krispies latexed to his face, prime evidence of pottiness apparently, I was filming out in the desert with Freddie, John and Morgan. We shot a sequence there, then sat under large parasols to shade us from the blazing sun.

There was a lull in proceedings and a silence fell on the little group, who were hardly able to breathe in the intense heat. Someone said, 'It's difficult to imagine winter in England at this moment, isn't it?' There was another pause and then I started to sing one of Shakespeare's songs.

> When icicles hang by the wall
> And Dick the shepherd blows his nail,
> And Tom bears logs into the hall,
> And milk comes frozen home in pail;

When blood is nipped and ways be foul,
Then nightly sings the staring owl
Tuwhoo! Tuwhit! Tuwhoo! A merry note!
While greasy Joan doth keel the pot.

When I'd finished there was another pause, then Freddie Jones said, 'I think I'm in love.' No-one said anything else after that. We were all trying to contain our energy for the afternoon's filming. Eventually we broke for lunch.

We were all sitting at the luncheon table, which was out of doors but tented over, when Leo joined us, all Rice Krispied up and looking, I have to admit, fairly potty. I mean, what man in his right mind would stick his breakfast all over his face? He started to tuck into the meal, which was excellent. To make conversation, I observed to him, 'Leo, while you have been away in make-up, Freddie has fallen in love with me.' 'Really?' Leo responded with interest. 'Yes,' affirmed Freddie through clenched teeth, 'and it's hell!'

Later that night, back at the hotel, which had a swimming-pool, I was sitting having a drink at the bar with John Rhys-Davies. Freddie, who'd been taking a dip in the pool, suddenly burst, dripping into the bar area. Fortunately the floor was tiled, but unfortunately, Freddie had omitted to pack his swimming trunks and Leo had lent him his. Freddie was tall and slim, Leo shorter and with an enormous girth. Freddie fixed me with a wild eye and said savagely, 'Do you think I'm made of STONE?' He stood there in a pool of water, the aforementioned trunks in no way concealing his modesty. I hurriedly averted my gaze and replied brokenly, 'I'm sorry, Freddie.' We kept this act up for the duration of the filming, much to everyone's amusement.

I was told that there was someone who really was in love with me on the set, the producer. Why I didn't respond, I can't imagine. He was a tall, handsome, charming, quietly intelligent American. I must have been mad. I've come to the conclusion that the thing that put me off was his power. I'm a control freak. I admit it freely. Anyway, I passed up on a really lovely man and I now regret it deeply.

I think it was around about the time when I got back from Spain that I went to Bristol to do an episode of *Men of Affairs*, which starred Warren Mitchell and Brian Rix and in which I played a Russian spy. I had to appear at their hotel room door, clad in the briefest of black leather outfits with high boots and announce myself. 'Good evening, I am Tanya Lens, your contact!' to which Brian Rix had to reply, 'Ah, our contact lens!' I ask you.

I made another film in Spain, a very small part indeed. A whore, in *Cannon to Cordoba*. I had to give George Peppard a bath and seduce him. We were filming in the studios in Madrid and the air conditioning had broken down. It was unspeakably hot. I arrived for my first scene and had just changed into a satin basque with fishnet tights and a great deal of make-up and hair. There was a knock on my door. 'Come in' I called without turning around. There was a pause, then the door swung open. Leaning, posed nonchalantly against the door frame, dressed entirely in western gear, gun in holster, cheroot clenched between teeth and cowboy hat tilted provocatively over one eye, which incidentally was gazing at me appreciatively, was George Peppard.

'Hi' was all he said. I responded with perfect old-world courtesy. 'How do you do, Mr Peppard. I'm Kate. I believe we have a couple of scenes together.' 'Yeah,' he replied without moving a muscle. The conversation ground to a halt. I pretended to busy myself about my dressing-room. He seemed nonplussed. Then he asked, 'Do you have anything to drink in here?' 'No, I'm sorry, only water,' I replied in a relieved voice. 'Okay, well look, er, why not come by my dressing-room. I've got a freezer full of stuff.' He began to exhibit signs of animation. Oh, God, I thought, not *again*. Can men think of nothing else! I seriously believe it's time someone invented the opposite of Viagra! 'It's awfully kind of you,' I said, politely, knowing full well it wasn't, 'but I have to go to make-up in a couple of minutes.' I was lying through my teeth. George took the hint and, heaving himself off the door frame, sauntered off to his dressing-room. I breathed a sigh of relief. What I find so extraordinary is that a lot of men, however unattractive, seem to think they are God's gift to women. As it happens, George Peppard was one of the more attractive of the breed, but did he honestly think that I would just come running? I noticed he was faintly hostile towards me on set, but I ignored it and got on with the business of seducing him! Which ironically was what was required.

A couple of days later, I was asked to join two of the producers for supper at the unit hotel. I acquiesced. I was sitting at a round table between the two of them. We had hardly begun eating when the guy on my left put his hand on my thigh under the table. I removed it. To no avail, it came back again, and so did the hand of the guy on my right! I put up with this grotesque behaviour for as long as I could, then I suddenly pushed back my chair and, putting my hand over my mouth, I gasped, 'I'm terribly sorry, I don't feel very well,' and fled up to my room. I sent a note of apology down to them explaining that something I had eaten had disagreed with me and hoping they'd forgive my sudden departure. I was thankful that my contribution to the movie was so small and that it was not long before I was on my way home again.

In 1979 I had my first crack at Cleopatra. Sadly, it was a mutilated version. *Antony and Cleopatra*, uncut, runs at 3¾ hours. I know because I've done it, at my second attempt in subsidised Rep. But the first time I played Egypt's Queen was at the Thorndike, Leatherhead, where the citizens need to get home to their beds, so the play had to be cut. Unfortunately, huge chunks that could easily have gone, were left and famous speeches were hacked to pieces. It was a very distressing experience. But I was glad to have done it. It gave me a blue-print from which to work and by the time I came to my third attempt, there was nothing I didn't know about her or the play.

Act II. Sc.II

My film parts were getting noticeably smaller. Fortunately, my stage career was thriving. I joined the Birmingham Rep. Company, one of the most prestigious in the country, to do two plays. The first was *Misalliance* by Bernard Shaw, in which I played the Polish aviatrix. She was also supposed to be an acrobat and in one scene I had to carry Alun Corduner off on my shoulders! My problem is that I give the appearance of being tall and strong, whereas in reality I am only 5ft 4in and very slight. Alun is not tall, but even at 5ft 9in, a dead weight on one's shoulders is not light! We were on an extended tour and most nights I managed it, but on one occasion, at a new venue, there was less room in the wings than usual and I had to turn to get off. In so doing, his forehead caught the grandfather clock and he sustained a nasty gash. I was horrified, but he, being the gentleman he is, brushed it off as a mere scratch. I had my doubts and when I saw him recently in *Topsy Turvy* being brilliant as Sir Arthur Sullivan, I looked anxiously at his forehead whenever he had a close-up to see if there was any evidence of a disfiguring scar!

The second play was T S Eliot's *The Elder Statesman*. Both plays starred the wonderful actor Paul Rogers, who had entranced me at the Old Vic when I was a teenager and used to frequent that hallowed place. I have never known anyone with more energy and charisma on the stage. I adored my scenes with him. In the T S Eliot piece, I played his daughter and he always used to joke that I was one of the two women he would leave home for! The other was Siân Phillips! His wife, Rosalind Boxhall was also in the cast and took it all in good part.

As a result of playing the Polish acrobat so successfully, the management invited me to take over from Susan Hampshire in *The Crucifer of Blood* in the West End. I finished the tour on the Saturday night and opened on the Monday at the Theatre Royal in the Haymarket, the oldest and most historic theatre in London. So there I was in dressing-room No.1, with my name lit up outside, the leading lady in a most marvellous production. I had to pinch myself again, as I had done on the set of *Great Catherine*, to make sure it was true! It was another play about Sherlock Holmes, played this time by Gerald Harper, with whom I had worked twice before. At the final dress rehearsal, Gerald broke his arm. Not only that, but the new villain got the sack for not being villainous enough, but apart from that everything went swimmingly! Somehow Gerald managed to play with his arm in a sling and the original villain, the brilliant actor John Quentin was persuaded to stay on until a replacement could be found. I suggested an old friend Frank Barrie, who learnt the part in record time, went on after a couple of days and was magnificent.

The director and author was Paul Giovanni. Working for him was the most marvellous experience. He was a true man of the theatre. It was a fantastic show. We actually had a ship on stage and a huge cataclysmic thunderstorm produced by sensa-surround. The noise and vibrations seemed to shake the building and one was frightened for the historic old theatre's survival! But I was assured that it was only an effect. I also had the best curtain call I've ever had. The curtains parted to reveal a completely bare stage, right to the back wall of the theatre, where I was standing in a scarlet velvet dress with my back to the audience, my hands tied with a belt of diamonds! I had to sweep down-stage and take a solo call to the music of Benjamin Britten. What more could a girl ask! I played the part for the six-month run and each night I thought to myself, 'Savour this moment, O'Mara, you'll never get this again!.' And I never have.

*   *   *

In 1980 we went straight into rehearsals for the West End tour of the Tom Stoppard play *Night and Day*. It had originally been mooted that I take over from Diana Rigg, who had created the part, but Michael Codron, the theatre management, said that I was not tall enough for the part. Oddly enough I was tall enough for the tour! Stoppard attended rehearsals. He had just returned from the States, where Maggie Smith had been playing the part on Broadway. We were using that version of the script and some of the dialogue had obviously been rewritten to accommodate Maggie's unique and quirky sense of humour. Not being possessed of her eccentric and brilliant talent, I naturally found some of it tricky. But when I mentioned this to Tom, he very sweetly, without a moment's hesitation, rewrote it for me. Stoppard, I think, is quite proprietorial about his leading ladies and he wrote to me often on tour to, as it were, keep me up to the mark.

In the cast with me were George Sewell and a young actor called Robin Sachs. I had first met Robin during the run of *Arms and the Man*, as he was one of Eleanor Summerfield's sons. He was now married to Siân Phillips, Peter O'Toole's ex-wife. As she accompanied us on many of our tour dates, I was able to get to know her much better and what a delightful person she turned out to be! We had a very happy tour staying at weird and wonderful 'digs'. The best time of all was when the entire company stayed at Auchterader House, a baronial hall in the highlands of Scotland.

It was a boiling hot summer and we spent the days sunbathing in the wonderful grounds and then driving to Stirling *en masse* to do the show. There was an hilarious black actor in the show who rejoiced in the name of Honeyboy Williams! Our host for the week, Iain Urquhart, an old Scottish chum of mine, at that time owned Auchterader House and let it out to various rich people for golfing holidays. We were all out lolling about in the garden one afternoon and Honeyboy, not having the same compulsion to acquire a sun-tan as we did, found himself alone in the house! The phone rang and Honeyboy, realising that no-one was around, had taken it upon himself to answer. King Constantine of Greece, who was on the other end, had the novel experience of hearing himself addressed variously as 'Mate', 'me old mate' and 'sunshine'. I don't think he ever got over it!

* * *

After that glorious summer of touring sedately around Britain, I spent the autumn being tossed on the boiling North Sea under grey leaden skies, the only sign of external life being the odd seagull that flapped despondently past the porthole. Both the seagull and the porthole were also grey. As we neared the north Danish coast, force twelve gales were the norm. Yes, I'm referring to *Triangle*, the BBC's first attempt to film a drama series using a documentary format. We were shooting on a working ferry that plied between Felixstowe, Amsterdam and Gothenburg, hence the 'triangle' of the title. It has to rank as one of the most unpleasant locations *ever*.

The boat itself was fitted out in the manner of a motorway service station! My cabin was *minute*. I had a bunk bed, a wash basin in which it was impossible even to clean one's teeth without bumping one's head, a shower in which one could not turn around, likewise the loo. I was subjected to this living hell for 27 episodes of *Triangle* and the powers that be could not understand why I had to leave the series. The only time it became bearable, was when we docked in Amsterdam and filmed on shore in civilised surroundings away from the common herd.

I repeatedly remarked that if we could shoot the series in a studio, like any normal drama, I would have been prepared to stay forever. But obviously the BBC were determined to make it on the cheap, so I left. As the series had been written for me, I was accused of being the proverbial rat that deserted the sinking ship. The fact that almost all the crew and a huge percentage of the actors all suffered from the most appalling seasickness, seemed not to sway their decision or affect their sensibilities. I was relatively fortunate, I was a good sailor, but some of my fellow actors suffered horribly. My leading man, Michael Craig had been in the Merchant Navy so was able to withstand the rigours of a force twelve gale. But Larry Lamb was pole-axed and we didn't see him for days at a time.

The make-up department, being situated in the hold, came off worst. I would go down for my 6.30 make-up call to find the girls lying prostrate around the floor, moaning. This happened day after day and I have to say I think their treatment was nothing short of barbarous and inhumane. The camera crew used to work in shifts, one lot on, while the other lot was throwing up and then changing places to allow the others to go off and be sick! Do you wonder I left the series with barely a backward glance? When the series was shown, it became notorious for the opening shot of me sunbathing, topless, on the deck under the obviously sunless, grey skies on the North Sea. The phone lines were jammed with complaints. I rest my case.

Back to civilisation and culture. In 1981 I went to Harrogate Theatre to play *Hedda Gabler* and met the very tall and extremely charming Mark Piper, one of the gentlemen of the theatre. We have worked together many times since and it has always been the greatest of pleasures. He is now married to the wonderful Sue Holderness, who plays 'Marlene' in *Only Fools and Horses,* and a more delightful couple it would be hard to imagine. I have no idea what my performance as 'Hedda' was like, but I do know that I had very little sympathy with the woman and thought her suicide at the end a total cop-out. But I enjoyed myself none the less, not least because on one Saturday night after the performance, I was approached by a truck driver who said he'd never been to the theatre before, but had come to see the show because I was in it. He made the whole thing worthwhile for me.

* * *

After nineteen years, I finally achieved an early ambition to go to the Open Air Theatre, Regent's Park and to play one of the most fascinating of Shakespeare's heroines, 'Beatrice' in *Much Ado About Nothing.* The reviews were most gratifying and one even compared me to Peggy Ashcroft, the ultimate accolade! 'Beatrice' is one of the most witty and sparkling of women and I adored playing her. My 'Benedick' was Gary Raymond, who had been in *The Crucifer of Blood* with me, playing my father! The dearest of men. Also in the cast was Sandi Toksvig. I think it must have been her first job on coming down from Cambridge. She was quite irrepressible and never drew breath. I am one of those actresses who likes to concentrate and get my thoughts together, get into character and generally centre myself before going on stage. Impossible with Sandi around! She would barge into my cubicle (dressing-room) as I was trying to fix my hat and natter at me ceaselessly. 'Sandi, shut up and go away!' I would say in exasperation. To no avail, she would continue chattering. I recall, that at the Charity Gala, which we always held at the end of the season to raise money for the Open Air Theatre, she supplied herself with a brilliant solo spot at the end, which she had written – it went on for ages and was completely above everyone's heads!

To my delight the management told me that they were going to mount the next season around me, if I was interested. 'I can't think why we've never employed you before,' remarked David Conville in a puzzled basso profundo, which was his usual timbre. 'I did try to persuade you,' I replied aggrievedly, 'three times. But you wouldn't have me!' 'Extraordinary,' said David baffled. I agreed that I would return for the season the following year. I was to play 'Katherine' in 'The Shrew' (again) and 'Titania' doubling with 'Hippolyta' in *A Midsummer Night's Dream*. I tell you, perseverance pays off! One should never give up on one's dreams.

* * *

Meanwhile in 1982 I had been asked to take over from Frances de la Tour in *Duet for One*. The set and the director were from the West End production. My leading man was Philip Madoc, a splendid actor with whom I worked before, up at Elstree. We were to do a massive tour of Britain and then go to the Zagreb Festival, followed by a tour of Yugoslavia. I took four weeks off to learn it, as it is a two-hander and *she* has 75 per cent of the dialogue. I was determined to know it and in fact be off the script by the first day of rehearsals. I knew it was my only chance and I did just that. I have found that it is impossible to get to grips with a part until one has got the lines under one's belt, so to speak. Then and then only is one able to make the dialogue one's own. I have to say, I found the play quite harrowing to perform. One had to get through so much emotion every night, not just dialogue.

On the Monday night in each venue, the theatre was invariably only half-full. Even regular patrons had looked at the pre-publicity and thought, 'A two-handed drama between a famous violinist who's got multiple sclerosis and her psychiatrist – no I don't think so.' On the Tuesday morning the crits in the papers would say, 'If you don't see anything else this year, you *have* to see *Duet for One*!' And that would be it, we would be packed out for the rest of the week. I remember one woman coming up to me in Billingham of all places and saying, 'I've known black despair like that.' (And frankly, living in Billingham, I'm not surprised!) But, the point is, women identified with the character of Stephanie; even though they would almost certainly have had no experience of a debilitating disease, they knew what it was like to be in total despair, with no possible means of escape. As Thoreau so astutely observed 'the mass of men lead lives of quiet desperation.'

We toured Britain for six months, before going to Yugoslavia under the aegis of the British Council. An unforgettable experience. In Zagreb, where we were the official British entry for the Festival (we won by the way), we found some highly articulate Slovene actors who were, however, very reticent to discuss politics with us, although, of course, we were fascinated. Zagreb was very sophisticated, whereas some of the more remote venues we played were very rough and ready. Drains, I recall, were the main problem almost everywhere. The all-pervading stench was overpowering and deeply unpleasant.

Being with Philip was a pleasure both on stage and off. For him, a foreign country presented no difficulties whatsoever. He is a polyglot. I'm not sure how many languages he speaks, but the minimum has to be nine. The really clever thing is that he knows the root of so many different tongues, be it Slav, Magyar, Greek or Teuton. In the same way that when once one has learnt Latin, which thankfully I have, one is then, after a little practice, able to make oneself understood in French, Spanish or Italian. Likewise, Philip took only a few moments to be able to communicate with the inhabitants of Serbia, Slovenia, Croatia and Macedonia. It made life very much easier and with his help, we were able to get around and order whatever was available with very little trouble. The only problem we had, was with the hordes of women he attracted everywhere we went.

Macedonia was an eye-opener. We were playing a new theatre in Skopje – well, everything was new, as Skopje had been devastated in an earthquake a few years earlier. The inhabitants had never seen drama before and had no experience of an English theatre company. To our amazement, when the curtain went up, we found the place was packed to the rafters. There were dozens of children in the audience and many women with babes in arms. I can't believe they understood much of what was going on, on stage, but I remember making a conscious effort to show my emotions more forcibly than I had in England. I gesticulated quite a lot in a desperate attempt to get them to understand Stephanie's predicament. The whole of the action (well, there is no action actually, both parties are sedentary almost throughout, with very few moments of activity) took place with me in an electronic wheelchair, which I have to say I became very adept at manoeuvring.

As I mentioned before, the speeches were huge and it required every ounce of concentration I possessed to get through the play. On the first night in Skopje, I had just started on a speech of about two pages long, when, suddenly, a tiny trap flap opened in the wooden stage and a head popped up. I faltered for a second, then went on, glaring at the offending object ferociously. The raised flap prevented the audience from seeing it, but my view was quite uncluttered. The next moment it disappeared. I heaved a sigh of relief – that is to say, I exhaled through clenched teeth and got on with the play. Just when I'd been lulled into a false sense of security, the flap popped open again and the head was back! I glared balefully at it, the sort of look Perseus went to great lengths to avoid from the Gorgon. My man would have put any Greek hero to shame. He wasn't remotely phased. He simply looked with interest at the proceedings on stage for a few moments, then disappeared from view. I was still talking, still getting on with my reams of dialogue.

I threw a glance across at Philip to see if he'd witnessed this outrage. For once, he seemed to be awake and was twinkling at me. Normally, he had a tendency to nod off during my really huge monologues and I had to shout his long-awaited cues, to galvanise him. But on this occasion, he was on the qui vive and plainly interested in watching developments. The head returned and I very nearly dried, but I knew just what I was going to do. I was going to kill the bastard! I was going to charge him at speed and decapitate him with my wheelchair! I waited for my moment. It had to be dramatically justified. I knew the place in the script where a move was indicated, it was usually across to stage right. To kill him I would have to go to down stage centre.

The moment came. I took off the brake and, fixing him with a gimlet eye, I pressed the electronic button that drove the chair forwards. I hurtled towards him with all the force I could muster and descended on him like one of the avenging furies. From gazing at me complacently, his look became one of extreme alarm. At my approach (which, because of the raked stage, was swift) he shot down the trap with alacrity. I arrived at the trap door, which was actually very small and blended in with the rest of the stage, but was just discernible. I parked the wheelchair right on top of it and sat there for the rest of the act. Admittedly I had failed to kill him, but at least I'd prevented any further egress on his part. The curtain came down and Philip burst into roars of laughter. I, on the contrary, was beside myself with anger. I stalked off-stage, found the stage manager and said quite simply that there would be no member of any crew allowed below the stage at any time during the show; otherwise I should not return to play the second half. My wish was granted and the rest of the evening passed off without further incident.

My memories of Yugoslavia were of grey buildings with horrid yellow neon lights, few shops and those that there were, seemed to be filled with cheap plastic wares. There was very little food anywhere. I lived on fried cheese and raw cabbage the whole time, but that didn't worry me, as food simply does not interest me. I eat because I have to, not because I want to. It was February and there was quite a lot of snow. I went and stood by the Blue Danube only to find it was grey. The whole country appeared grey and weighed down with impending doom – until we got to Split on the Adriatic coast, where suddenly we were in a different country. It was warm and beautiful and we were greeted by the sight of Diocletian's Palace, glinting in the sun in Roman splendour.

When we got back to England, there was still a further leg of the tour to do. We opened it at Canterbury and I suddenly realised that I had to go back to my old performance for an English audience. Eventually, we finished and I took to my bed for a week with flu. I suddenly got a dramatic phone call from a theatre in Scotland asking me to go up that very night and open in *Duet for One!* The actress playing Stephanie had had a nervous breakdown at the dress rehearsal and could I please take over. Fortunately, my flu had left me with virtually no voice and I croaked down the phone at them. I was terribly sorry that it was a physical impossibility and I just couldn't do it but my ill health was a blessing in disguise! I was quite upset that I couldn't help them out and almost contemplated rousing myself from my sick bed until they added, by the way, they were using the original script, which of course was *not* the one that Frances had used in the West End nor, indeed, the one we had used. That decided me: streaming cold, no voice to speak of (!) *and* a totally different text, not to mention a different actor. No, it couldn't be done. I sank back into my pillows thankfully and fell into a deep sleep.

* * *

Once I was fully recovered, I devoted all my energies to learning the two parts I had been allotted in *A Midsummer Night's Dream* at Regent's Park. Having already played Katherine in *The Taming of the Shrew*, that was already stored in my memory bank. It is odd the stuff one remembers and the lines one jettisons as soon as a job is finished. On the whole, Shakespeare is retained by the memory, dormant, for most of one's life and requires very little revising for it to spring back into life again. People are always asking actors how they remember all those lines. I'm not sure I know the answer other than I learn them until they're coming out of my ears! The lovely, red-haired actress, Adrienne Corri, gave me that advice when I was about seventeen. She said the secret of good acting was to know the lines so well that one didn't need to consciously think about them, they just come out unbidden as 'twere. I believe she's absolutely right, for then, they seem spontaneous, as though one has just thought of them, which will make them appear totally natural.

There is no easy method, one simply has to sit down with script in front of one and *push* the words into one's brain. The satisfaction derived from them remaining there after a while is enormous. I usually learn the very big speeches first! Then when I arrive at them, instead of facing one's Waterloo, I think, 'Oh, it's all right, I know this bit.' Some people I know have 'photographic memories.' I'm not one of them, although I do know exactly at what point I am on the page. Occasionally, I use mnemonics to help me, but on the whole, it is telling the story that does the trick. Anyway, I sat down and pushed Titania in, as she was by far the bigger of the two parts. It was lovely doubling the Queen of the Fairies and the Queen of the Amazons. One was able, on the one hand, to show the feminine, sexy, amoral side of woman and on the other, the pragmatic, earthy, and more masculine. I think the double works really well. There is the parallel of the worldly court and the mirror image of the other-worldly court.

Christopher Neame, an eccentrically brilliant actor, was my leading man for the season. He later went to the States and played a regular character in *Dallas* and a notable villain in a *Die-hard* movie. He had been in the series *Colditz* and so made a splendid Petruchio as well as doubling Oberon and Theseus. 'The Dream' was a truly magical production. After an initial hiatus, Tim Goodchild (one of the most talented of all theatrical designers) and I persuaded David Conville to do an Elizabethan production of the play. It is thought that Titania and her fairy court were an oblique nod to Elizabeth I and that there is even a subtle reference to Mary Queen of Scots in the text. David was keen to set it in the Indian Raj era, but both Tim and I loathed the idea and between us we urged him to rethink. This he generously did.

Richard Digby Day, a wonderful director who at that time was running The Nottingham Playhouse, had decided to set 'The Shrew' in forties Italy. I, being a purist, was deeply unhappy about this, but there was nothing I could do but go along with the idea. Fortunately, Richard always manages to make the text crystal clear, so I shrugged my shoulders and got on with it.

It was the Queen's Silver Jubilee Year and a visit to the Open Air Theatre, Regent's Park, was one of the items on the Royal agenda. It is a well documented fact that England's most famous subject, William Shakespeare, is not the most favoured of entertainments of England's Queen. So I was not requested to perform for Her Majesty. The third play in the season's repertoire was chosen instead. *The Dark Lady of the Sonnets,* a short one-act play by Bernard Shaw, is an amusing piece, in which Shakespeare himself breaks into the Royal Palace at Whitehall and has an encounter with Elizabeth I. It would have been an ideal entertainment for Her Majesty, had not an almost identical incident taken place a few days prior to this event – in real life! It was too late to change the arrangements. Programmes had been printed, invitations had been issued. The evening had to go ahead as planned.

As the leading lady of the company, I had been delegated to 'look after' the Queen backstage in the Green Room. Backstage at Regent's Park is pretty rough and ready, as one would expect of an Open Air Theatre, especially in England, a country renowned for the unpredictability of its weather. In the old days, tents and duck-boards were the order of the day backstage. But since the Lloyds Bank sponsorship scheme had rebuilt the auditorium, things had improved somewhat, even for the actors. There was the gentleman's end and the ladies' end in a long, low, single-storey hut with corresponding loos. (For this relief, much thanks!). Sandwiched in between these two corridors of cubicles, which is what the dressing-rooms consisted of, was a Green Room. It featured a number of ex-sofas and chairs, a couple of ex-coffee tables, a sink, a water heater and numerous shelves stuffed to bursting with theatrical impedimenta. Here the company would foregather, before, during and after the show. Meetings were held here, line-runs and note-sessions. It was an agreeable area full of conviviality and occasionally, actors being emotional creatures, there were displays of exuberance and unconfined hysterics.

The elements are one of the hazards of working out of doors. They are always the unknown factor. Sometimes, indeed often, it can be cold and wet. As night draws on, it can be truly freezing. 'I'm going out now, I may be some time.' We used to quote Captain Oates' famous last words when leaving the warmth of the Green Room to venture onto the greensward! At other times, on a boiling hot afternoon, there is often the very real danger of getting sunstroke! Or worse, falling asleep on stage! This may seem unlikely, but it happened to me on more than one occasion in *A Midsummer Night's Dream*, when I was playing 'Titania, the Queen of the Fairies'. In one scene, 'Titania's' fairy helpers have to lead her to her bower where they sing her to sleep. This gives 'Oberon, the King of the Fairies', the opportunity to drop the juice of a magic flower into her eyes. When she wakes she will fall in love with the first object she sees – as it turns out, 'Bottom' the weaver, with his ass's head. Cue for much hilarity.

The problem was that the scene before I was supposed to wake was quite a long one and the sounds of actors' voices, somewhat removed, the humming of the bees and the heat of the sun all conspired to the drowsiness of the afternoon. The first time I fell asleep for real on stage, I was truly frightened as I awoke just in time. I begged Berwick Kaler, who was playing 'Bottom', to sing very loudly and as near to me as possible, but even so my first lines 'What angel wakes me from my flowery bed?' were often very accurate!

It was during this season that the horrific bombing of the bandstand in Regent's Park took place in which six soldiers of the Royal Green Jackets were killed. I always used to walk through the Park past the bandstand which was a few hundred yards away from the main entrance to the theatre. I loved to stop and listen to them on my way in. It was very shocking but we were told that the show would go on as usual. We had a matinee the day after it happened and I couldn't believe that anyone would turn up to see a show, a comedy at that. But they did. In fact, we had a very good house. It was a grey, misty day; there seemed to be a pall hanging over the Park and the smell of death was everywhere.

However, for the auspicious occasion of a Royal Visit, the whole place had been cleaned within an inch of its life, a new temporary loo, installed at a discreet distance from the hoi polloi for Her Majesty and a table and chair set up in the Green Room, on which was placed a very large calf-bound book awaiting the Royal signatures. The presentations backstage were to take place before the performance and we were all in a high state of anticipation. Julia Goodman, an ornament of the profession, who was attending purely as an invited guest, was backstage adjusting her make-up. She decided to go to the loo at the very moment plain-clothes policemen arrived with sniffer dogs to seek out any unwanted incendiary devices. The result was that she remained locked in during the entire proceedings and wasn't able to emerge until about three quarters of an hour later, thus missing all the fun.

With Julia safely out of the way, the Royal Party duly arrived and were ushered into the Green Room where the actors were waiting to be presented. I was at the end of the line, because I had to look after the Queen after the presentation. David and his adorable wife, the late actress Philippa Gail, were introducing the actors one by one, first to the Queen, then to the Duke of Edinburgh. Christopher Neame, who was standing next to me, had found the excitement too much and had been to the bar in advance of the presentation. As he was virtually a teetotaller, this was a very bad move. Even after one glass of mulled wine, the staple diet for the patrons at Regent's Park, being unused to alcohol, he was already paralytic. I heard him jabbering incoherently when the Queen asked him a perfectly ordinary question.

I was appalled, but reckoned that she was probably used to this sort of thing. She gave up on him as he was making no sense and came to me earlier than anticipated. I hardly fared any better. She asked me about the costume I wore as Titania (except that she pronounced it Tytaynia as though it were some sort of metal alloy). Thank God, I just managed to stop myself from correcting her pronunciation and we discussed the merits of my frock for some minutes. I was glad that I'd worn a dress of clear turquoise as, when I looked into her eyes, I noticed that they were of exactly the same beautiful hue. Having exhausted the sartorial theme, I then asked her if she would be so kind as to sign the visitor's book. I'd been instructed that this was to be the order of play. By this time, Chris Neame was talking nonsensically to the Duke and David Conville was giving him a ferocious stare from under thick, black, bushy eyebrows and Philippa Gail, who was party to this surreal exchange, was wearing a fixed grin.

I guided the Queen over to the table, sat her down and handing her a pen, asked her if she'd be so kind as to give us her autograph. 'Where would you like me to sign?' she asked with interest. To my horror, I found myself suggesting that under where 'Elizabeth R' was printed might be a convenient place! She did so with a flourish.

David and the Duke, having by now decided that any further 'babbling a green fields' from Chris Neame would prove unproductive, had moved on only to find an empty space where I should have been. I heard David say in his best Brigadier tones, 'And here we have Miss Kate O'Mara, Sir, our leading lady, very talented actress – Kate, er Kate, where are you?' 'Excuse me, your Majesty.' I apologised to the Queen and darted back to my place at the end of the line. 'Hello,' said the Duke jovially, 'Where did you pop up from?' 'She's been talking to me dear,' observed the Queen airily without looking up. I had a few minutes chat with the Duke about performing in the open air. He, it transpired, had the edge on me as he'd been to Epidaurus, the open air theatre in Greece and I hadn't. I made a point of remedying this omission at the first possible opportunity on my next visit to Greece!

Eventually, both signatures were done and everyone was free to go to the auditorium for the show. By now Chris and I were so overwrought that I virtually had to carry him to his seat in the front row of the dress circle and I appreciated for the first time, the true meaning of the phrase 'legless'. The next forty minutes or so were spent by the audience not so much watching the play, but watching the Queen watching the play to see how she took it. I have to confess, I stole the odd side-long glance to see if I could gauge her reaction. There was nervous laughter from the audience at all the Shavian, cheeky, anti-Royal humour, but the parallel with the intruder who sat on her bed but a week before, must have been too close for comfort, for I never saw her smile once.

* * *

While still mid-season, Richard Digby Day asked me to go to the Nottingham Playhouse and play 'Cleopatra' for him. I jumped at the chance to play Egypt's Queen again, particularly as the previous experience had been so unsatisfactory. Richard said he wanted to do a completely uncut version. This pleased me enormously. He also mentioned that he wanted to do it in modern evening dress. This did not please me at all. I tried to talk him out of it, but he was adamant, saying that it was essentially a 'chamber piece'. This is true of the scenes in Egypt and indeed the Senate in Rome, but the play also contains the wonderful stage direction 'The Roman army crosses the stage'! And of course there is the Battle of Actium, which takes place at sea. But I desperately wanted to do the play again and the Nottingham Playhouse had always been regarded as one of the top regional theatres in Britain. He also asked if I would play one of the most famous of all female comedy parts, Millamant, in the Restoration comedy *The Way of the World*. It was an offer no actress could refuse.

The Regent's Park season lasts in all, counting rehearsals, for five months. One plays in all weather and a terrific feeling of camaraderie is thus engendered. It is usually very sad when a company breaks up at the end of a run, although in the acting profession it is often inevitable that one will work with the same actors again, sometimes not for years, but the nature of the business is such that one is able to pick up where one left off. To my delight, a couple of the actors would be joining the 'Cleopatra' cast. But mostly they were new to me. Playing one of 'Cleopatra's' servants was Gregory Doran, a very pretty young actor. He was the messenger who brings the news to Cleopatra that 'Antony' has married 'Octavia'. She goes berserk and almost kills him. There were nights when I used to get carried away and belabour poor Greg unmercifully. He has since become a famous director, most particularly with the RSC. He was also in *The Way of the World* with me, but in spite of being aware of my ability as an actress, he has not employed me, I notice! Maybe I shouldn't have hit him so hard!

Malcolm Sinclair, a superb actor who had been with me in *Misalliance*, was playing 'Octavius Caesar' in the show and brilliant he was too. Douglas Hodge, who had been in the season at Regent's Park playing very small parts, suddenly came into his own. He, too, was playing a servant (everyone had to play dozens of different parts as it is a cast of thousands!) and on his first entrance into the play, comes to Antony to tell him that his wife is dead. Well, Dougie came on and said the simple words, 'Fulvia, my lord 'is dead.' That's all. But it brought the rehearsal room to a standstill. We all held our collective breath. There was something about the way he said it. The utter truth of his delivery, that was so compelling, that every actor believed at that moment that 'Fulvia' had not only lived and was a very real person, but that she had indeed died. We all, as one man, looked to 'Antony' (played sublimely well by the actor Ian McCulloch) to see how he would take the news, such was the power of the acting between the two men. I was very fortunate indeed to have the support of so many fine actors.

The same applied to the play which followed, *The Way of the World*. My leading man was Frank Barrie, who had just come from playing the same part, Mirabell, at the National Theatre, opposite Geraldine McEwan. A tough act to follow! Also in the cast, apart from Dougie Hodge and Greg Doran, was Hilary Tindall who had been my predecessor in *The Brothers*. She and I had hit if off immediately when we worked together in television and now here we were, sharing a dressing-room at Nottingham.

It had been a tough rehearsal schedule, because I was rehearsing all day and playing 'Cleopatra' at night. *Antony and Cleopatra*, uncut, runs for 3¾ hours and we had two matinees a week. That meant 7½ hours on stage. On one memorable occasion we did three performances in one day, a schools morning matinee having been inserted into the schedule, so that time I spent 11¼ hours on stage. No joke, I can tell you. I was so tired during rehearsals for *The Way of the World* that I used to take cat-naps in the rehearsal room. One time, I fell asleep on top of an upright piano! I have since adopted this form of sleeping arrangement, because it means one is out of the way and not likely to get trodden on by a passing actor!

Hilary at that time was being harassed by the Press. We had heard that they were likely to turn up at the Stage Door on the Saturday afternoon, so as to get a photograph and a story in the Sunday newspapers. We decided to try to trick them. Hilary was taller than I, but not much. We were both brunettes and of a similar build. We were also about the same age. Accordingly, while she slipped into the theatre via the front of house, I drove up to the Stage Door in her car. I was clad in Hilary's very expensive cashmere coat, her suede boots, her Hermès silk scarf and her large sunglasses. She always had very good 'classical taste' and despaired of my Bohemian ways! I parked the car near the Stage Door and got out, slamming the door behind me. I heard a series of echoing slams as the various members of the Press witnessed my arrival and got ready to pounce. I then did what I considered to be a very passable imitation of Hilary's rather swaggering walk!

Up to the Stage Door I strode pursued by calls of 'Hilary,' 'Miss Tindall,' 'er, Hilary, could we have a word?' 'Miss Tindall, can we have a photo?' etc. etc. As I reached the Stage Door I turned round and lowered the sunglasses. 'Can I help you?' I asked airily, knowing full well that they were beyond help. The battery of cameras that were pointed in my direction were lowered in disappointment. 'Good afternoon, gentlemen,' I said affably and went in. We had pulled it off! Sadly Hilary died a mere ten years later, but I hope she's up there still chuckling to herself. I had found Millamant very difficult to learn and on the whole I prefer not to have to do two enormous parts concurrently. I am sure it was partly because I was giving my all to Cleopatra, but I struggled with the lines for *The Way of the World*. Congreve is not the easiest of writers; his language is brilliant, but dense. I had done only one other of his plays, *Love for Love*, at Watford, years previously, but that was a less complicated plot. One of the crits said, 'Miss O'Mara speaks her lines as though she has only just thought of them.' How right he was!

* * *

My son, meanwhile, had spent several years at the Royal
Shakespeare Company, learning everything there was to be
gleaned about the theatre. Dickon worked in every department,
so that now he can design, build, paint and light sets. He can rig
and de-rig, do the sound, run the show from the prompt corner.
He has acted on stage and I often went to see productions he had
worked on, only to find him appearing on stage, and he'd never
told me. While he was at the RSC he met the adorable actress
Jenny Agutter and was with her for several years. He eventually
accompanied her to Los Angeles where he started his own set
construction company. They were both there when I arrived in
1985 to do *Dynasty* and we all shared a house together. This was
tremendous fun and worked surprisingly well. I was very upset
when their relationship finally came to an end, as I had grown
very fond of her.

* * *

As a result of playing 'Cleopatra' opposite Ian McCulloch,
Richard Digby Day, our director, decided that we had to play
'Macbeth' and 'Lady Macbeth' as well, but with a difference. It
would be just the two of us! This way, he claimed, without 'all
those tedious lords and thanes,' the Macbeths' relationship and
its deterioration would be under the spotlight. The play, thus
truncated, would form the second half of the entertainment. The
first half would consist of anecdotes, reportage and stories, some
possibly apocryphal, of all the bad luck associated with the play.
It was to be called *An Evening with the Macbeths.*

The first half would be about an hour long. We would perform
in full evening dress, recounting with humour and a slight air of
urbane condescension, an extraordinary melange of facts. When
we had finished we would then announce to the audience, that
having heard all about the play, would they please repair to the
bar and down a few stiff drinks, because after the interval, things
were going to get serious! We were going to do the play for them,
just the two of us! This pronouncement was always received by
the audience with slightly nervous laughter. They must have
wondered what on earth they were in for.

While they were refreshing themselves, we got ourselves togged out in eleventh-century gear, to be as far removed as possible from our former sophisticated selves. The lights dimmed alarmingly, there was the sound of wind howling across the heath, followed by the eerie disembodied voices of the three witches and then Ian went into the first big soliloquy. He had been a magnificent 'Antony', whom he had played as a weary old lion, a soldier who is tired of fighting and is totally infatuated with the 'Queen of the Nile'. Now, he played the younger, ambitious, energetic soldier with a keen hunger not for a woman, but for power. It was an inspired performance.

However, before *An Evening with the Macbeths* could be realised in 1983, I was cast in a revival of *The Rehearsal* by Anhouilh, which was to be directed by Gillian Lynne, the brilliant choreographer of *Cats*. It was to star Leslie Caron, the gamine French actress, Dinsdale Landen, an eccentrically brilliant actor, the wonderful Peter Jeffrey and Lalla Ward, a young actress who had tremendous vulnerability and who had been Tom Baker's assistant in *Dr Who*. The set, which was all mirrors and the costumes, which were cool colours and divine, were by Carl Toms, one of the top designers in the theatre. The production was destined for London, so everywhere we went we were billed as 'Prior to London'. We never got there however, for various reasons. The play was almost entirely miscast. Leslie Caron, although a delightful actress, spoke her lines, naturally enough, with a heavy French accent. The rest of us played our parts in our own English accents, which was obviously odd and inconsistent. The play is set in France, but the adaptation was, I thought, uninspired. The music was by Stephen Sondheim, why, I cannot say.

Gillian, whom I adored, used to do a physical warm-up every day before rehearsals which was a form of torture, although Leslie, being a trained ballerina, sailed through the proceedings. But, in spite of this company activity, the show was not a happy one. We packed out wherever we went, but the reviews were damning. One described Leslie's performance as a cross between a linguaphone record and the Queen's Christmas

Broadcast and also said the production was so leaden, they seriously doubted whether the motorways of Britain could sustain a prolonged tour!

There was a huge scene in the middle of the show which was a two-hander between Dinsdale Landen and Lalla Ward. Peter Jeffrey and I would betake ourselves off to an empty dressing-room, turn off the tannoy and read scenes from Shakespeare together to retain our sanity. At one point, Trevor Nunn turned up to give us all notes at Gillian's behest. At another time, Gillian came into my dressing-room and told me that it had been decided that I should take over from Leslie Caron and then they would re-cast my part. Then and then only would the management contemplate taking the show into the West End. Well, as so often before, I was doomed to disappointment and it never happened.

This is par for the course in this profession. I have been summoned into the head office of Columbia Pictures and informed that they were going to put me under contract, but they didn't, Universal, and The Minish Organisation made similar noises but to no effect, so did Warner Bros. and Paramount. Jack Hawkins wanted me to meet the director Henry Hathaway and to that end, invited me over to dinner at his house. I was just getting ready, when the phone rang and Jack's wife informed me in a cold voice that my presence would not be required! What happened there? Who knows?

* * *

For the previous few years I had been sharing my life and my house with Steven Howard, a sports journalist with an impeccable theatrical provenance. His grandfather was the film idol Leslie Howard, his father the actor Ronald Howard, his uncle, famous for being Jimmy Edwards' much-put-upon assistant master, the actor Arthur Howard and most notably his cousin, the charismatic leading actor at the RSC for many years, Alan Howard.

Steve had no pretensions in that direction and was reasonably happy as a staff reporter and occasionally features writer. His only frustration being that whenever he tried to infiltrate Shakespearean quotes or even 'long words' into his reportage, they were ruthlessly excised by a sub-editor. Without one realising it, 'dumbing down' had begun subtly even in those days, courtesy of Rupert Murdoch. Steve was a happy-go-lucky sort of chap, permanently affable and good-humoured. Unfortunately, his preferred place of recreation, like others of his tribe, was the pub. I, who had suffered at the hands of an alcoholic father, went to great lengths to avoid pubs and indeed alcohol. However, Steve was good company, had had an excellent education, so we rubbed along together for several years.

After the failure of *The Rehearsal* to transfer to the West End, it began to dawn on me that my career was not going so well as I would have liked. After *Triangle*, television seemed to have dried up and although I was always on a short-list for one film or another, someone else would get the part. One of these was in a James Bond movie. I have no idea which one. I just knew that my photo had been sent out to Sean Connery on a yacht somewhere and I was 'hot favourite' for several weeks. Huh! If you believe that, you'll believe anything! Anyway, that didn't happen either. Apparently I was too short. Well, they have to come up with some excuse. So I went on yet another tour!

* * *

It was called *The Exorcism* and was a horror tale with a very strong moral slant. In it with me were Norman Eshley (a romantic leading man on television for many years in various sit-coms), Doug Fisher and a girl I hadn't seen since she was in her early twenties, Vivien Heilbron. The author of the play, Don Taylor, was also the director. It was a spooky piece to perform. I had to go into a trance towards the end and then wake up as someone else! I had the most horrifying speech in which, occasionally, I even used to frighten myself!

Vivien and I used to drive everywhere together and share digs, which on a long tour makes life much more pleasant. At least it's supposed to. Good digs are not easy to find and more often than not, it is a case of trial and error. One particular cottage we booked was definitely an error. We were somewhere up North, possibly Ashton-under-Lyne or Chesterfield. It was winter and bitterly cold. There was no heating in the cottage and the sheets were damp. I attempted to light a few twigs and pieces of coal, but they too were damp. We sat huddled around its weak glow trying to warm our fingers around cups of packet soup.

We were reluctant to go to bed as Vivien was convinced we'd get frostbite in our extremities during the night. She said she had a feeling that they turned black before dropping off and she had no wish to wake up in the morning with black feet. 'There's a Red Indian tribe called the Black Foot,' I volunteered helpfully. 'You could always join them.' Vivien gave me a withering look. 'I'm not sure that they'd welcome an amputee, unbidden, into their midst with unbridled joy,' she retorted scornfully. 'No, you may be right there,' I conceded. 'I believe they're renowned for their stealth.' 'I rest my case,' she said with finality and so saying, she turned on her heel and exited up the tiny staircase. I should mention here that in those days, we *all* called them Red Indians. I was not being deliberately offensive, merely accurate. That was how we spoke then.

A few moments later, Vivien made an entrance at the top of the stairs. She was wearing a polo-neck sweater, pyjamas, dressing gown, two cardigans, a pair of socks and on top of these, a pair of bed socks, a shawl, a scarf, a pair of woolly mittens and a hat with a pompom on it. 'I'm going to bed,' she announced briefly and so saying retired for the night. 'Sleep well,' I called after her, but my words had a hollow ring to them. I followed suit shortly afterwards and climbed into my damp bed, but could not stand it for long and climbed out again and went downstairs to spend an uncomfortable night in an arm chair. I awoke early with a stiff neck and feeling terrible!

I came to a decision. I got my suitcase, packed all my belongings, tidied the place, cleared out the grate and then revived myself with a pot of tea. At eight o'clock I set off for the nearest phone box – we didn't have mobile phones in those days and there was no phone in the cottage – and contacted the owner of the cottage and informed her that we were leaving. She was furious. I told her that she had our deposit but that we were not prepared to pay a penny more, as the accommodation was not up to standard. I said I would report her to the Tourist Board, the Theatre and just about everyone else I could think of. I had had a ghastly night and was in a high old rage and I never content myself with two words where a hundred will do. I ranted for some time, slammed down the receiver and trudged back to the cottage.

I was in the middle of loading up the car with my gear when Vivien, who liked to get her full ten hours in the arms of Morpheus, appeared looking startled. 'What's going on?' she demanded. 'We're leaving,' I replied tersely. 'But, we can't, we've paid for the week!' she protested, her Scots heritage rising to the surface in an unwelcome manner. 'No, we haven't, nor are we going to. I've checked us out.' Vivien took this in and regarding me as though I had suddenly assumed the mantle of Flora MacDonald, she said, 'What on earth did she say?' 'Well, she was fairly unpleasant, but it's done now.' 'But where are we going?' she demanded. 'Davy's coming up to stay for a few days, you remember.' 'We're going to the nearest hotel to the theatre,' I said firmly. She gasped. 'Yes, I know we can't afford it, but if we both go down with pneumonia, they won't be able to do the show – there's only one female understudy, you recall.'

My reasoning won the day. 'Anyway, it'll be nice for you and David to have a few nights in an hotel,' I added. David Rintoul, Vivien's partner of many years, was also Scottish and I privately doubted that he would regard this extravagance with equanimity. The extreme warmth of the hotel which greeted us on our arrival there, more than made up for any misgivings we might have had and dispelled all lingering qualms. If anyone is under the delusion that the life of an actress is glamorous or that touring around the country sounds like jolly good fun, I should now like to disabuse them of this entertaining fiction, born of the 'we could do the show, right here in the barn' lore of Hollywood musicals of the pre- and immediately postwar era.

Some weeks later, Vivien and I were on our way to the Sheffield area on a bleak dark, rainy, Sunday evening. We were hoping to find a petrol station fairly soon as we had almost run out. The radio was on in the car to give us comfort. It was news time. We listened attentively to take our minds off the fact that we were travelling on a thimble-full of fuel. The newscaster was warning us of a man whom the police wanted to question, regarding several murders. He was dangerous and the public was advised not to approach him. The newscaster was quite adamant about this last point. The man had been seen in the Sheffield area and would possibly be hiding in a barn or out-building in the surrounding countryside. They mentioned the name of a village where he was thought to be heading.

Vivien had been consulting the map all the while, having been appointed navigator. 'How funny,' she observed without any noticeable humour, 'that's exactly where we're going.' 'Fancy that,' I replied, trying to sound only mildly interested. The red light on the fuel gauge was now on permanently and making plaintive noises. 'Yes, all right, all right,' I said irritably to it, 'we're on the outskirts of Sheffield. There's bound to be a petrol station any minute now!' And so there was, in the nick of time. The car ground to a halt right by the petrol pump. 'Phew,' we both exclaimed in unison. 'Just made it!' We filled up.

'Where now?' I enquired as we left the town and headed towards the country. It was absolutely dark, but Vivien was a good map reader. We turned off the main road and headed up a lane. 'Are you sure this is right?' I asked doubtfully. 'I can't see anything that looks like human habitation.' 'I can just discern the outline of mountains,' she said hopefully. We had booked into an old cotton mill and it definitely said in the brochure 'set in the glorious hills of Edale.' I said, 'This *can't* be right. There are no signs anywhere.' We were in the middle of a network of country lanes, any one of which could lead to Edale. 'We should have started out earlier. It gets dark so quickly at this time of year,' I added. 'Do you think he's there already?' said Vivien tentatively. 'Who, David?' 'No, the Fox.' This was the nickname the Press had given the wanted murderer.

For a moment we sat in silence contemplating the awful prospect of arriving at an unknown deserted cotton mill in the pitch dark. 'I tell you what,' I said after a moment, 'we'll pretend to be lots of people.' 'How do you mean?' 'Well, for God's sake we're actresses,' I replied. 'We'll assume different voices, as we get out of the car and slam the doors several times. He'll think he's outnumbered and not attack us.' 'But we won't know where the door is and he might shoot his way out if he panics and thinks we're going to discover his hiding place.' I had to admit that the scenario was decidedly grim. We looked at the map again and decided to take the next turning we came to and hope for the best.

We set off again, found a turning and took it. It led to a dead end at the foot of the side of a mountain. Then the car broke down. 'What's happened?' asked Vivien in a matter of fact way. Although she had learned to drive, she preferred not to and was not car-minded. 'The gearbox has seized up,' I said trying to sound as though it was an everyday occurrence. The car was an automatic one and we were well and truly stranded. 'Ah,' observed Vivien picking up my tone. 'Now what do we do?' 'Get out and try to get help,' I replied briefly sounding like Arthur Lowe in *Dad's Army* when caught in an insurmountable situation. 'Fine,' she said with equanimity and glanced at herself in the rear mirror to check that her appearance passed muster for a social call. We got out of the car slowly and braced ourselves against the freezing cold air.

At that moment, a figure loomed out of the darkness and approached us. We both stood transfixed and rooted to the spot. He had a torch. He let the beam fall on my face. 'Kate O'Mara?' he asked in astonishment. 'Yes,' I said falteringly. 'Good lord,' he said with joyful enthusiasm. 'Do you remember me? We used to be neighbours when you lived in Twickenham – oh, this is my brother,' he added, as another man loomed up. 'Sir Galahad and Sir Lancelot, I presume,' I cried joyfully, 'this is my friend and companion, the actress Vivien Heilbron!' 'A most welcome sight!' she said, 'it's the greatest of pleasures to meet you both.' We explained our predicament.

In no time at all, we had transferred our luggage to their car and a few moments later were pulling into the drive at Edale Mill. The lights were blazing forth from the old building. Inside David was already ensconced and had lit a fire. 'We bought crumpets earlier,' I cried triumphantly. Our two heroes and saviours had arranged to have my car towed away by the local garage. They now joined us for a glorious tea around a large scrubbed pine table with blue and white china, steaming Lapsang Souchong, toasted crumpets dripping with melted butter and honey! A happy end to a somewhat stressful day.

* * *

Another of the rigours of touring is that in some of the more out of the way places, it is difficult to obtain items that one can purchase with ease in London. I had developed what I considered to be rather fetching silver streaks in my hair. Girls were paying fortunes to have them put in, but I had them naturally. However, the consensus was that people liked me as a brunette, so I was obliged to cover them up with assorted hair rinses. I had read somewhere that elderberries made an ideal natural hair colouring and as one week we were staying in a cottage surrounded by elderberry trees, I decided to try it.

We duly picked a basket of the berries. I stewed them on the gas stove and then realised I had no thickening agent to make the stuff stay on my head. I decided to improvise with self-raising flour. The result was that when I massaged it into my hair, my head resembled a blueberry muffin. The flour, having been activated by the heat of the fruit, had become a purple dough! Thank heaven I was playing a bohemian part on stage at night, as I had aubergine hair for a fortnight.

After the tour was over, I went home for Christmas and the New Year. I had absolutely no work, and no prospect of work. My agent told me frankly that he was unable to get me work, that people simply didn't want to know and that my only chance was the States, since they appreciated glamour out there. I realised that the glory days were over. I went on tour with my mother, who was still pursuing an active career. The play was *The Ghost Train*. This was the first time we had ever worked together and although I was only playing a small part, I had taken the job so that I could chauffeur her around the country. I had replaced Nyree Dawn Porter, with only three days' rehearsal. She in turn had taken over from Fenella Fielding who had left the show. During my brief rehearsal time, which amounted to about half an hour each day, the other actors kept saying, 'Let's cut to Kate's entrance,' or 'let's just do Kate's bits,' so that although I knew my lines, I had absolutely no idea of what preceded them or indeed came after them before the next lot.

My mother, who by this time was getting progressively more deaf and very blind, was on this occasion of no help whatsoever. On my first night, I found myself sitting next to her, upstage away from the main action, listening desperately for my next cue, which I hoped to God I would recognise. My mother leaned towards me confidentially and murmured under her breath, 'Can you nudge me when my cue comes?' I turned on her with a look of horror and disbelief on my face. 'What!' I whispered back. She became confidential again. 'Can you nudge me when my cue comes?' she repeated. 'Listen!' I hissed savagely, in a stage whisper, 'How the *fuck* do I know what your cue is? I haven't a clue what *mine* is!' I needn't have worried though. Blind and deaf she may have been, but when her cue came, she heard it all right and was up and charging off down-stage to join in the action! I think she enjoyed me driving her around the countryside. It was spring and we visited heritage sites on our Sundays off and had a thoroughly good time. A memory I cherish.

* * *

In the summer of 1984 I returned to Regent's Park once more to play one of the 'Merry Wives of Windsor'. David Conville directed and naturally had to set it in Victorian times. Yes, it's the only one of Shakespeare's plays which deals with the middle classes. It isn't about royalty or the aristocracy, and even Sir John Falstaff, who features, is made the butt of everyone's fun. But the Victorians were a very different kettle of fish from the Elizabethans. As Mistress Ford, I had some fairly sexually overt lines and I found them impossible to say, clad as I was in a crinoline and ringlets with not an inch of flesh showing anywhere. I had always seen the 'wives' as plump, rosy wenches with plenty of cleavage, their sleeves rolled up, their hands covered in flour. So, every time I had a raunchy line to speak, I found myself compelled to let my hand fly to my mouth as though appalled at what I'd just said. The trouble is, directors never think these things through. I decided against the ringlets and tried to make her more basic, by doing my hair in a bun in the nape of my neck.

Dora Bryan was in the show and stole it single-handedly. As far as I'm concerned, the old adage of 'never work with children and animals' should read, 'never work with children, animals or Dora Bryan.' She was quite simply devastatingly brilliant! She made all the Elizabethan word play which to modern ears was gobbeldy-gook, totally comprehensible. The audience understood every word. Or thought they did.

Richard E Grant was also in the cast. Philippa Gail, who was playing the other 'Merry' wife, and I despaired of him. 'That boy needs a kick up the bottom!' she confided to me one afternoon at a matinee. I agreed wholeheartedly. 'Wet' didn't adequately describe his performance. I used to say to him as we were all waiting to go on, 'For God's sake, Richard, get on that stage and give it some welly, so that we don't have to come on and pick it up off the floor, where you've just left it!' He never got any better in spite of my bullying. At the end-of-term Gala, I 'glammed' myself up for the occasion and was covered in make-up, hair, false eyelashes, sequins and rhinestones. I bumped into Richard as we were about to go on. He gasped, grabbed me by the waist and said, 'Why Kate, you're beautiful!' I was highly amused. Actually, it's amazing that he still speaks to me after the way I treated him. But he does. And he seems to be doing all right without my help!

That autumn, Ian McCulloch and I finally managed to get *An Evening with the Macbeths* on at Colchester. It was a resounding success and further dates were promised. But my life was about to change dramatically.

* * *

In January 1985, I opened a letter one bleak morning. It purported to be written by the girlfriend of the boy I had given

131

up for adoption nineteen years previously. My heart stopped. My worst fears had been realised. The law concerning the children of adopted parents had been changed the year before and I had hoped and prayed that my son would not seek me out, as I knew no good could possibly result from such an encounter. But worse was to come. The letter informed me that he had already been to the Press and was quite prepared to go again. The girl begged me to see him. It would transform him, she assured me, as he had been consorting with an undesirable crowd. It was a touching letter, but the underlying threat was unmistakable. I was out of work, my relationship with Steve had been in pieces for some time, I was at a low ebb and I didn't know how I was going to cope.

4

'What we really need is someone like Kate O'Mara – only younger'

The weeks that followed were horrendous. For four days after receiving the letter, I was unable to move my left arm. It seemed to be paralysed. I suppose I must have been in a state of shock. Then, once I got the feeling back, I started to tremble and shake uncontrollably. It was probably just as well that I wasn't working. I realised there was no escape from the situation. I had to meet the boy. My dear friend Patricia came to the rescue. She offered her flat as a rendezvous and it was all arranged. I arrived at the appointed hour and then again lost all feeling in my left arm. 'I can't move my arm,' I told her. I saw a look of extreme alarm cross her face, but she hastened to reassure me.

There was a ring at the front door and she came back a few seconds later with someone who bore no resemblance to either me or the father. I started to shake again. It was like a bad dream. Patricia left us alone together. Summoning all my strength, I tried to explain to him why I had had him adopted. He didn't seem interested. I told him of how, at the time, I had been destitute, desperate and abandoned. He just looked at me. The whole meeting was distressing and ghastly. I realised it had been a mistake, he didn't want to listen, or try to understand. He just sat and stared at me in an unnerving way. I got the impression that he just wanted money – I thought he'd been put *up* to it and just wanted to be part of what he imagined was my glamorous lifestyle.

Rather foolishly, I allowed him to come to my home. At that time Steve and I were living in a very old semidetached cottage in Surrey. It was tiny. 'This isn't where you live, is it?' he asked in disbelief. He was plainly expecting some huge Georgian mansion. Like so many members of the public, he was under the delusion that actors and actresses earn lots of money. At this particular point in my career, it so happened that I was absolutely broke and was driving some beat-up old car. I never have glamorous cars or clothes and my dwelling places are always modest in the extreme. But people don't understand this and clearly he didn't either. His visit was a disaster.

I began to dread answering the telephone. He would ring me constantly. I don't know what he really wanted, but I always felt threatened. It was a nightmare. I started to refuse to answer the phone. Steve would take the calls for me. The boy told him that he'd been to the Press before and that he would go to them again. I told him unequivocally that if he went near the Press, I would never speak to him again. Well, he went to them, again and again and again, last time as recently as two years ago. I was devastated and I have had no further contact with him. I daresay many will think me heartless and uncaring. Any mother will know and understand the awful pain and distress I experienced when I had been persuaded, against my better judgement, to offer him for adoption. The thought of having my own private grief and despair which I had nursed secretly in my heart for nineteen years paraded for people to pore over was more than I could bear. I had managed to keep it a secret from my own parents, even from my sister. I had wanted to spare them the pain of *my* pain. I realised that one way to escape from all this was to remove myself from the public gaze.

I made a decision, I would give up acting and try to get a job as an assistant to a director. I sat down and composed a letter that I proposed to send to the directors of various repertory companies in the UK, offering my services. No sooner had I done this, when my agent rang and said, 'You've just been offered four episodes of *Dr Who*, playing the Queen of some planet or other. I've told them you'll do it, money's crap of course, but that goes without saying, anyway you're doing it.'

I accepted my fate and found myself once again working with my old mate Colin Baker. He and I had been sparring partners in *The Brothers*. I had enjoyed my scenes with him enormously and was looking forward to working with him again.

In fact, we had come across one another on several occasions. The first time was in 1970 at the Yvonne Arnaud Theatre, Guildford, in a good old-fashioned play called *The Holly and the Ivy*. Colin was not actually in it; he was understudying the part of the son. I should mention that this part was a very large one: huge two-handed scenes with the father, big scenes with the aunts, the sisters, etc. etc. Colin appeared the first day of rehearsals with the female understudy, worked for one morning and then the two of them went off to do something else – a studio production, I think, but still attached to the theatre. The point is that we never saw either of them again until the fateful day when the actor playing the son was 'off' with food-poisoning, gastric flu or something.

Whatever it was, he was at home in bed and Colin, who had, at best, an extremely tenuous passing acquaintance with the text, was 'on'. He came to me just before the curtain went up. Neither of us was on until about half an hour into the play. He was on first, and then I made a dramatic entry towards the end of the first act. I started to go through Colins' lines with him. He did not know them. I went as far as I could, then on he went. I listened apprehensively for a few moments. After hearing him struggle for a while, I decided I couldn't bear it and turned the tannoy off. Finally, I was called to the stage where I found a lot of people looking extremely strained and white at the knuckles. The second act found us all on-stage in a little family group, with Colin lying on the floor stretched out in a nonchalant manner. I witnessed the 'actor's nightmare' at first hand.

This is a well-known phenomenon that happens to every actor and actress. The dreams take various forms. One is about to make one's entrance and either one has no idea *what* the play is, or one *knows* the play, but can't remember *any* of the lines, or one *used* to know the lines and if only one could lay one's hands on a script, one could revise in time before going on! I have spent dreams, frantically scouring a theatre for a costume, a script or *some* indication as to what the play might be. The extraordinary thing is that none of the other actors present in the dream will help one, nor do they seem to be in any way perturbed by one's panic. A psychologist would doubtless dismiss them as 'anxiety dreams'. Whatever the underlying cause, it is a tremendous relief to wake and find oneself in one's own bed!

Well, all of this is what happened to Colin, except that it wasn't a dream. It was a living nightmare! I recall him lying there in a pool of sweat, somehow getting through it, while we all tried to help him out where we could. Afterwards, I thought to myself, if he can survive this, he deserves to succeed!

* * *

I enjoyed playing the Rani in *Dr Who* in 1985. She had supposedly been at University with the Doctor and was herself a Time Lord. The great advantage of playing power-crazed people (and the Rani wanted to rule the Universe, in fact *any* Universe and any number of Galaxies) is that one can be as extreme as one likes in the big scenes, because being totally fictional and science-fictional to boot, there are no rules of conduct. One assumes that a creature such as the Rani, who is a scientist, is totally amoral and prepared to sacrifice all in the cause of science. It is interesting playing ruthless characters, they are motivated purely by self-interest and get off on power. I'm a bit like that myself, although I would like to think I have *some* redeeming features!

I had a fairly alarming experience while on location for *Dr Who*. The Rani is supposedly the mistress of disguise, and in this episode had transmogrified into an old crone. The make-up department had made a latex mask for me that was a wrinkled and ravaged version of my own visage. Liquid latex had been painted on to my face and left to set. The result was suitably grotesque. I was given a straw with which to breathe through my nose and told not to panic!

One morning on location in the Black Country, cradle of the Industrial Revolution, we were filming my first episode of *Dr Who*. In the make-up caravan at about 6.30 on a dark and chilly morning, my latex mask was being fitted onto my face. Attached to it were wisps of long grey hair. My mouth was blanked out and my eyelashes powdered. I was clad in mid-nineteenth-century clothes – long skirt, boots, petticoats with shawls over my shoulders, mittens, a mob cap and more shawls on my head. Well, at least I was warm. I was glad of my bundle of old clothes when I stepped down from the caravan into the early morning air. The make-up girl had suggested that I grab a spot of breakfast while waiting to be called to film.

I never eat breakfast, but thought a cup of hot tea would be welcome, so I made my way to what I could see was the mobile canteen truck. To my surprise, I found that people were brushing against me and in some cases, roughly pushing me out of the way. I have always been used to a certain amount of deference on a film set. On the whole, I have found film crews to be the most affable and overly polite bunch of men. (It is only relatively recently that women have managed to infiltrate this male technical preserve – women have traditionally been make-up and hair artists and continuity girls). Of course, I was unrecognisable. I began to wonder whether the courteous, respectful treatment I had always received on a film set was due to my status and maybe people thought I was an extra and perhaps extras were always subjected to this lack of consideration. But then I saw some young girls receiving smiles and right of passage from technicians engaged in the normal hustle and bustle of setting up.

I joined the queue at the canteen truck. Several people pushed in front of me. I finally managed to get a cup of weak tea, but not before a member of the kitchen staff had demanded ungraciously of me what I wanted. It was pointed out to me with barely concealed irritation, that the tea was self-service from an urn on an adjoining table. I took a polystyrene cup and poured it. I found a piece of plastic that passed for a spoon and put in plenty of sugar to make up for the weakness of the tea. I searched around and, seeing an upturned oil drum, sat down thankfully. 'Sorry, luv, need that,' and it was wrenched unceremoniously from under me by a passing crew member. It gradually dawned of me that it was not just because people did not recognise me that I was being treated so carelessly, it was because people thought I was an old woman. I wondered whether my mother, who was always playing what she called 'bundles', was subjected to this indignity on set. Eventually, I gave up and went back to the make-up caravan for warmth and to await my call.

We started filming at 7.30 a.m. and I had some fairly unpleasant scenes where I had to pretend to put maggots into an actor's mouth! The maggots were a heaving, glistening mass and smelled revolting. I had a make-up change during the morning, when my mask had to be removed and my normal self was revealed, but I was still wearing my rags. The big transformation came at midday. I was taken off to the wardrobe caravan and put into tight black, aubergine and bronzed leather pants, matching plunging jacket and thigh-high heeled boots. I had hair down to my waist and my most glamorous make-up. Transformed, I stepped out of the make-up caravan once again. I was immediately surrounded by men. Someone brought me a chair, someone else produced a plate of lunch 'all vegetarian, because I know that's what you like,' yet another person submitted a cup of tea – in a proper cup and saucer. The contrast was total and revelationary. I decided there and then that I would never get old if I could possibly help it!

This all happened in 1985 and things have generally improved for women, largely thanks to Joan Collins, who made being an 'older woman' acceptable, but only the other day I read a review of a film featuring the ever-youthful Catherine Deneuve, whose beauty transcends the advancing years. It read, 'Mlle Deneuve is a credible sex-object in spite of her sixty odd years.' I rest my case!

In spite of my inauspicious beginning, I found filming Dr Who immensely enjoyable. It has an atmosphere all its own, probably due to its enduring popularity, the affection it engenders in the public's hearts and its undeniable cult status. I was later to do more, but my first efforts in 'The Mark of the Rani' were my favourite episodes.

Interval

It is possibly because I am able to learn lines quickly, or that producers know that I am totally reliable and won't let them down, or simply because I have a reputation for rising to a challenge, that I am always being asked to take over a part from some other actress, at *very* short notice. One such occasion had happened a few years before and it was about to do so again! Previously I had gone to bed early one evening, when the phone rang and the silky smooth tones of Rod Coton, Bill Kenwright's right-hand man of many years standing, was heard making polite enquiries as to my health and circumstances. I assured him that all was tickety-boo.

'Are you doing anything at the moment?' he asked casually. 'Well, actually I'm in bed, as it happens,' I replied cautiously. I'd received phone calls of this nature before, and knew from experience that they were inevitably the prelude to an intense acceleration of feverish activity. 'Ah,' he sounded relieved, 'well, in that case, would it be all right if we biked round a script this evening?' 'Ye-es,' I said warily, 'what is it?' 'Er, well, it's a thriller, Francis Durbridge in fact –' 'Oh,' I said without enthusiasm. 'I've done him before.' 'Good, good,' said Rod, waxing enthusiastic, 'this one's called *House Guest* – look, why don't we pop the script round and you let us know what you think?' 'Okay,' I agreed.

The script arrived in a very short space of time; the leading female part was a film star whose son has been kidnapped. I liked the part and, at the time, I had nothing better to do. Besides the money they were offering was quite high. Suspiciously high, if I'd thought it through! Also, my agent had not been contacted.

I read the script and phoned Rod back. 'Yes, all right. I'll do it,' I uttered the fatal words. I've never been able to resist making a quick buck. 'Oh marvellous,' he sounded overjoyed. 'When is it, and where?' I thought I ought to get down to practical details, as plainly my agent was not going to be involved. 'Well, er, we'd like you to go to Birmingham tomorrow.' 'TOMORROW!' 'Yes, well that's where it is playing at the moment. It's better that you rehearse in the actual set.' 'But tomorrow's *Friday*, Rod.' 'That's right,' he agreed. 'But why can't I start on Monday?' 'Because that's when you open.' 'WHAT?' Rod, having played his cards, returned to his silky-smooth dulcet delivery; he, like Bill, had been an actor in his time. 'You block it through tomorrow in Brum at the Alex, come back, you've got the weekend to learn it, dress rehearsal Monday afternoon, then open Greenwich in the evening.' He made the whole thing sound totally reasonable and utterly normal. Shirley Ann Field had left to do a film in Ireland and I would be replacing her.

I was, for once, speechless. But I can never resist a challenge and so I found myself on a train to Birmingham the next day. Bill Simpson, the original 'Dr Finlay' and Mark Eden, seen latterly in *Coronation Street* (as lorry driver Wally Ranole), were my two leading men. Both darlings. I came back and started to learn the part on the train on Saturday. I pushed the lines in on Sunday. I went over to Mark's place in Balham, where he took me through the whole script, until I knew it. This was kindness itself, although not entirely altruistic! Thrillers are notoriously difficult to learn, consisting almost entirely of questions and answers that are often non sequiturs.

On Monday afternoon, I found myself at Greenwich Theatre. It was boiling hot, but I'm fond of the theatre at Greenwich. It's a good space to play. Bill had somehow managed to replace Shirley Ann Field's name with mine at very short notice. I was wearing my own clothes and sharing a dressing-room with a bunch of actresses I'd barely met. I had managed to get two more copies of the script, one of which I placed stage-right, the other, stage-left. I kept the original open in my dressing-room. The point being, that although I knew *my* part, I wasn't at all sure as to what happened before or after my scenes or in what order the other scenes occurred. Anyway, although I have to say, I was fairly frightened, nay, terrified, I somehow got through it and played it quite happily for a six-week season.

* * *

So, it was about to happen again. This time, my agent called me and told me that although it was Friday and rehearsals were due to start on Monday and everyone realised it was terribly short notice, but they knew what a 'pro' I was, so they wanted to send me a script and where should they send it? 'They?' I queried. 'The Kenwright Organisation' replied my agent crisply. 'Well, I'm going to the theatre tonight,' I said dubiously, 'so there won't be anyone here to . . .' 'Which theatre?' he interrupted, as he had the Kenwright office on another line. 'The Mermaid,' I replied. After a further exchange with the other phone he said, 'There'll be a script waiting for you at the Stage Door of the Mermaid Theatre before the show. Read it tonight when you get home and if you want to do it, you're to go tomorrow to meet the director in Camden.' 'It's either feast or famine,' I remarked to myself. The reason for this last observation was as follows.

Maude Spector, the much loved and revered veteran casting director, who had been instrumental in giving me my first film break in *Great Catherine*, had been in touch with my agent regarding casting for *The Colby's*, an American TV series which was to be the spin-off from *Dynasty*, which was then the most high-profile TV show in the world. So on the Tuesday of that same week I had toddled off to Park Lane to meet the American casting director. In spite of having just completed *Dr Who*, my bank balance was at an all-time low, partly because I'd been out of work but mainly because the BBC were famous for paying actors far less than anyone else. But, of course, in those days, they had a terrific reputation. In *those* days.

The truth of the matter was that I had precisely £300 in my account. I knew that if I was to be in with a chance of getting something as glamorous as a Hollywood TV series, it was absolutely necessary to 'look the part'. My mother had always instilled this into me. She had a very low opinion of director's and producer's imaginations and always insisted that one went along looking as near to what was required as possible. Reluctantly, I went to a little boutique I knew which specialised in fashionable yet classic garments. I was taking a huge risk, but it had to be done. Taking a deep breath, I spent every last penny that I had on a little Valentino number. I felt terrible, but I had looked in my wardrobe and knew that there was nothing there that would even vaguely pass muster. I dug out some very high black heels, bought two pairs of glossy black tights (in case one laddered) and hoped that fate would look kindly on me.

It was a scorching day on the Tuesday. I arrived early in Park Lane and stood in my Valentino outfit on the corner of Hill Street, watching various women of my own age as they went in. 'You're wasting your time,' I said under my breath, 'this job is *mine.*' Well, it wasn't as it turned out, or at least not this one. But, what to me was something even better, was. It was then *my* turn to go in. It was lovely to see Maude again, who looked exactly as I remembered her. The American casting director was charming and *very* keen. He seemed to think I was *exactly* what they were looking for and could I come back on Thursday and put a short test on film? Absolutely, I most certainly could and I left with high hopes, jubilant that my sartorial investment had so far been justified. Of course, I would have to wear the same outfit for the test, but that couldn't be helped.

On Thursday, the rain was torrential, so I put a full-length black plastic mackintosh over my outfit, pinned my very long hair into tiny pin curls all over my head, covered these with two head-scarves, wore waterproof boots and carried my high heels in a bag and arrived at the sound studio in Soho looking like something out of an Italian post-war movie (*Bitter Rice, Bicycle Thieves* etc, etc). The girl at reception looked at me as though I had crawled out from under a stone. 'Can I help you?' she asked doubtfully. 'Yes, please, I've come to test for *The Colby's.* Could I do my hair in the Ladies?' I asked as humbly and winningly as I could. The look she gave me said quite plainly that in her opinion, no amount of grooming, hairdressing or even a full blown make-over would enhance my chances of getting past the studio door, never mind into Hollywood.

She indicated the appropriate door and I executed the quickest of changes.

I emerged five minutes later all legs, hair, cleavage and glowing skin, but most particularly hair. A huge cloud of the stuff swung and floated around my head like a nimbus. My short skirt and high heels showed my glossy slim legs and trim ankles off to perfection. My Valentino jacket plunged almost to my navel and was nipped in at the waist to make the most of my figure. The only objects marring this vision were my boots, my mackintosh and a polythene bag in which my shoes had been carried. I demanded peremptorily that she look after these unsavoury articles for me forthwith. She sat there, her mouth agape and nodded her assent dumbly.

A few moments later, I was summoned to do my test. I started the proceedings with one leg in the air as though smoothing on my tights – I got the idea from the poster of *The Graduate*. I later heard that it had gone down a storm in LA. Thanks to my early dancing classes I have always been quite pliant, so my leg was up high in shot. I got through the scene, giving it my all. When I had finished, the casting director got very excited, asked me if I had a Green Card and when I replied in the negative, assured me that this would not be a problem, as they would be able to get one for me. I left the studio cock-a-hoop, feeling it was in the bag. Had I known then that sixty girls had been short-listed and eight of those sixty had tested, I daresay I would not have been so sanguine. I simply couldn't believe it when my agent called me to say I hadn't got the part, but I'm running ahead of myself.

Having tested on the Thursday, I went to the Mermaid theatre on the Friday evening. We were going to see *Breaking the Silence*. It starred Steve's cousin Alan Howard and Jenny Agutter; my son Dickon was doing the sound. I collected the script (in case you've forgotten, the one from the Kenwright Office!) from the Stage Door before the show. It was an American piece called *Light up the Sky* by the brilliant writer Moss Hart. After the show, we all went out to supper, Alan, Jenny, Steve, Dickon and myself. Alan noticed I was clutching a script and asked what it was. I told him. 'I was asked to play the director in that a year ago,' he said, 'but I wasn't able to do it. It's a very funny play.' 'I believe Bob Stephens is playing that part now,' I said, as that much I had gleaned. 'What have they offered you?' he asked with interest. 'The ice-skating star,' I replied. 'Best part in the play,' he said with conviction, 'do it!'

We had enjoyed *Breaking the Silence* a great deal and had had a really good evening in the theatre, so we sat over our meal for quite a while, discussing the play and the production. It was very late by the time we got home, but, naturally, I had to look at the script as I was supposed to be meeting the director the following day. So I sat up until the early hours, reading avidly. As soon as the character of 'Frances Black', the ice-skater, appeared, I knew it was a peach of a part and that I would adore to play it.

* * *

Accordingly, the next day I set off for Camden, not a part of London with which I am familiar, but I managed to track down the director, Keith Hack, who had made his name directing Glenda Jackson. I read for him and he seemed reasonably pleased with my rendition. Clutching the script which he had told me to keep, I went home and waited. Sunday came and went and I had heard nothing. At midnight on Sunday, I called Bill at his home. 'So I didn't get it then?' I asked tentatively. 'Of course you got it,' he replied immediately. 'You start tomorrow morning, Her Majesty's Theatre. Rehearsals, ten o'clock.' 'Nobody told me,' I said, rather aggrieved, thinking how I'd been on tenterhooks all day. 'Nobody gave me my call.' 'Didn't they? Well, they should have done,' he said firmly. 'See you there,' he added. 'Night.' And he was gone.

So off I went the following morning to find myself in the company of a truly magnificent cast – the glorious Robert Stephens, the wonderful Maxine Audley, the Broadway actor Robert Morse (who was playing my husband), Gary Waldhorn, Patricia Quinn and Hannah Gordon. My part had originally been earmarked for Maureen Lipman, it turned out, but she had gone off to do a TV series at the last minute. When I had been unable to do a further leg of *Night and Day* for Bill, Maureen Lipman had taken over from me. Bill's reasoning had been, 'If Maureen can play Kate's parts, it follows that Kate can play Maureen's parts.' It doesn't follow at all actually, but I was jolly grateful to have such a humdinger of a part!

We opened at Leatherhead and Maxine and I went down a storm. We had them rolling in the aisles. We were doing a double act and were perfect foils for each other. I was cast completely against type as the dumbest of blondes (except I was now playing it as a redhead!) and Maxine was the streetwise seen-it-all, done-it-all, no-holds barred, tell-it-like-it-is showbiz big mommy of them all! And she was magnificent! One ace after another, forehand smash down the line, backhand skimming the net, you couldn't fault her.

Everyone's hero, Robert Stephens, was mesmeric as the director. I had always idolised him since his early Old Vic days and I had not, as yet, recovered from the fact that he had come to see me play 'Beatrice' in 'Much Ado' at Regent's Park and had sent round a highly complimentary note afterwards. From him, praise indeed. I floated on air for days afterwards. The three of us garnered most of the reviews. But then, we had the best parts. That glorious redhead Patricia Quinn, so memorable in *The Rocky Horror Show*, was playing the secretary brilliantly in an Eve Arden sort of way. She later married Bob Stephens which delighted us all. They were a divine couple.

I'm jumping ahead again, but there is a good reason for this. Everything happened at once. We had only been rehearsing for a few days when I got a visit from one of the girls from my agent's office. She arrived during my lunch break to inform me that Hollywood had called. They wanted me to go out to LA and test for *Dynasty*! Of course, it was impossible. I had already started rehearsing the play. My then agent, Michael Ladkin, was on holiday in Portugal and there were a lot of tortured phone calls from the poolside. It was a huge opportunity, but it couldn't be done. Once one has turned up for rehearsals for a play, even if one hasn't signed a contract – which I hadn't – the very fact of one's presence in that rehearsal-room indicates that one has made a commitment. In any case, I didn't want to leave the play and I had no intention of reneging on a contract, even if it hadn't been signed. So, I had to turn Hollywood down.

I got a call from LA over the weekend. It was from the casting director, Tony. 'Katy, hi there, how are you doin'?' 'Hi Tony, I'm fine thank you.' 'Listen, Katy, we want you out here. They just adored your test. They want to meet you and . . .' 'Er, Tony, you know I'm doing this play, don't you?' 'Katy, this is not a problem. We can buy you out. Let me talk to your producers . . .' 'No Tony, you don't understand. I'm contracted to do this play. I can't break my contract. I would be black-listed.' Long pause. 'Katy, I don't think *you* quite understand. You have the chance of international stardom here!' 'Tony, believe me, I *do* understand and don't get me wrong, I appreciate very much what you are saying and the chance I'm being offered, but I really can't come to Los Angeles, not until I've finished the play at any rate. Please, you *do* see, don't you?' Another long pause. 'How long does your play run?' 'Until October.' 'Katy, I'd really like you to think this over.' 'Thank you, Tony. I will.'

The next night I had a phone call from Maude Spector, practically in tears. Hearing her upset, I started crying as well. She repeated more or less what Tony had said the night before, that they were prepared to buy me out of the play, that they would get me a visa and work permit, how they'd adored my test, etc. etc. I don't think Maude could believe that I was actually turning down a chance to play a major part in the biggest TV series in the world at that time. But I was. I came from the world of the theatre, where a 'gentleman's agreement' was sacrosanct.

We opened at the Old Vic. Maxine and I received reviews that were nothing short of euphoric. So did Bob Stephens. I put Hollywood behind me, no point in dwelling on that now. This was where I belonged, in the theatre. And I was playing the Old Vic, that hallowed place where I had come, as a girl, to see Richard Burton as 'Henry V', Paul Rogers as 'Petruchio', Paul Daneman as 'The Bastard' in *King John*(!). Maxine had been in that production and here I was sharing a dressing-room with her. Bob Stephens had to leave the cast for a prior commitment.

We were all very disappointed, but dear old Peter Wyngarde stepped in and was brilliant.

Then, to my amazement, word came from Hollywood again. They didn't need me out there to test. They would take me on trust and they would wait for me. I was to fly out on 15 October and start work the following week playing Joan Collins' sister in *Dynasty*! As my mother was so fond of saying, 'There you see? God *is* good to little actresses!' Well, he certainly was. The management was informed. 'But we were thinking of picking up the option of the extra week,' they insisted. Michael Ladkin said, 'If they want you, they'll have to come to the tarmac at Heathrow to get you. You're leaving on that plane on the date they first agreed.' And so it came about that Patricia Quinn took over my part for the last week of the show, which had been tagged onto the end. I promised Bill that when I got back from Hollywood I would do *Light Up The Sky* for him again, in the Wet End. And I did.

Act III. Beginners to the stage please

My arrival at LA Airport was unpromising. I was regarded with deep suspicion by the immigration officer – suspicion bordering on intense personal hatred – and, for one awful moment, I thought I was going to be denied entry into the country. He found it necessary to enlist the aid of his superior officer, who muttered that his fears were unfounded. As I stood there nervously awaiting my fate, I wanted to tell them that, far from being an undesirable alien, I could show them stacks of pornographic fan mail proving beyond doubt my eminent desirability. He asked me the nature of my work.

'I'm an actress,' I said, curbing the impulse to add, 'But it's open to debate.' The look he gave me was chilling. I also resisted the urge to jolly things along by saying, 'Is that a gun in your pocket or are you just pleased to see me?,' as I realised that it was indeed a gun in his pocket and this boy was clearly not into older women.

After what seemed an eternity, he snapped my passport shut

and, with a look of deep contempt, gestured to me to get out of his hair. I joined my agent, Michael Ladkin, who was looking apprehensive at the baggage collection point. As indeed he might – the vision of mega-dollars having temporarily gone out of focus before his very eyes.

Things got better after that. I signed my first autograph for a charming porter, who thought I was the bee's knees. I mentally apologised to President Reagan's portrait, as I passed it, for my extreme impudence in presuming to invade his territory (the immigration officer, I was now convinced, was trained to look into people's souls and knew that I was an unwilling visitor).

We waited on the pavement for our car to pick us up and I had just had time to observe sights and smells which reminded me of Tangier, when a white house on wheels drew alongside and we scrambled aboard. We did not avail ourselves of the numerous amenities on offer (television, cocktail cabinet, telephone, gymnasium etc.), but stared bleakly out of the smoked-glass windows at the gargantuan hoardings lining the freeway.

The Beverly Hills Hotel is an old-fashioned establishment done out in very dark green, which I found forest-like and reassuring. One expensive hotel is very much like another on the inside, so once in my room I drew the curtains, shut out the palm trees and turned on the TV set. To my utter delight, after trying about fifteen channels of junk, I found a programme about music and had about 45 minutes of Scarlatti, Viotti, Clementi and various other Baroque babies. This, plus the fact that it poured with rain all Monday, softened the culture shock somewhat. Michael made several phone calls, then we met for a drink in the Polo Lounge.

I slept fitfully for almost twelve hours, then tried to ease the tension in my back by soaking in a hot bath. I went down to breakfast and joined Michael who was already seated at a table. The dining room was adjacent to the Polo Lounge, but was really a sort of loggia that looked out onto a patio overhung with the gnarled and twisted branches of a tree. The whole effect was one of pleasant shade and foliage.

Thus refreshed (I only had tea), we took a taxi to the less expensive part of town to get me some heated rollers, as the security staff at Gatwick had confiscated my butane gas-powered curling tongs. I also needed an alarm clock since I had no way of knowing the time, particularly as my internal clock had gone haywire. The sleazy tawdriness of the area appalled me: everything was brash and tacky. I managed to get the articles I wanted and beat a hasty retreat to the hotel.

There were messages waiting for us from my American agent, informing us that after an initial meeting with him over lunch, my presence was required at the studio to meet the writers and one of the producers. I would also be needed in wardrobe. Michael told me to put on a dress, as this was considered de rigueur. I obliged and, feeling wildly over-dressed, took a cab with him to the American agent's offices, where we were welcomed enthusiastically. With Harry (your softly spoken, cultured American, silver-haired, suntanned, impeccably dressed), who runs the New York office, was his right-hand man in charge of the LA office. He buzzed in and out of the office answering vital calls and sending telexes, then finally rushed off to a meeting that could no longer be denied his presence. After meeting the rest of the office staff we went to lunch, where we sat in a booth on a leather banquette and Harry and I exchanged pleasantries. I've been a vegetarian for years and don't like to eat too much anyway. They could manage a vegetarian sandwich, but brought me one big enough for ten people! I consumed less than one-tenth before we set off for the studio.

There I was taken up to the office of Elaine Rich, who actually ran the show. She turned out to be a thin, tense, attractive woman in her fifties. She was absolutely charming to me but I would hate to incur her displeasure, let alone her wrath. She took me to meet the writers, a husband-and-wife team who thought up the storylines. They proved to be darlings: he a thin, gawky, soft-spoken, retiring man with pale brown, almost beige, wavy hair, and she a Junoesque bouncy brunette who was vociferous in her welcome. She admitted to identifying closely with 'Alexis' (the character Joan Collins played), and they both confessed that they made it up as they went along.

After being given a cup of coffee (of which I was allowed two sips) and a brief synopsis of my storyline (I mentioned that I thought Cassandra a wonderful name – it fell on stony ground and I'm stuck with Caress) I was dismissed to wardrobe, where a sweet girl, Breezie by name, greeted me with a dazzling smile and a rail full of some of the most hideous frocks I have ever seen. I tried on the least offensive, a creation in lime green satin and magenta taffeta, topped with a brown organza meringue. The door opened and the designer, Nolan Miller, appeared.

'Stunning!' he said. 'Just terrific!' and approached me, deft fingers twitching. He shoved the material this way and that, pinned it in here and pulled it out there and, having made it his own, declared it fit for the cameras.

Elaine was summoned. She strode in through the door and shrieked: 'She can't wear that! It's too, too . . .' Words failed her.

A person of uncertain gender then oozed into the fitting room, covered in gold trinkets and baubles and having apparently, absent-mindedly placed his sitting room rug on his head. He took one look at me and uttered the ominous words, 'Joan wore that on a Sony commercial last week.'

'I knew it,' squawked Elaine.

'Are you sure?' ventured Nolan, keen to get back to more important matters.

'Positive,' he said, relishing his role as Nemesis, 'I know because I did her hair!.' And, having ruined everyone's after-noon, he oozed out again.

The offending garment was ripped from my back and I was then shoved in and out of various other monstrosities. With each new frock, I was scrutinised and commented upon as though I was not present. I began to feel like Alice in Wonderland, with Elaine as the Queen of Hearts yelling: 'Off with that dress!' Whenever there was a lull in the proceedings Nolan, as the Mad Hatter, desperately tried to placate her. Poor Breezie was definitely the March Hare, going demented trying to make something work, and I noticed that Michael had gratefully assumed the role of the Dormouse, quietly nodding off in the corner. It was finally decided that there was nothing suitable and Breezie and I would have to go shopping the following day.

At this point Bob, the make-up man, arrived. Charming, unassuming, softly spoken, humorous and slightly portly, he was like a dozen other make-up men I've worked with, a reassuring, familiar figure. He drew me to the fitting-room mirror under the lights. Looking like Nancy Reagan after a bad night, I told him to brace himself and do what he could. He said not to worry, he would make me look gorgeous.

Michael and I were glad, at last, to be able to get back to the hotel as jet lag had hit us. So we flung ourselves into our studio car (a relatively modest chariot) and were whisked off to the hotel, where we soon called it another day. It was, to my delight, pouring with rain.

After breakfast, Breezie arrived and we all three set off shopping. We spent all morning in every expensive boutique and department store in LA, ending up in Giorgio's – a very exclusive shop, where they were playing thirties music and a marble and copper bar was dispensing both free coffee topped with cream and cinnamon and ice-cold beer. We partook of their bounty and I tried on a ravishing black velvet number with black grosgrain ruffles around the shoulders, set off by diamond and sapphire necklace and earrings. Armed with that and other tasteful garments culled from our morning's travail, Breezie returned to the studio and we went back for a late lunch.

Then a bizarre character came briefly into my life. Michael had met her last time he was in LA and was by way of being her London agent. She was about 35, blonde and reminiscent of an early Dyan Cannon. She skipped up the entrance steps to the hotel and bounded, light as thistledown, into the lobby (a girl clearly used to appearing in television commercials for vitamin pills or shampoo or something healthy). She squealed with delight on seeing Michael and embraced him enthusiastically. He then introduced me and she gazed at me with skin aglow and eyes shining.

'Oh, are you my friend?' she said excitedly. 'Yes, you are my friend, I know it!' she exclaimed without waiting for a reply.

Then she clasped me to her for what seemed an eternity. I disentangled myself after what I thought was a decently polite interval.

Michael said, 'This is Kate's first visit to LA . . .'

'Be a happy guest,' breathed this vision. 'Know yourself, fill your space and be a happy guest.'

'OK,' I said, keen to finish the conversation and put a lot of space between myself and this dizzy blonde. But she didn't let up.

'In this world of ours,' she continued, 'we have to know our time and what we are and when our time comes, we have to fill our space, we have to be at peace with ourselves and our space. Be happy, my friend, be a happy guest.'

I gazed wildly round the lobby for a means of escape and, finally, I turned to Michael. 'What the hell is she talking about?' I said, trying to make it sound humorous. Rude, I know, but she was beginning to get to me. Michael laughed in an embarrassed way and I decided to leave them to it. 'I'm sorry, jet lag,' I said, and beat a hasty retreat.

I spent the rest of the day going over my lines and catching up on sleep, as I had a 4.30 call the next morning. Even though I now had my alarm clock I was taking no chances, so I called the desk and asked for an early morning call. 'Pardon me?' said the operator politely. I repeated that I would like an early morning call. 'You wanna make a call in the morning?' She seemed surprised. 'Oh, you wanna wake-up call, fine.' 'Thank you.' 'Surely.'

I slept fitfully again, but was up by the time I got my 4.30 'wake-up call'. At 5.30 I was at the studios. They pulled my hair off my face and gave me very little make-up. I then had to get into my prison garb – a shapeless garment in grey with a long skirt and high neck and some really naff, flat, Mexican, plaited leather shoes – and was taken downstairs to the set. Here, I was introduced to what seemed like thousands of technicians, all very friendly, and the director, an ex-actress named Betty Maguire.

My 'gaoler' was a Mexican actor, who was keen to go over the lines with me. This was just as well, as he plainly did not know them and in any case I was nervous. We got onto the set and rehearsed; Betty seemed pleased, suggested a couple of things and then called for the stand-ins. She then decided she wanted to do a very complicated opening shot which would take ages to light, but she was determined and so there was a hiatus of about an hour. Finally, we got the first shot done and the second with Juan blowing his lines every time. Fortunately, I had my wits about me by this time and was busy learning the names of at least twenty of the crew.

We were setting up the third shot when a very pretty, very thin blonde suddenly appeared in front of me and clasped my hand. This proved to be Linda Evans, who played 'Crystal'. 'I've just come to say hello and welcome,' she smiled, 'and to see if you were all right.' She was wearing blue jeans, a pale blue shirt and white fringed moccasin-type boots and had two rollers in her hair at the sides. She looked and was enchanting. A few set-ups later, John Forsythe (Blake Carrington, her husband in the series) wandered onto the set – also, he claimed, to welcome me.

John Forsythe used to greet me each morning by quoting from Shakespeare, 'Good morning, Kate, for that's your name, I hear.' I would reply in kind. It's a quote from the opening speeches of the encounter between 'Kate' and 'Petruchio' in *The Taming of the Shrew*. I thought it sweet of him as he obviously wanted to put me at my ease, establish a rapport and make me feel at home. We got on famously. He was a true gentleman and a lovely man. We were given lots of scenes to play together as I was playing his ex-sister-in-law in the series. They were most enjoyable.

By this time, thanks to Betty wanting fancy shots and the 'gaoler' blowing his lines, we were two hours behind schedule. Not a very auspicious beginning, I thought. However, we finally got the last shot done and then I went off to make-up to have myself made glamorous, as we were having more costume fittings in the afternoon. Bob, the make-up man, made me look fine and I decided to leave my own preferred make-up details until the next day, when we were shooting my first 'entrance' as 'Caress'. The hairdresser was called Lynne – a very nice girl who took me on, as Gerald decided that coping with Joan was about as much as he could handle.

When I was almost glamourised, Linda Evans popped her head around the door to pass a few complimentary remarks, then she was gone. A few moments later the door burst open and Stephanie Beacham, an old mate, appeared. In about five minutes flat she managed to give me a rundown on her new lifestyle, code of behaviour at the studio and her two phone numbers (her place at Malibu as well as the one in town) before she too buzzed off.

I had been given the use of Diahann Carroll's dressing-room, the walls of which boasted framed nominations for various awards, letters from two members of the Kennedy Clan and other such memorabilia. I was in the throes of casting a jaundiced eye over all this when Bob put his head in and said, 'Would you like to meet your sister?' 'Rather!' I enthused.

I heard him go two doors along (Linda Evans had the dressing room next door) and repeat the question. There was a sort of squeal followed by a rat-tat-tat of determined high heels on a hard, shiny surface, and the next moment Joan Collins was asking if she could come in and sit down. She was clad entirely in cream – trousers, shirt, scarf, shoes – and gold, and wearing not a scrap of make-up. She looked stunning. Her hair was scraped back off her face and secured with an elastic band.

Joan flung herself onto the black leather sofa and asked me how I was getting on. Did I know anything about the storyline? She was somewhat alarmed, she said, about her background being revealed. She'd been playing 'Alexis' as having a rather good upbringing and if now I was about to reveal otherwise – well, it was a bit throwing to say the least. Where was I staying? She looked surprised when I told her. Were 'they' paying? 'Good Lord, yes,' I said. 'Good,' she said. I told her I thought she was wonderful in the show – and meant it – and she seemed pleased.

She thought it would be a good idea if I had an affair with 'Dex' (her 'boyfriend' in the series) – that would stir things up a bit, she thought. Suddenly, she could hear her phone ringing in her room. She let out another squeal and leaped up. 'I must go – I've a dozen messages to take. I can't wait for our first scene together – they're all longing for it – the Battle of the British Bitches,' she laughed. 'The BBB!' And she tore off down the corridor. A little while later I bumped into her and Linda, both fully made up and dressed and both looking glorious, Linda in black and white and Joan in red.

The first encounter of the 'British Bitches' began inauspiciously. It was an eating scene. Joan is very good at these. She is an extremely accomplished film actress and has 'business' for the camera down to a fine art. On this occasion she had decided that she should not do all of the script but improvise the opening sallies. Also she had decreed that we should be eating *crudité*, thus enabling her to punctuate her remarks with a decisive and appropriate crunch of gleaming, white, perfect teeth on a stick of celery or an unsuspecting radish. The director called 'action' and she opened the unscripted pleasantries. Naturally, I had absolutely no idea what she was going to say and braced myself for the fray. 'Well, Cassie darling,' she began, 'it's a lovely surprise to see you again, and looking so well, too. I must say, you're very slim. Have you been on a diet?' 'Yes, as a matter of fact I have,' I countered. 'You ought to try it sometime,' I continued, giving her the benefit of a cheeky grin and twinkling eyes. 'Cut!,' called the director. We went back to the script after all!

Working with Joan was very rewarding. She is a consummate professional. However, there was one occasion when, to my immense surprise, I arrived on set to shoot one of our many scenes, to find that she was not ready. This was so unlike her that I thought she must be ill. We all waited and waited. Apologies kept being made by the first assistant director and still we waited. Finally, we heard a commotion from the entrance to the set and sobbing and sounds of distress. I heard Joan exclaim, 'Nobody knows what it's like, living in this goldfish bowl. My life isn't my own!' She was obviously very upset. I don't know what had happened but I suspect the strain of being the world's most popular television actress and all the high-profile exposure and attention that position entailed, had finally got to her and her usual composure had cracked. To her eternal credit, she pulled herself together and after apologising to me – played the scene superbly.

155

Then there were more costume fittings. I was put into the gorgeous black number and Nolan Miller was called. 'Well, it is just sensational!' he said.

Elaine Rich was summoned. She stopped dead in the doorway and put a hand to her brow. 'What is this?' Nolan turned away, exasperated. 'Oh, my Gahd!' he said. 'For heaven's sake, if we have to worry about what every other woman in the entire cast is wearing . . .' 'No, just what Joan wears, she mustn't have the Joan Look!' There followed a heated debate, after which the divine black dress was removed from my person, never to be seen again – except, I imagine, on Joan.

After this, they fished out a little swathed gold lamé number with matching frilled shawl. Again Elaine was called, again she had a turn and said Joan had worn something similar. 'Yes, but that was four years ago,' said the despairing Nolan. Another fierce argument ensured, which ended with Nolan almost swearing on oath that the one Joan had worn was nothing like this one. Elaine accepted this reluctantly and we all went our separate ways.

When I got back to the hotel, I went to my room where I watched *Yes Minister* and *The French Lieutenant's Woman*, which I had not seen before, not being a cinema-goer. I then did a good session on my lines for the next day and went to bed. I was beginning to get over my jet lag by now, so was able to wake up at the proper time and joined Michael for breakfast. I then washed my hair and set it as – incredible though it may seem – they didn't have facilities for hair-washing at the studios. Warner's studios look much like Elstree at first glance, only they are painted a hideous mud colour all over. And the dressing-rooms are tiny – not like dear old ABPC (Associated British Picture Corporation) or Pinewood, where one had an enormous sitting-room with a bed and private bathroom or, at least, a shower and loo. Not a bit of it. Here, there was only a public loo, which I find quite extraordinary.

We were on location in South Pasadena and I had a late call. So off I went with my driver, who gave me a conducted tour and was most informative. We arrived at City Hall in Pasadena, which has Baroque pretensions, and I sought out the make-up trailer. No one was ready for me, so I went to my own trailer and waited, going over my lines again. Finally my hairdresser arrived and said she would Carmen my hair. This she did, and very well too. She was a pretty, quiet, shy girl who knew her job. Soon after this, they announced that Betty had got ahead of schedule and we were all moving to the next location. So the second assistant director – a really nice, jolly, bouncy girl called Kerry, who was full of beans and also very good at her job, Bob, Lynne and I all piled into a car and were driven there.

The new location proved to be a most beautiful house, set in lovely grounds at the top of a sweeping drive and surrounded with trees. It was built in 1902 in a sort of quasi-Queen Anne style, but with the odd Art Nouveau touch here and there and occasionally a hint of Spanish influence. However, despite these mixed origins, the overall effect was one of quiet, subdued splendour. There were superb antiques everywhere, lovely if obscure oil paintings, an old gold silk carpet, parquet flooring and chandeliers. A fountain was playing in the inner hall and there was a small staircase, down which I was to make my first entrance.

After I was made up, I did my first rehearsal with my hair in curlers and in my make-up robe and slippers – both provided by the studio. I then walked back through the gardens to my trailer and changed into my gold lamé number with the frilly shawl and gold high heels. I was given a bronze necklace and earrings, my hair was tarted around and backcombed and lacquered, tweaked and teased within an inch of its life and I was proclaimed ready for my grand entrance. I caused a minor sensation on the set – but technicians are the same the world over.

The actor with whom I was playing the scene was a tall, distinguished-looking man in his late fifties; he was very good, had obviously worked in the theatre and played the scene really well. However, when it came to his close-ups, he too started blowing his lines. I deduced from this, that the problem is that actors simply don't get enough practice out there and therefore lose confidence when under pressure. When we weren't shooting the scene, we retired into a cool conservatory (it was boiling outside) and went over our lines there. We finished the scene about 5.45 and I was driven back to the hotel, where ABC TV rang inviting me to a 'Dynasty/Colbys' bash.

More wardrobe fittings! I went to the studio and tried on a snazzy little red suit for my first scene with Joanie, at La Mirage. It was nipped in at the waist to fit me snugly – the skirt was made less flared and pads were put in the shoulders to give me the current Hollywood look. Breezie had also managed to get the most wonderful grey, wool trench-coat, that was several sizes too large. It was ruthlessly reduced to my size and looked divine. I prayed that it would meet with the approval of the Red Queen and the Mad Hatter. A runner was despatched, and several minutes elapsed as, apparently, they were looking at the daily rushes.

Suddenly, Elaine was at the door. She came rushing in and kissed me on both cheeks, exclaiming that my scene in the gold lamé dress was a triumph. It transpired that screams of delight had gone up in the viewing room on my first appearance. After this (in my opinion) excessive display of emotion, she discovered that she loved the red suit and thought the trench-coat adorable. Nolan appeared and agreed wholeheartedly. Dear Breezie was flushed with triumph.

I spent the rest of the day getting ready for the 'Dynasty/ Colbys' 'do'. At seven o'clock, Michael and I were downing our pre-bash drinks (mine a Virgin Mary, which the Americans do superbly well) to allay our nerves, then went out to our waiting limousine. We arrived at the Beverly Wilshire and climbed out into a sea of people, popping flashbulbs and throngs of reporters. I knew they were not interested in me and I was just slipping in, I thought unnoticed, when suddenly a lone photographer yelled my name. There was nothing for it – I had to turn and pose, before following Michael into the hotel.

We entered a room full of glittering people – not one of whom we knew. We grabbed a drink and then found ourselves accosted by a number of people, who were all ecstatic about my rushes – as the producers were among those who were eulogising, we allowed ourselves to feel optimistic for the first time.

After this we all drifted into dinner. More or less everyone else was there, though, including Ricardo Montalban, whom I had been given to understand was playing my boyfriend. Among the 'Colbys' I spotted David Hedison, whom I had worked with in 1970. We had done a TV play for Anglia directed by Alvin Rakoff, in which I had played Richard Johnson's wife and David had played my American lover. He didn't seem too pleased to see me among the present throng.

I found my table in the dining room and we all sat down. After the starter, one of the producers got up and made a speech and introduced the other producer to the assembly. He chuntered on for a while about this and that, then the ABC representative got up and the whole thing turned into a mutual admiration society song of praise. After this, the first producer decided to introduce each member of both casts to the multitude. I prayed that I wouldn't be included in this mass exposure, but to my horror I heard an introduction that began with, 'The newest member of the *Dynasty* cast, an English actress . . .' and saw the spotlight swinging over in my direction. Michael pushed me to my feet, so I bowed and smiled hopefully to the room and caught a glimpse of Kirk Douglas glancing over in my direction and politely joining in the general applause. The whole ghastly scene easily surpassed my worst nightmares.

The rest of the evening passed off without incident and I had time to notice that Katherine Ross (a 'Colbyite') had cut off most of her beautiful auburn hair to shoulder length and had it permed, and that Linda Evans was wearing a red evening suit with a black leaf-like design in sequins over one shoulder. I chatted up the writers who were sitting next to me at our table and was very thankful when Michael suggested that, as various other people were leaving, we might as well go too. The food was fairly inedible – as is always the case at these functions – and in any case, we were sick to death of the 'Dynasty' theme, which the band had played almost continuously for most of the evening.

As we were leaving, Nolan came up to me with the veteran actress Barbara Stanwyck, who was in *The Colbys*, on his arm and congratulated me on my rushes. Then he said, 'Barbara, I'd like you to meet Kate O'Mara. Kate, this is Barbara.' Miss Stanwyck took my hand and said, 'Barbara?' Nolan said, 'No, *you're* Barbara. This is Kate, she's playing Joan's sister.' 'Who's Joan?' enquired Miss Stanwyck, non-plussed. 'She plays Alexis.' 'Alexis?' wondered Miss Stanwyck, totally baffled. 'Oh, never mind,' said Nolan wearily. 'I don't know who anyone is' Miss Stanwyck complained with desperation. Nolan led her away, a beaten man who was exhibiting all the signs of having spent a lifetime of coping with difficult women.

We came across Diahann Carroll on our way but she totally ignored me, so we made our way to the front of the hotel, where we found a dispirited little group of extremely famous people all waiting anxiously for their limousines to come and whisk them off into the night. Our turn came sooner than the rest and we sank back into the plush upholstery with a sigh of relief.

The next day Michael had hired a car and was determined that I was going to see the Californian coastline, so armed with a map and with me as navigator, we set off for Malibu. This was a vast disappointment and reminded me of Shoreham-on-Sea in the sixties after a particularly hectic visit from the Mods and Rockers. On the way, we made a mental note of the whereabouts of Stewart Granger's abode (he had invited us for supper as Michael represented him and was going to pay his respect) and then drove on to Venice, which was even worse than Malibu. Michael appeared enchanted by the place, but I don't know when I have encountered anywhere more dirty, tawdry, sleazy, full of junkies, con-men, reprobates, mindless alcoholics, tramps and charlatans. The rejects of society – the misfits of the world.

Michael said, 'Isn't it fascinating? I wouldn't mind living here.' I replied, 'Listen, you can see this any day of the week at throwing-out time at any pub in the country and save yourself the air fare.'

Michael was unconvinced and we spent most of the day wandering up and down among this motley crew. He insisted that we have a drink on Malibu Beach in a fairly ghastly sort of café. The best part was gazing out of the picture windows, watching the gulls and sandpipers and suddenly seeing a school of dolphins disporting themselves in the waves, which reminded me of Cleopatra's lines in her eulogy about Antony after his death:

> ... his delights
> Were dolphin-like; they show'd his back above
> The element they liv'd in ...

This made me homesick again and I gazed out to sea, trying not to think of dear Will Shakespeare and our mutual love of the English countryside and trying not to cry.

Finally it was time to go to Stewart Granger's, who made us very welcome. He had cooked enough food for ten people and we did our best, but it was quite an effort! He gave us cheese on toast as an appetiser. Then cold asparagus with an amazing vinaigrette sauce. Plus avocados. Followed by spaghetti bolognaise with a special alternative sauce for me, a sort of ratatouille. Then chocolate mousse and strawberries and cream. I managed to eat a little of everything but not without a great deal of difficulty. He is not a man to be thwarted.

Stewart, known to his friends as 'Jimmy', still handsome, witty, amusing, fascinating, with a confidence bordering on arrogance, made a charming informal host. The corridors of his apartment were crammed with photographic evidence of his once staggering good looks and superb, tall physique. There were shots of him in *Beau Brummel*, *The Prisoner of Zenda*, *King Solomon's Mines* and a dozen others. He was a good actor, too, but never recognised as such. I remember him in those films and thinking him the most handsome man I had ever seen with the exception, perhaps, of Errol Flynn. And I remember crying at the end of *Beau Brummel* and *Young Bess*, and the sadness remaining with me for ages afterwards.

'I wasn't a bad-looking chap, was I?' he said heartily, as he showed us around his flat. I suddenly realised that I had seen every one of his films – and told him so, which pleased him. I even managed to quote a line he had said to Peter Ustinov in *Beau Brummel* and this plainly delighted him.

Immediately outside his bedroom door was a life-size photograph of himself in bathing trunks taken on a yacht, bronzed and young and beautiful (and knowing it!). 'Ah, yes,' he said, laughing. 'I show this to my girlfriends and say, "Now take a good look at this chap. Then close your eyes and imagine he's the fellow you're in bed with".'

Michael had to leave Hollywood and go back to England. All my agents turned up at the hotel for a party for casting directors – they were giving themselves awards for casting! (I mean – PLEASE!) I happened to be in the lobby just as the lunch was finishing and bumped into my new agents, who instantly grabbed the opportunity and managed to introduce me to every important casting director in the business in the space of half an hour (they were waiting for their limos to collect them and in high good humour, being slightly pissed). The casting directors were all very charming but only politely interested in me, until my agents let it slip that I was a new regular in *Dynasty*, whereupon they all became riveted by me and paid me a great deal of attention.

As I was responsible for my own transport to the studio, I had a cab standing by and arrived in beautiful time to do my first scene with Joan and Gordon Thompson, who played one of Joan's sons, 'Adam Carrington'. I even had a chair with my name on it on set – something that had not happened to me for several years. Bob did a good job on my face; he was gradually catching on and taking my advice as to what needed doing to make me look presentable – I hoped to get my make-up the way I wanted it by my third episode.

Joanie was very sweet to me. She had invited me to a party at her place, which, as I was going home at the beginning of the week, I should have to miss. We had no exchange of dialogue in this, our first scene. It really consisted of me watching her covertly over breakfast at La Mirage – she unaware – and being spotted by Adam doing so.

When we broke for lunch, she and I had photos taken together for the *News of the World* the coming Sunday, 3 November. She chatted to me in a most friendly manner all the while. So far, so good. Elaine also came onto the set and congratulated me on having my options picked up. I was never in any doubt about this eventuality, but then, if I had known there were sixty girls up for this part, I might not have been so sanguine about that either. Eight were eventually tested on videotape. Stephanie Beacham actually had to do a test in Hollywood as well. At least I was spared that.

There was no canteen or restaurant at Warner Bros and most people sent out for food, but I had been overlooked. So I changed out of my red suit and black hat, put on my jump-suit and wandered out into the blazing sunshine to find the catering truck, which was behind the *Love Boat* stages. They had been making *Matt Houston* there until a few months ago. I finally found the truck and asked politely for a banana sandwich with brown bread, if they had it. The catering manager stared at me and said, 'How's that, sister?' I repeated my request and he said, 'Aw, got ya, you wanna banana on wheat – comin' up! Whaddya wan on it?' 'Just banana, thank you,' I replied timorously. He shook his head disbelieving, but made it just the same!

A special delivery arrived on the Friday afternoon from the studio. They had written me in another scene at La Mirage, also to be shot on Monday. I was very pleased, because it showed they seemed to have some confidence in me.

I spent the evening watching TV. American sit-com series are far, far better written than ours – they are wittier, sharper, funnier and do not rely on contrived situations for their plots. I saw, in quick succession, about five which were obviously long-running favourites and they were all excellent. As a great treat, I ordered hot chocolate in bed and listened to Benjamin Britten and did the *Observer* crossword. I read the paper from cover to cover. Little did I realise as I sat there in bed in Hollywood, that soon I would be doing exactly what I dreamed about in the theatre, running my own company.

Act III Sc.II

But before any of this could happen, I had to face the worst trauma of my life. I had been accounted a success in Hollywood. My options had been picked up and I was making good progress. I was gradually becoming acclimatised. I resigned myself to the eternal sunshine and tried to put memories of grey skies and soft rain behind me. It was no good longing for the English countryside; I had made my bed and I must lie in it.

My first episode was due to be shown in England and everyone was agog. So far, my contribution to the series had gone down very well at the studios and they seemed pleased with me. To my great delight, one day returning from filming, I received a phone call from England from Patricia, my great friend of many years.

'Oh, how wonderful to hear from you!' I exclaimed joyously. 'No, it's not wonderful at all,' she said, her voice shaking with emotion. 'What on earth's wrong?' I asked, alarmed, thinking someone must have died. 'Oh, darling,' she sobbed, 'that boy has gone to the Press and they're going to put the story all over the newspapers to coincide with your first episode.' My heart lurched. 'Oh God, no, no, no' I cried. 'We've been to a lawyer, to try to take out an injunction to get it stopped, but it doesn't look hopeful.' I'd never heard her so desperate or unhappy. My world started to spin out of control. 'My parents,' I said. 'Yes, I know, your parents,' she echoed. 'The shock will be overwhelming for them. Are you going to tell them?' 'I'm going to have to, they have never known about it, never had the slightest suspicion.' 'Oh God,' she exhaled, 'well, your mother will cope somehow, she always does, but what about your father?' 'It'll kill him,' I said sombrely, little realising how prophetic my words were to prove.

We discussed in detail a statement I would make to the press, all to no avail, as they totally ignored it. I rang my mother and simply said, 'There is a ghastly story coming out in the news-papers tomorrow. You are to disregard it entirely. Don't read it. Whatever you do, don't let my father see it, he'll never cope with it. But I don't want you to see it either. It all happened nineteen years ago. It's done now and there's nothing anyone can do. So don't go near a news agent until it's all blown over.' 'No, all right dear,' replied my mother shakily. 'What's it about?' she asked tremulously after a moment. 'You don't want to know. I deliberately kept it from you at the time and it's better it stays that way,' I replied tersely.

The next day, it was front-page news in every tabloid. By that, I mean screaming headlines. Being in the States, at least I was spared the sight which would have severely traumatised me. Needless to say, some so-called 'friend' of my father showed him a copy. He *was* traumatised and brought it home to show my mother, who, without glancing at it, tore it up and threw it on the fire. But the damage was done. My father suffered a mini-stroke and made the first of many stays in hospital, which resulted two years later in his death. My mother suddenly had a fibrillation of the heart, which led to a blood-clot on her left eye. This healed in time, but left scar-tissue which ultimately meant that she became virtually blind and, indeed, was registered as such. All because this boy had done what I had begged him not to do.

So far as I was concerned, I thought my life was over. I sobbed ceaselessly for three days in my apartment. I received a phone call from the studios, asking me to speak to *The National Enquirer*. I said I couldn't possibly. I couldn't talk to anyone about it. It was too distressing, too painful. They made sympathetic murmuring noises and said how sorry they were, but it would be better to grant the paper an interview, otherwise they would publish a concocted story. Very reluctantly, I agreed. I needn't have bothered. The 'interview' they published was nothing to do with me, not a word of it was true, it was entirely made up. They had interviewed a 'friend' of mine, they claimed, who had told 'all'. As I had never mentioned a word of it to a soul, this was plainly a fabrication.

The 'story' went round the world. The thing I had most dreaded had happened. My worst nightmare had been realised. Although the studio had been sympathetic, I knew I had blown my chances of 'making it' in the States. In those days, scandal of that sort was terribly damaging and one's chance of surviving it virtually nil. I did manage to last another season with *Dynasty*, but my image had been tarnished. I had been publicly humiliated worldwide. If this was the price of fame, well, it was too high. I couldn't afford it. I would go back to England and lick my wounds. I would return to the theatre where I belonged and lead a civilised life again, where the audience come to see one because they know they are going to have an enjoyable evening's entertainment. They wouldn't have been salivating over the prurient horrors of the tabloid Press.

* * *

The rest of my time in Hollywood passed more or less without incident. Angharad Rees and Christopher Cazenove, who had been cast as 'Blake's' long lost brother, 'Ben', had moved out to LA with their children and were renting a magnificent house in Bel Air with a pool and a view over the city. I caught up with lots of British chums. For most weekends, Chris and Angharad would entertain and very generous they were too. At their many parties I met up with Pierce Brosnan and his late wife Catherine, Judy Parfitt and her husband Tony Steedman, Laurence Harvey's widow, Paulene Stone, Miriam Margoyles, David Suchet, Sue Lloyd and her late husband Ronnie Allen. Louise Jameson and Ann Bell all turned up.

Hollywood taught me a lot. I had already learned self-reliance, my childhood and teenage years had taught me that. What I learned in my twenties and thirties was a rabid self-belief. I had to. Then I had a small child to bring up on my own. I had to succeed. My son depended on me for his survival. In Hollywood, I acquired the art of self-promotion; in other words I learnt to be a saleswoman and the product I was selling was me. It takes a lot of courage to sell oneself. One has to be certain that one can live up to people's expectations and that is where, of course, the self-belief comes in. When I go on stage, I am mentally saying to the audience, OK, this is what you've been waiting for, here I am, just sit back and enjoy yourselves. That's easy, because I am hiding behind the character I am playing. In real life, one has to have the same attitude using one's own personality.

That's what LA taught me. People there are so up-front, extrovert, ebullient, some might say downright pushy. In England we tend to be laid-back, reserved and modest in the extreme. Self-deprecating even. A sort of 'I can take-it-or-leave-it' approach is the norm. In the States, it is quite the reverse, a 'I-gotta-have-it' attitude prevails. I think quite a lot of this rubbed off on me while I was out there. I found that one gets nowhere by fading into the back-ground, but I have to admit pushing myself into the forefront of the action does not come easily to me.

I was given very good scenes to play and was fortunate to work with some of Hollywood's finest character actors and directors. There was a constant flow of visitors to the set. *Dynasty* was at the height of its fame and people came from far and wide to watch the filming. On one such occasion, I was playing a scene seated on a high bar stool at the cocktail bar in La Mirage. Opposite me, serving behind the bar, was a young actor playing the bar-tender. He was unbelievably good-looking as only happens in Hollywood. We were starting the scene with the camera behind me, shooting over my shoulder on this Adonis. I would have been quite happy to have done the whole scene that way, as he was far prettier than I was. Nancy, the director, a lovely lady, was very good at her job and we were soon ready to go. We did a final rehearsal, then Nancy said, 'Don't turn round, Kate, don't turn round.' Well, of course, I was immediately consumed with curiosity and dying to look behind me. But I did as I was told and we shot the scene, but Nancy was not happy and gave the young actor some acting notes. 'OK,' she said, 'let's go again, don't turn round Kate, don't turn round,' she added, murmuring in my ear.

By now I was agog, but resisted the temptation to look. Finally, the scene was done and the camera was moving position to behind the bar, to do the reverse shots on me. At last I was able to see what the fuss was about. I turned round and there, sitting *en masse*, was the Royal family of Monaco. I was delighted. I always like having an audience to play to and I hate to say it but my performance definitely improved after that. Later, I was introduced and found them all charming. *Dynasty* certainly attracted worldwide attention and for me it regenerated my somewhat flagging career, of that there is no doubt. To this day I still get fan-mail from all over the world, most particularly from the United States, Scandinavia and Germany. It seemed I was popular with the public in the States at the time, too popular, I suspect. I heard from one particular source that my days on the show were numbered, due to the determination of a fellow-member of the cast. However, those rumours were not unfounded and my agents were informed that my option for the third series was not going to be picked up. They were suitably appalled and indignant. They knew I had a following and that my episodes had been exactly what the public wanted. Like me, they smelled a rat.

I had been in an almost unique situation in LA. I was starring in the top TV series, yet to the Americans, I had no track record. When going for interviews with casting directors I was treated politely, but without evident warmth. In England, everyone knew me. I seldom had to go for auditions, but when I did, I was treated respectfully. I went for a movie while I was in the States, starring Shirley McLaine and Charles Dance. I had to wait in the outer office with a cross-section of other actors and actresses of all types and ages. The receptionist on the desk had been appallingly rude to me, so I was not feeling my most confident. When I finally got in to meet the director, casting director and producers, there was no easy familiarity to break the ice. I was about to sit down to engage in exchange of pleasantries with the powers that be, when I suddenly realised that the female casting director was standing by my side with a script in her hand saying, 'Are you ready?' I hastily got to my feet realising that formalities had been dispensed with and I was to plunge straight in.

I read the part, that of a British aristocrat, fluently. If you can't read with aplomb after the number of years and the amount of experience I've had in this profession, you might as well give up and go home. They all seemed suitably impressed and I was summarily dismissed. I was just starting to descend the staircase when the casting director came hurrying after me. 'Kate, that was fantastic. You got the part!' 'What already?' I gasped. The

Americans certainly didn't hang around. Yes, I'd got the part all right, but I didn't want it. In my opinion it was far too small, one tiny scene. I turned it down. The trouble is, when you're riding high, you think you rule the world.

* * *

I was sitting in the house I was renting with my friend Jenny Agutter, gazing out at the brown scorched landscape that was the lower regions of Griffith Park. It was situated somewhere below the famous Hollywood sign and painted a rather interesting shade of yellow ochre. I had now come to the end of my current story-line in Dynasty and had been informed by the studio that my services would not be required again until the end of the series, when I would possibly be in four episodes. This meant kicking my heels in Hollywood for a couple of months. I had been offered a couple of television roles, neither of them particularly exciting, and a new play at the Mark Taper Theatre. The latter held some interest for me, although I wasn't that enamoured of the part.

Suddenly, the small green plastic frog by my side burped several times. In other words the phone was ringing. I picked up the offending animal and held its gaping mouth to my ear – I always felt slightly ridiculous addressing my remarks down the throat of this idiotic instrument. The voice on the other end was my agent ringing from London to tell me that I had been offered the parts of either 'Goneril' or 'Regan' in *King Lear* with Sir Anthony Quayle's company, Compass. Was I interested? And, if so, which of the two parts would I prefer to play?

I had always had rather a hankering to play 'Goneril', the elder of the two sisters. I thought that she was possibly the more interesting character for me to play, since I would normally be more natural casting for 'Regan'. 'Goneril' is married to a good man and, I feel, has become corrupted over the years, whereas 'Regan' seems to me more of a psychopath married to an equally bad, mad husband. For although it is 'Goneril' who suggests that 'Gloucester's' eyes are put out, it is 'Regan' who is actually there when the ghastly deed is done.

I accepted the job with alacrity and requested a meeting with the studio bosses to inform them of my decision. They seemed puzzled, not to say perplexed, that I could possibly prefer to go home to England, to go on tour with a classical drama instead of remaining in Hollywood to earn the big bucks. This altitude has mystified countless people whom I have spoken to, journalists and public alike. For me, there was simply no choice. I have always had a philosophical attitude towards money: I have this fundamental belief that I will always manage to find it from somewhere, but that my soul needs constant attention.

About this 'ruling the world' business, an example of what I mean occurred during rehearsals for *King Lear*. As I said, I had been given the choice of playing either of the two monstrous sisters, 'Goneril' or 'Regan'. I read through the play twice, speaking first 'Goneril's' lines aloud, then 'Regan's'. In my view there is not much to choose between them in terms of villainy. The difference lies in their birth and choice of husband. 'Goneril', being the elder, is naturally the one with the most authority and, being an elder sister, I felt most familiar with this aspect of her character, that of a woman who issues orders in a blunt way, yet absents herself from the carrying out of these orders, which to me is more interesting. She is also more dominant and straight-forward. The fact that she despises her husband for his goodness shows the extent to which her power has corrupted her.

The deciding factor for me in choosing which of the two sisters to play came with the speech which begins 'Milk-liver'd man!'. 'Goneril' contemptuously berates her husband for his lack of manhood and I thought this exactly summed up her character, that she is in fact more masculine than he and goes on to make preparations for war. Accordingly, I decided that 'Goneril' was the character to whom I was better suited and informed my agent so. Imagine my dismay, therefore, when, on arriving at this point in the play during rehearsal, the director suggested that we cut the speech! I could hardly believe my ears!

The women's parts in most of Shakespeare's plays are, with a few notable exceptions – for example 'Cleopatra', 'Rosalind' and 'Queen Margaret' – far smaller than the men's. To cut what, for me, was the best speech in the play, not to mention the one which is the most revealing of her character, was tantamount to heresy. I said so in no uncertain terms, but the director, Don Taylor, with whom I had worked before on his play *The Exorcism*, was adamant. I gave him what could only be described as a withering look, flung my script on the floor and said calmly, 'Find yourself another actress!' and left the stage.

I ran up to my dressing-room, my heart pounding and sat at the dressing-table, my head in my hands in despair. What had I done? I had just chucked in a part I desperately wanted to play. I had left Hollywood to do it, giving up at least another four episodes of *Dynasty* which, to me, was worth $80,000. I had accepted this job because of my love of the theatre and, most particularly, of Shakespeare. I was working for £500 a week, a fact which all the newspapers had regarded as beyond belief and, indeed, foolhardy. But I'd done it now. My accursed temper had reared its ugly head and now I'd lost everything.

About ten minutes elapsed while I sat there, trembling with rage and terror. Suddenly, the door opened and Don Taylor came in. He was full of apologies and said of course I could keep my speech if it was so important to me. I immediately burst into tears and flung myself into his arms. I sobbed my apology for my outburst and explained my reasons for my ultimatum. At the time I hadn't thought of it as such, but in retrospect, I became aware that I had more clout than I realised. Compass needed me. I was now an international star. They were hoping that people would flock to see *King Lear* – and they did!

* * *

Exactly six weeks later, a little troop of strolling players could be discried toiling up the side of a mountain, albeit a small one, in the Derbyshire Peak District. The air was bitingly cold – in fact it was freezing and underfoot there was a great deal of slithery mud and the occasional snowdrift. I had already fallen flat on my back twice in the murky slime, had been almost up to my waist in icy water and had left my ears a couple of miles further back, on what looked like an ancient track-way. I was the only woman on this little expedition, which consisted of nine members of the *King Lear* company headed by Peter Woodward, who was playing 'Edgar' in the production. We had opened the previous week and were determined to enjoy our Sunday off. Woodward's idea of enjoyment was to drag this disparate little group of thespians on a ten-mile routemarch across wild, unwelcoming terrain. He, however, was not among those present, but if one shaded one's eyes and gazed ahead, he could be discerned as a speck on the horizon, occasionally turning to burst into a frenetic display of semaphore, urging us onwards. About halfway through this ordeal, after we had all passed through the pain barrier, Woodward very obligingly sat atop a little knoll to wait for us to catch up with him. Thankfully, we collapsed and partook of various bits of survival food, nuts and chocolate and the like.

After this brief respite, he fell in beside me as we tramped along, arms swinging and getting into the rhythm of the whole thing. Suddenly, he said 'I'm thinking of starting a theatre company. Are you interested?'

Now, I am not a woman to be easily disarmed. I pride myself on being able to rise to any occasion, however preposterous. 'Yes,' I retorted immediately. 'I'll ring my solicitor tomorrow and put my house on the market.' Peter threw back his head and laughed immoderately. 'I'm serious,' I said. 'I'll do it.' And I did.

* * *

Six months and a great deal of trauma later, we opened *The Taming of the Shrew* at the Alexandra Theatre, Birmingham. I think it was probably the most exciting night of my life. The next day we got the sort of notices that one dreams about and the British Actors' Theatre Company (BATCO) was born.

Given my background – five generations in the theatre, it had long been a cherished ambition of mine to start a theatre company. But without the American experience behind me, I doubt if I would ever have achieved it. Americans seem to be bursting with self-confidence and this is something I learnt from them: that anything, but anything, is possible if you believe in it.

Self-belief and self-esteem are two of the most important assets if one is to survive, let alone succeed, in this bizarre world. Setting up a theatre company requires a monumental amount of determination, hard work and that essential total self-belief. Like any other business venture, it is necessary to research the market, find the product and then persuade people that they want it. Providing that one aims for excellence and the workmanship is of a high quality, one is in with a chance of success.

They were heady days, those early times during our very first production. We were breaking all the theatrical rules. For a start, we had no money. We had borrowed a lump sum from the bank to set up the production and were relying on the small guarantees we had from each theatre to pay the actors' wages. I was permanently armed with a needle and thread and a thimble and could be found, at any time of day or night, frantically sewing yet another Elizabethan costume. With amazing foresight, Peter had purchased a set from *The Prisoner of Zenda*, in which he had appeared at Chichester two years previously. This was revamped and repainted to accommodate our view of Padua and Verona in the late sixteenth century. The costumes were bright and colourful and so were the performances.

The one thing that audiences all over the country and, indeed abroad, have commented on is the high energy level of our productions. This was established in our first 'Shrew'. I had worked on two productions of the play previously and so was very familiar with the text, having very strong ideas about how we should stage it. We did not use a director for our first venture and the combined artistic input of the company was extraordinary. Wonderfully imaginative and anarchic ideas flowed constantly and we all found it a most exhilarating way in which to work. It was difficult and contentious, of course, but ultimately rewarding, because what the audience saw when the curtain went up was the actors' collective realisation of Shakespeare's play. Even when we do use a director with our productions, we are now so used to expressing our own ideas, that the actors' input has become a major, integral part of our work.

These ideas go right across the board and if I feel I am right about something I want to add to a production, I will fight tooth and nail to get it done. One of these obsessions gave rise to 'The Pink Hat Incident' occasioned by a brilliant comic performer, Nicholas Day, after an incident in Brighton. He was giving a superb performance as 'Tranio' in that first BATCO production of 'The Shrew', but I like to think that I have contributed in a small way to his considerable expertise.

For most of the play the character has to dress up as his master and we had the idea that he should borrow his master's very, very best suit of clothes. Thus it was that Nick was an Elizabethan vision in cream leather and strawberry pink suede. He was wearing make-up and earrings and looked superb. However, for my money, I felt the whole ensemble should have been topped with a wonderful Elizabethan hat. Nick disagreed: he felt he looked fine the way he was and didn't need to worry about the hat. He had, however, said that although he was enjoying the part, he felt that something was missing. I knew precisely what it was. It was that pink hat. And I was determined that just such a hat would be found.

After the matinee performance at the Theatre Royal in Brighton, I whisked out into Hannington's, the local department store, and to my great joy found a length of strawberry-pink silk that exactly matched the hue in his costume. I then rushed to an antique market and found some glorious, dusty-pink feathers, including a piece of drooping osprey. Quickly, I rustled up one of those Elizabethan pancake-style hats out of the pink silk and sewed on the feathers so that they stuck out at right-angles, in a manner potentially lethal to any passing fellow actor. The drooping osprey I positioned so that it fell slightly over the left eye. I pinned a bright, jewelled brooch where the feathers were stitched and presented Nick with this confection. He was amazed and delighted and wore it that night, bringing the house down. He was profuse in his gratitude and credited me with having supplied the missing element from his otherwise splendid performance.

I am very particular about the way my actors look on stage. If they are going to be brightly lit, I think it is essential that they look superb, otherwise there is no point to any of it. The audience come to see, as well as hear, a show and they must not be disappointed.

When we were doing Vanbrugh's *The Relapse,* we had some fabulous costumes. My leading man, Richard Heffer, looked superb in almond-green silk: ruffles at the neck and wrists, long, blond, curling hair tied at the nape of the neck and wonderful, thigh-high leather boots. Richard is a fine figure of a man and he looked a dreamboat. Unfortunately, he was persuaded by one of his fellow actors that the boots did not look right and that the proper way to wear them was turned down at the knee. I made an entrance to find the man with whom I was supposed to be madly in love, wandering around the stage in what appeared to be a pair of milk pails. It threw me quite badly. I almost dried and certainly fluffed. I became completely riveted by this ghastly apparition and played the scene with inwardly mounting fury at the sight of this travesty.

At the end of the scene, I stormed into his dressing-room and let rip. To my enormous surprise, he let rip back at me. I am not used to this and it almost took the wind out of my sails, but having found a good sparring partner, I went for it. We both screamed, yelled, shrieked and shouted at each other for about ten minutes. Indeed, it was said that the row could be heard on stage, even though we were a couple of flights up in a remote dressing-room. Most dressing-rooms are remote in many of the big theatres, since theatres are almost always designed without any thought for the actors' need to get to and from the stage for quick changes. Conditions backstage are, on the whole, fearful, even in very modern theatres, where in many instances they seem to have forgotten that there are actors. In one infamous case, a brand-new theatre was designed and completed without any dressing-rooms for the actors at all. What they thought all those people in the very comfortable auditorium were coming to see, God alone knows. But I digress . . .

Trembling with fury, Richard and I then had to go on stage and play a passionate love scene. It is conceivable that this particular encounter had rather more emotional content than usual. It is to his lasting credit that he reappeared on stage with the boots properly pulled up and that he has not only forgiven me for my ridiculous outburst (which I have to say in my own defence, was simply because I wanted him to look good), but he has also shown signs of extreme friendliness towards me. Later on we even did a nude bed scene together in *Howard's Way* when he was cast opposite me again!

* * *

Talking of nude scenes, I've had to do my fair share and several spring to mind. I think my first was with George Maharis in *The Desperados*. I have to say I felt quite inhibited, but George didn't seem to mind a bit and, in fact, was quite enthusiastic! Then came my exposure on stage in Iris Murdoch's *The Italian Girl* at Wyndham's Theatre, when I had to lower the top of my nightdress for Richard Pascoe. It used to unsettle the audience dreadfully and affect the following scene, so I began to cheat it, so that the lights were dimming before my top was down. I got caught out one matinee when the director, Val May, was in front. He came round afterwards, furious with me, so I had to reinstate it. Then, of course, there was my unscheduled strip for Paul Scofield in the wings!

In the Hammer movie *The Horror of Frankenstein* in 1970, I had a nude bed scene with Ralph Bates and I knew that the studio bosses had let the stills photographer onto the supposedly 'closed set', but I managed to thwart his efforts by sticking Elastoplast over my nipples and other private parts! He was not best pleased. In the same year came a TV play with Richard Johnson and David Hedison, called *Man about a Dog*. Again, I had a nude bed scene in which David managed to protect me from the camera by lying on top of me most of the time! I made a film in 1974 called *Whose Child am I?* in which Paul Freeman and I, playing husband and wife, had to make love (for what seemed an eternity) for the cameras, first thing in the morning! Never easy. My next bed partner was Colin Welland in a TV film called *Machine Gunner* (1976), which co-starred Leonard Rossiter. There was quite a lot of Colin, even in those days, and there has never been much of me, so I was utterly swamped! After that came that deck scene in *Triangle* which was the opening shot of the series and featured me topless in a bikini, or some of it and produced a storm of protest. The switchboard at the BBC was jammed for ages afterwards.

The biggest storm of all was over an infamous, although entirely innocent, poster for BATCO's production of *Antony and Cleopatra*. Useless to point out that it was the fashion for Egyptians to go topless in the early years of the first millennium, or that many of the portraits of 'Cleopatra' show her as a very independent woman and obviously having burnt her bra! The poster featured me cradling the dying body of 'Antony', played by Bernard Lloyd. We had decided to set one of the early scenes in the play in a bath house. It is a very sexy scene, in which 'Cleopatra' is reminiscing, with her two hand-maidens, about 'Antony' and she imagines that she sees him on his horse and how she wishes that she were that horse so she might bear his weight on top of her! The Elizabethans left very little to the imagination and entered into the spirit of Ancient Rome and Egypt with unbridled enthusiasm. We thought the poster very suitable for conjuring up the sybaritic view of Egypt that Shakespeare had in mind. But people went about sticking bits of adhesive paper onto me to make me decent! One of the newspapers even published a cartoon celebrating the event! Nowadays, I dare say no-one would bat an eyelid. Anyway it paid off with *Antony and Cleopatra*, we were packed out for the entire tour. It is interesting to see the different views of the public. There are those who are up in arms at the baring of any flesh and those who will go to any lengths to be present at that baring! Or are they the same people?

*   *   *

'The Relapse', which BATCO toured in 1988, featured a host of popular names: Roy Marsden, who had made female hearts flutter as 'Adam Dalgeish'; John Challis, the gloriously naff 'Boysie' in *Only Fools and Horses*; Michael Thomas, hilarious as the estate agent in *After Henry*, Peter Adamson, famous for being 'Len Fairclough' in *Coronation Street* and infamous for a case to do with child molesting that had been brought against him while I was away in Hollywood so I had no knowledge of it. Thus I found myself in the midst of a maelstrom of debate and put in the firing line on the radio, live. I was asked, point-blank, why I was employing a known paedophile. I hadn't the faintest idea what the interviewer was talking about or to whom he was referring. It was a horrid moment and I must have sounded a complete idiot, or a complete innocent. What people in Britain don't realise is that anything that happens here is of no interest whatsoever in the States. Americans regard us as very small fry indeed. This piece of news had eluded me altogether. When I finally realised that they were talking about Peter, I replied, rather haughtily, that I employed actors whom I thought 'right' for the part and judged them by their talent and not on the rumour or hearsay of their private lives, although, of course, I abhor anything to do with child abuse.

Also in the cast was Sabina Franklyn, a delightful actress, and Richard Heffer, who had been a heart-throb in *Colditz*. With this starry cast we toured the provinces with enormous success, then had an offer to bring the show to London to the Mermaid just for the 1988 Christmas season. My agent, Michael Ladkin, was appalled. He said, 'You're opening the very week that no-one goes to the theatre, in a Restoration comedy that no-one wants to see, at a theatre no-one can ever find! You must be *mad*!' I said, 'Michael, I can't let my actors down. They're all expecting to work over Christmas. I *have* to do this.' 'I wash my hands of you,' he replied firmly.

This was not the first time an agent of mine had said this to me. In fact, I seem to inspire this 'Pontius Pilate'-like activity in quite a few people, as it has been said to me on a number of occasions by various different people. It's all down to my hubris, I suppose. My flying in the face of the odds. But as it turned out, we packed the place. I recall going on stage on the first night and raking the auditorium with a calculating eye, trying to gauge the size of the house. It seemed pretty full. Then I pulled myself together. 'For

Christ's sake, Kate,' I mentally addressed myself, 'there are national, not to mention international critics out there who are judging you as an actress. They have no idea that you're the producer of this show, so pull yourself together and give the performance of your life!' Thank God it worked. The bill for publicity alone came to £94,000! We didn't make any money, but we did break even and everyone received their full pay at the end. The entire cast had agreed to go into London on the Equity minimum, on the understanding that they would be 'topped up' if we took enough money at the box office – which we did, but it was an alarming experience, a nail-bitingly close call.

We did not do it, however, with *Macbeth*, through no fault of ours. After a brief tour of Britain, which started at the 1989 Arundel Festival, the production played the Almagro Festival in Spain, with enormous success, then went on to Denmark under the aegis of a Swedish entrepreneur. Unfortunately, he declined to pay us at all, so we had to use our profits from *Antony and Cleopatra* to cover our debts. A real tragedy, as we had been doing so well.

* * *

I had filmed another *Dr Who* story, playing my arch villainess 'The Rani' again. She had made quite a hit with the 'Who' aficionados and I was even made into a chess piece! My 'Doctor' this time was Sylvester McCoy, in fact 'The Rani' was responsible for transmogrifying Colin Baker into Sylvester. His assistant was played by Bonnie Langford, whom I had to pretend to be! I can think of no two people more dissimilar than Bonnie and myself. It is one of the most difficult tasks I've ever been asked to accomplish. My android helpers were called 'Tetraps'. They were strange, one-eyed, hairy beasts who lurched about performing whatever ghastly deed I required. My punishment at the end of that particular story, 'Time and the Rani', required me to be hung upside down in a cave like a bat. This I did uncomplainingly – well, to start with. Then, after a while, I began to feel decidedly peculiar and said so. They turned me the right way up again and to everyone's horror, most particularly mine, under my eyes were specks of blood where the blood-vessels had broken. The studio nurse was summoned. She insisted that they cease and desist filming me upside down, otherwise the damage would be permanent! So then I was hung the right way up and *the camera* was turned the other way up and a wind machine was employed to make my hair fly upwards!

The hazards of film-making are many and I've suffered many a physical discomfort in pursuit of my art. On one such occasion, however, I was fortunate, but my stunt double was not. I was playing a leading guest role in *Dempsey and Makepiece*, in an episode which was being directed by its star, Michael Brandon. I was playing a police officer and had a lot of gun-toting to do. (My friend Patricia was always jealous of me because of this tendency of mine to get parts which required me to tote a gun – 'I never get to tote a gun,' she used to wail.) The fact of the matter is, there is something quite 'butch' about me which makes me look as though I'm equal to any situation.

In this instance, my character, 'Joyce', I think her name was, had to suddenly see the villain of the piece – played by my old mucker mate, Richard Johnson – driving off in his Jaguar. 'Joyce' had to aim her gun at the windscreen and then he had to drive straight at her. She had to bounce onto the bonnet of the car, be thrown off and killed. We shot the first bit of the action, which involved me lying on the bonnet, then jumping off and running backwards. They then reversed the film to make it look as though I'm running towards the car and being hit. I can never believe that this method actually works. I had to do it once before in a seventies episode of *The Champions*, so I was familiar with the technique and I have to say, on seeing the finished scene, it really *does* work. So, as I say, we'd done the first bit. Then it was the turn of my stunt double, Dorothy Ford, to do the really tricky and dangerous part of actually bouncing on and off the car. She did it brilliantly. Too brilliantly. As she flung herself on to the car, her head hit the windscreen and knocked her unconscious and she fell to the ground.

Everyone thought it a fantastic stunt, until we realised she was not responding to the unit's applause, which always greets a

Above: George Maharis and me in *The Desperados*, a Western for Columbia Pictures.

Left: Peter O'Toole and me in *Great Catherine*.

(Author's private collection)

Richard Easton and me pictured offset for
The Brothers. (Jim Monk)

Above: The Purser and the Captain (Michael Craig) at loggerheads on the bridge in *Triangle*. (Ronald Grant Archives)

Below: Chatting up Ronnie Barker in the 'Charlie Farley' section of *The Two Ronnies*. (BBC Archives)

Peter Woodward and me at the launch of The British Actors Theatre Company at the Old Vic in 1987. (Author's private collection)

stunt well executed. She was lying, senseless, on the ground. Immediately people ran to her side, an ambulance was called and she was rushed to hospital. She was all right, it transpired, but had suffered a broken cheekbone and various cuts and bruises. I felt terrible, and that it was my fault that this had happened to her. The next day, I was not called to the studio, which was just as well, as I spent it at home throwing-up, an emotional reaction I'm sure to the events of the previous day. This custom of applauding the cast, or the crew, or the stuntmen and women on set, is, I'm sure, where a little bit of the theatre has crept into the film business.

While working on *Dynasty*, Chris Cazenove and I had quite a long scene together in a restaurant. Being good little professional British actors, we rehearsed our lines off-set to make sure we were word-perfect. Then they were ready for us on-set and as usual for the master-shot, they filmed the rehearsal. Time was money. *Dynasty* was an extremely expensive series to make, so every second saved was a dollar earned. Chris and I sailed through the scene. The director said 'Cut' and to our amazement, the crew broke into spontaneous applause. We hardly dared look at each other. We'd heard about things like this happening in Hollywood. But they had usually happened to Bette Davis or Spencer Tracy. The director was thrilled. The camera moved position to do the close-ups on Chris. Again we coasted along. Again at the end, applause. We couldn't believe it and stole covert looks of wonderment at each other. The director was over the moon.

The camera was moved again to cover *my* close-ups. We were on a roll by now, but surely there couldn't be any more applause. But there was. The director was ecstatic. I must say, it's really very nice to have appreciation from time to time. One so seldom gets it in England. However, we soon realised that it was not our acting which was provoking such approbation. It was, quite simply, that we'd got through each set-up in one take! Because of the pressure on the *Dynasty* set, one was led to believe that this seldom happened. It was nice to think that we hadn't let the side down, that we Brits were considered to be pros, but secretly, we wished we could have claimed it was for our brilliant performance! Mind you, with the sort of dialogue we were given, we'd have been hard pushed to pull that off!

* * *

After a matinee during the opening week of *The Relapse* at the Richmond Theatre in 1988, I was told I had a visitor. The man turned out to be Gerry Glaister, a dapper little man, who single handedly had been responsible for *The Brothers, Airplane, Trainer* and latterly *Howard's Way*. On my arrival back in England he had approached me about doing *Trainer*, but horse-racing is a sport of which I don't altogether approve and I had declined. This provoked another display of 'Pontius Pilate'-like washing of hands from Michael Ladkin, my then agent. But Gerry had not given up. He came round to congratulate me on my performance and to offer me a humdinger of a part that was to be specially written for me in *Howard's Way*, that of 'Laura Wilde'. I accepted with alacrity.

I had actually watched *Howard's Way* and thought it excellent. The bulk of it had been shown while I was away in the States, but my chum Patricia, who featured largely in it, had brought me up to date by showing me all *her* scenes from forty episodes, one after the other and omitting everyone else's! Confusing, but I got the gist. She was still in it, which was a bonus.

It was while I was still on tour with *The Relapse*, that it was announced in the Press that I was joining the cast of *Howard's Way* 'to rescue the sinking soap' said the glaring headlines. This was quite untrue. For a start, *Howard's Way* was not a 'soap' but a drama series. It was also highly successful and certainly not in need of 'rescuing'. I was simply going to inject a new plot-line into the series.

The trouble with a long-running series, especially ones that are centred around a family unit, is that there are only so many story lines and variations that can be introduced and played out, before the situation loses credibility. The usual course taken by script-writers is to introduce a new character to stir things up and generally act as a catalyst for the 'regulars' to bounce off, or cross swords with or have an affair with, or at least a flirtation. This

182

was exactly what had happened to me in *The Brothers* and a highly successful ploy it had proved both for me and the series. My sparring partner had been 'Paul Merroney', played by Colin Baker. He had been superb as the cold, calculating and quite unmoveable, ruthless accountant of the 'Hammonds', the family haulage firm around whom the series was based. Our scenes together were electric. The script writers catered for our contrasting personalities with relish and I was fortunate to have wonderful scenes to play.

In quite a different way, the same thing happened in *Howard's Way*, in which I was cast opposite Stephen Yardley, whom I had encountered, briefly, years before, in *Softly, Softly*. 'Ken Masters', played superbly by Stephen, was the highly objectionable, oily, self-satisfied, common, ambitious, ruthless con-man, who was convinced that women found him irresistible. Stephen played him brilliantly and to the hilt. Playing scenes with him was a joy! It was inspired casting on the part of the producers.

One of the most remarkable coincidences on *Howard's Way* was that whenever we went on location for the filmed sequences – on the Solent down in Southampton and off the coast of the Isle of Wight, the weather was glorious. The sun shone relentlessly and on cue. The sea was a millpond and filming was a real pleasure. I have nothing but happy memories from the show.

* * *

My career was thriving again, but my love life, as usual, was in disarray. I had grown accustomed to this. For the past few years, I had lurched from one unsuitable lover to the next. The reason they were unsuitable was nothing to do with them, but with me. I'm not suitable for anyone! I am autocratic, impatient, overbearing, intolerant, unsociable, irascible and altogether thoroughly disagreeable. A bit like Beethoven really, except without the talent! I am very susceptible to flattery, however, and if I see a young man mooning about, I take pity on him and then off I go again, on another pointless semi-relationship. At least, I used to. I've given up entirely now. But, back in the eighties, after

I had split up from Steven Howard, I took up with an assortment of younger men, the disparity between whom says much for my catholic taste, if nothing for my discernment.

I have turned down most of the few really nice, good men that I've encountered and gone, unerringly, for the dysfunctional, maladjusted, insecure bastards every time. One simply cannot always put it down to bad luck. And, in any case, one either has a successful career or a happy home life. I don't think one can have both. I think one has to make a choice and, without a doubt, I have opted for my career every time. But, naturally, being with the wrong partner can lead to a great deal of unnecessary pain. After Steve and I went our separate ways, I had an affair with a leading member of an extreme left wing political group. He was handsome and charming and had a most beautiful voice. He also had another girlfriend and had no intention of giving her up. He said he didn't believe in monogamy. I said I didn't believe in having one's cake and eating it! To no avail. He persisted in keeping us both on tap!

Keith Baxter, the marvellous actor and a great friend, witnessed my distress when we were in adjoining dressing-rooms at the Globe Theatre on Shaftesbury Avenue (now the Gielgud). No.1 and No.2 dressing-rooms have interconnecting doors. Keith was in No.1. He stood, posed, against the architrave of the door for some time watching me as I sat sobbing into my make-up tray. Eventually he said in sonorous tones, 'Amputate, darling, amputate.' He was absolutely right. Mopping my eyes, I went to the backstage phone which, for once was working (they're almost always out of order or need emptying or something) and made the fatal phone call. We didn't have mobiles in those days – well, actually we did, but they were things that were suspended from the ceiling and danced and tinkled in the breeze. I felt better after I'd had the courage to excise him from my life. I was unhappy, though, because I had been very fond of him. I later heard from a mutual friend that he'd been heartbroken! He subsequently decided that monogamy was a desirable state after all. It's nice to know that one can perform these little social services from time to time!

I seemed to attract men who'd been married before and were still licking their wounds from the encounter. I fell in love with one of these. He was 6ft 4in and a charismatic actor. He still sends messages of affection to me, which is nice. I'm always being asked why I go for younger men. The truth of the matter is, I don't. *They* go for *me*. If I had a choice, naturally, I would prefer a man of my own generation. We would have the same points of reference, a similar hinterland of common historical experience. But, and it's a very big but, they don't go for me. They wouldn't look twice at me. What *they* want is a nineteen-year-old or something similar, particularly if they're just out of a second or even third marriage. What they don't want is more of the same. As one grows older, one acquires so much 'baggage', emotional baggage, I mean. It's very hard to enter any relationship with a 'tabula rasa', one cannot but be influenced by one's past experiences; one's attitude to life is coloured by them.

* * *

Our 1989 production of *Antony and Cleopatra*, although highly successful and financially rewarding to boot, was not a happy experience. I was *not* getting on with my leading man, Bernard Lloyd. A brilliant actor, whom I had first met years previously when he had worked with my mother at Stratford East, he didn't like my interpretation of the role. I played her for all she was worth, volatile, tempestuous, changeable, romantic, sexy, child-like, noble, dignified, skittish, spoiled, majestic, tragic, witty – you name it, I tried to incorporate it somewhere. Shakespeare had, after all, written of her 'infinite variety' and that's what I tried to live up to. At first, Bernie and I had got along famously. We had hit it off straightaway and things seemed to be going swimmingly. Then came the stumbling block.

There is a quarrel scene between the two lovers early in the play. He is threatening to abandon her which, of course, he does later on and she, realising she has gone too far with her display of childish temperament and provocative needling, begs him to hear her excuses. There are two ways of playing this exchange. He wanted me to be measured and stately. I preferred to play the impetuous girlish version, knowing she'd gone too far. During rehearsals, we got no further. We both hung on grimly to our own interpretation and neither of us would give way. In fact if we hadn't both been so pig-headed, we could have alternated the playing each night. Bernie didn't like my performance – at least he didn't at the time, but he has subsequently admitted to mutual friends that he thought it one of the best 'Cleopatra's' he has seen. However, at that point he'd decided he wanted an intellectual 'Cleopatra', but I claim that is *not* how Shakespeare describes her.

We went round the country in this unsatisfactory state of affairs with Bernie and I virtually not speaking to each other, except on stage of course. I was thankful when he died in my arms on the monument! Then I'd got the rest of the play more or less to myself! But it wasn't only 'Antony' who died each night. My unhappiness was compounded by the fact that my father was dying at home. Somehow my mother was coping. He'd had one stroke too many and was lying, semi-comatose, in hospital.

My mother used to visit him every afternoon to bring him the latest news and try to entertain him. 'I've just done another matinee for your father,' she'd say to me on the phone, 'It went quite well, not many laughs mind you, maybe it'll go better at the next house!' My mother's whole life was one long theatrical analogy. And why not: 'All the world's a stage and all the men and women merely players. They have their exits and their entrances.' My father was about to make *his* exit, but my mother was determined to keep him alive until I got home from tour and for Christmas. She was adamant that he must come home for Christmas. How she thought this could be managed, I can't imagine. He could barely move and when I saw him he looked almost skeletal, like the grim reaper himself.

There was a young actor in the cast of *Antony and Cleopatra*, very talented and very handsome. His name was Richard Willis. He had, I was told, separated from his wife and was not intending to return home after the tour. We were sharing 'digs' in Brighton and he was due to audition for Giovanni in *'Tis Pity She's a Whore* for Dundee Rep. He claimed he was having difficulty with the part and didn't feel he was up to it.

'Nonsense,' I had replied crisply. 'You can play it standing on your head. I'll take you through it.' I have great faith in my powers of encouragement and so coached him thoroughly in the scenes. The upshot was that he got the part and somehow felt I'd been responsible for his success. We had a brief affair to celebrate his triumph and then the tour ended and we went our separate ways. I have to confess, I thought no more about it.

I got home to my little cottage in Richmond and put the whole thing out of my mind. I went to see my father in hospital. I was shocked by his condition. My mother was, as usual, giving a sparkling performance but his eyes never left my face. 'Not much of a house,' observed my mother humorously. He died the next day.

5

'Well, I suppose we could always try Kate O'Mara'

I spent Christmas trying to help my mother cope with my father's death. Although their marriage had been anything but happy, they had still been together for 50 years. As always, she was philosophical and, although partially blind and almost deaf, was soon off to do another play on tour! The theatre was her life and that was how she got through any crisis. It was her survival kit. Over the years I've tried to emulate her and make it mine. It has always worked. It doesn't happen on a film set or in a television studio, only in a theatre. There is something about the smell of a theatre, a mixture of size and grease paint, that grabs me every time. I feel as though I've come home and I can cope again. I learnt this from her. There she was playing Miss Marple. God knows how she did it. I only hope I shall be able to follow her example when my turn comes.

I was walking up Richmond Hill one day soon after my father's funeral, when I heard my name being called out. It was David Pinner, a shining light among young playwrights in the British theatre in the sixties. I had met him in Rep. in Newcastle-on-Tyne in 1963, where we had been in *The Merchant of Venice* together. He had been a very bumptious young man, claiming that he would be England's next Shakespeare! He wrote me some poetry describing my beauty! Unfortunately, I have only a few lines of the first verse left, but it is spectacular. His first play *Dickon*, which he named after my son, was staged at Greenwich with Joseph O'Connor in the title role. He then had considerable success with *Fanghorn* which starred Glenda Jackson and *The Potsdam Quartet*.

Since then I'd lost track of him and although he had published several novels and his plays had been seen, his personal prediction for himself remained unfulfilled. We met up for lunch and I was able to recount to him the debacle of *Macbeth* and how the company was now out of funds. Peter Woodward had done another 'Pontius Pilate' on me and more or less washed his hands of it. I can't blame him. He had worked tirelessly, virtually running a one-man office. He had also been in *Antony and Cleopatra* playing Octavius Caesar, a superb performance! And his 'Macbeth' was the clearest I've ever seen. However, the company had been put to bed and, after all the blood, sweat and tears, not to mention money I'd invested in it, I was heartbroken.

David immediately suggested that I do a small-scale production instead, using the Orange Tree Theatre in Richmond as the venue. Accordingly, we put the idea to Sam Walters who, like Bernard Miles at the Mermaid before him, had had a dream and later seen it realised, due entirely to his own vision, determination, relentless hard work and boundless energy. I had seen many early productions at the Orange Tree Theatre and knew it to be a marvellous space: A room above the pub, where wonderful work had been created. David had a play *The Last Englishman*, which he was keen to see staged. It was about William of Normandy and Hereward the Wake, but so far had only been done on radio. I am a sucker for anything historical, so it appealed immediately. We arranged to have a reading the next evening.

To my immense surprise, I had heard from Richard Willis, which I had simply not expected. He had expressed a wish to see me again. I readily agreed. The next evening David came round to the little eighteenth-century cottage I had bought, finally, at the top of Richmond Hill. When I returned from the States, I had been reluctant to buy anywhere and subsequently had rented three properties from the Duke of Northumberland. But various friends advised me to get back on the property ladder as soon as I could. It wasn't good advice, as it happens, as the market was about to crash. But I was safe enough in Richmond, an area which seems to hold its market value.

I gave David supper and we settled down to reading *The Last Englishman* aloud. We were about half-way through, when there was a knock at the door. The cottage was tiny and the front door opened straight into the living room. I opened it. On the doorstep stood Richard. He was not alone. He had numerous suitcases with him. I knew he was off to Dundee to do the Jacobean tragedy, for which he had successfully auditioned, with my help. I assumed he was on his way to a station somewhere. I invited him in and he was obliged to sit and listen to the rest of the play-reading. We all agreed that *The Last Englishman* was a suitable vehicle for the Orange Tree and plans would be put into action immediately.

David departed and Richard then asked if he could stay for two weeks until he went to Dundee. I'm very easy going about people moving in and out. I have always lived my life along Bohemian lines and more or less take everything as it comes. I could not possibly foresee the result of this particular visit.

There was just time to mount David's play before *Howard's Way* kicked off again. We had a superb leading man in Geraint Wyn Davies, who was a star in Canada and had apparently given a memorable *Henry V* at Stratford, Ontario. He was a splendid 'Hereward', with the same sort of looks as my 'Antony', Ian McCulloch, very tall, well put together, blond and charismatic. Although the play did well at the box office, it was not a critical success. Critics, on the whole, seem not to like quasi-historical plays. I love them!

I had to go to the first read-through of *Howard's Way* on the morning of the day we opened at the Orange Tree. Nobody could believe that I was quite calmly sitting there, chatting away during the coffee-break, when I had a first night looming over me. But one gets used to these things over the years.

By this time, Richard had gone to Dundee and I thought I'd seen the last of him. I couldn't have been more wrong. He came back during the run of *The Last Englishman* and moved in with me.

By now, I was renting another of the Duke of Northumberland's properties, this time in Shere in Surrey. I had found the little house in Richmond too easy for the Press to monitor. Somehow, God knows how and I have never discovered to this day who tipped the Press off, it had become known that Richard was staying with me and we had been doorstepped mercilessly. There was no back door to the cottage in Richmond, but Richard had eluded their vigilance by climbing over the roof tops of adjoining properties and leaping to the ground, an amazing physical feat, but one to which he'd become accustomed, as he'd done it every night in *'Tis Pity She's a Whore* – a huge leap on stage from a pillar that must have been twenty feet high. God knows how he'd done it without breaking something.

Well, he'd escaped, but I was trapped, so we moved out to a little cottage at the end of a dark lane, with a ford which one had to cross to gain access. Fortunately, we enjoyed a fair amount of privacy there. But the Press did a huge *exposé* one Sunday which very nearly brought the relationship to an early demise. The newspaper had managed to publish two photographs of two different actors, neither of which was Richard. The headlines were lurid and insulting and the whole incident unpleasant in the extreme. However, we survived it somehow and after the play at the Orange Tree, I went back to filming on *Howard's Way*, which was hugely enjoyable.

*   *   *

It was when I was in the middle of the first series of *Howard's Way* that the remains of the Rose Theatre were being excavated. Ralph Fiennes sent out a rallying call to all actors and actresses to foregather on the site to try to stop the developers filling in the site and building an office block on top of it. The idea that anyone could contemplate such an act of vandalism was unthinkable, but apparently sites of historical importance – in this case an

Elizabethan theatre where Shakespeare and Marlowe had themselves played, the very cradles of our culture – were insignificant
by comparison with financial gain. No wonder our society is in
such disarray when greed overrides all else. The very stage
where the world's greatest literary genius, a man revered
internationally, actually played and had his plays produced!
That anyone should even contemplate filling it in and losing it
forever, shows one the sort of mindless barbarians who roam the
corridors of power in Westminster – too unintelligent to realise
the potential of the site which could have raised revenue for the
Exchequer as another tourist attraction.

I went along to the site as soon as I had finished work and
found any number of my fellow actors already there. We were
joined at intervals by Judi Dench, Peggy Ashcroft, Alan Bates and
Ian McKellen, to name but a few. We all did scenes from
Shakespeare to entertain the considerable number of members of
the public who had gathered. Peter Hall spoke during the
evening and said, memorably, that it was akin to the Greeks
building a car park on top of the Parthenon! Simon Hughes, the
Liberal Democrat in whose constituency of Southwark the site
was situated, was on our side of course. I spoke to him for a while
and found him informed, articulate and with his heart in the
right place. He addressed the gathering with an impassioned
plea for the Government to reconsider its outrageous proposed
act of calculated vandalism. We all spent the night at the site and
formed a circle of prone bodies, lying on the ground, to stop the
lorries gaining access to it when they arrived early the next
morning. Fortunately, the weather was extremely warm and
clement.

The archaeologists had been allowed to excavate what they
could before the lorries moved in; so they were working against
the clock. I had been invited by one of the team of archaeologists
to go down on to the area they were excavating. I was only one
of two or three actually allowed down there and I consider
myself fortunate indeed to have been given such a privilege. The
leader of the archaeological team helped me down and, to my
incredible joy, I found myself standing on the very stage on

which Shakespeare himself had stood! I confess I wept freely, completely overcome with the emotion of the occasion and the thought that it was going to be lost forever. Later on I was interviewed on television by a visiting camera crew, who had turned up to find out what was going on. I was unable to contain myself and cried again. The TV audience must have thought me very sentimental, but to me it represented everything that is wrong with our society.

The actor Brian Cox was among the many famous people who turned up to lend their support to the venture of rescuing the Rose. With him came his son, Alan, then a mere boy. His father was very amused to find that when we all 'turned in' for the night, his son was 'tucked up' with me, Patricia, Julia Goodman and Vivien Heilbron. 'That's my boy,' he said proudly, gazing down at us as we all snuggled up together to attempt to get some sleep. Not easy on the hard ground with only our jackets for cover.

The lorries turned up early the next morning, but we were ready for them. We formed a barricade around the site to prevent them gaining access. Some of the actors were so eloquent in their explanation of our presence, that one of the drivers signed our petition! We all stood holding hands around the submerged pit that was, to us, the holiest of holies. Both Judi and Dame Peggy made speeches, as did Ian McKellen and numerous others. The lorries were turned away, the day was won – for the moment. We, who had kept the vigil, had had hardly any sleep and I was feeling pretty ropey. But I was supposed to be filming on the Solent that afternoon, so at ten o'clock I bowed out, made my excuses and left. I found my car where I had left it – one did in those days – and it was intact in spite of the fact that it was south-east London!

I was due in make-up at one o'clock at the Polygon hotel in Southampton, known affectionately as the Dead Parrot. This was the unit hotel for the series. With a thumping headache and looking like the wrath of God, I hared down the M3 and the M27 and walked into the make-up room at exactly five to one. It was another boiling hot day and, as I was in a boat at sea, I begged the director to let me play the scene in sunglasses, which he did. I dosed myself up with painkillers and got through the afternoon's filming.

The next time I turned up at the Rose Theatre, which was on my next Sunday off, the whole thing had turned into a three-ring circus. There was a marquee, a stage had been rigged up, Vanessa Redgrave and Timothy Dalton were performing in costume, Brian Cox was giving an extract from *Titus Andromicus*, a Russian actor, a leading performer in his own country, gave an impassioned speech in Russian, not a word of which did we understand and yet so full of eloquence and emotion was he, that we understood every word he spoke. It was truly moving and wonderfully uplifting. There was a brilliant political satire sketch which featured Philip Voss as Nicholas Ridley. A pop song was specially composed and recorded. We all sang along with the group who had recorded it. I still have the CD, but dare not play it as it is too upsetting. Tony Quayle made an inspired speech which had me in tears, as I had not seen him since *King Lear*. I went up and claimed him afterwards. He was overjoyed to see me. He died a few weeks later.

As a finale there was the recorded voice of Laurence Olivier doing the 'Once more into the breach' speech from *Henry V*, reverberating around the makeshift auditorium. All to no avail. The Government ignored the entire profession, as well as the countless numbers who had sent messages of support from around the world. The developers moved in and building began. The only concession that was made was that the site was encased in a sort of air bubble effect to preserve it. I understand the office block only has a life of 50 years, so, if I manage to live to 101, I shall be able to see the Rose Theatre again!

* * *

After the final episodes of *Howard's Way* were filmed, rumours abounded that the BBC was going to make a spin-off with Stephen Yardley and myself, based around our characters. Sadly, this did not happen. It is an extraordinary thing about television programmers. They can never see when a situation has potential and they absolutely loathe it when a programme becomes popular, or worse still, when actors become household names and the public clambers for their return. People are always stopping me in the street and asking why they don't see me on television any more. I always say, 'Write to the people at the top.' The fact is, that if the public are anything to go by, I would always be on television.

One weekend, David Pinner and I went down to East Sussex to visit Christopher Fry, the wonderful playwright whose *The Lady's Not for Burning* must rank as one of the twentieth-century's great plays. Our mission? To persuade the great man to co-write a play about *King Arthur* that David and I were keen to put on. We had a fascinating meeting with Fry, who turned out to be absolutely on the ball, his mind and his eyes as sharp as ever. But in spite of all our persuasion, he declined to oblige, insisting that we write it. In the end, I wrote it but not for another ten or so years. It was wonderful to meet him, especially as I was to feature in a revival of one of his plays a couple of years later. We left, uplifted and inspired, despite him having refused us.

* * *

In 1990 Val May, who at that time was running the Yvonne Arnaud Theatre, Guildford, rang, asking me to do a play for him and had I any ideas? I am always being asked, 'Do you have a play you'd really like to do?' and my mind always goes a total blank. It did on this occasion, so Val, after a few days deliberation, came up with *Who's Afraid of Virginia Woolf?* It had been made into a film starring Elizabeth Taylor and Richard Burton, Sandy Dennis and George Segal. It is the story of a tempestuous marriage in which the two main protagonists, Martha and George, play out a fantasy life and attempt to destroy each other in the process. It is a terrifying play and yet immensely entertaining. Martha, the part I played, is a grotesque monster but vulnerable as well. A justifiably famous play, but I secretly was of the opinion that it was hardly Guildford fare. I also thought that Elizabeth Taylor had been brilliant in the movie and doubted that I could produce a performance to compare with hers. But Val persuaded me otherwise. Well, I thought, I'll just have to play her as a thin monster. 'Martha' is definitely overblown and voluptuous. She's over the hill and past her best. In the play she's 52 and that was exactly the age I was when I played her, but of course, it's always better to be older than the part and the most difficult thing of all is to play older.

Val cast Francis Matthews as 'George' and he was sensational and surprised a lot of people who had hitherto thought of him as a light comedy actor. What nobody seems to realise is that 'light comedy' is the most difficult thing to play. Far, far trickier than high drama or great tragedy. Fran Matthews is, indeed, a fine comedy actor and, therefore, a highly accomplished performer. His 'George' was mesmeric. I hadn't worked with him since *Paul Temple* years before. He hadn't changed and was still a delight to work with. Richard played 'Nick' and very well too.

Val had an unusual idea for 'Honey'. He imported Charlene Tilton, of *Dallas* fame, over from the States – a wonderful publicity gimmick of course, but as it turned out, an inspired piece of casting too. A delightful girl with a very charming daughter, Cherish, who, although only about ten at the time, was mature beyond her years and at our first meeting over lunch in the restaurant at the Yvonne Arnaud, removed a flower from the vase on the table and presented it to me, completely taking the wind out of my sails!

Charlene was a product of the Actors Studio of great renown and had been carefully taught to take a great deal of time to consider what she was going to say, before she actually said it. Val was having none of this. 'Charlene, darling, you must pickup your cues, you must come in with your line without a second's pause.' I think I saw a look of pure astonishment come over Charlene's face, but she did as she was told. It took a week or so before she got into the swing of it, but my God she did it! She worked like a Trojan and I saw her transform in under two weeks from a 'method' actress into the best of British. She learned how to act in the English manner and pulled off a stunning performance. I was lost in admiration and wondered, if the situation had been reversed, whether I would have been able to learn to perform in the 'method' style of acting in less than a fortnight! The production, surprisingly, was very successful and the Guildford audience flocked to see it.

* * *

Richard and I moved to an eighteenth-century farmhouse in Sunbury. Well, it had been a farmhouse in the days when Sunbury had been in the depths of the country. I was then propositioned about doing two things I'd never done before. Firstly, to write a book and secondly, to appear in my first pantomime! The book was to be a 'lifestyle' tome, sort of helpful hints to my fellow-women. I decided to call it *Survival Kit*, but the publisher thought otherwise and named it *Game Plan*, which was ludicrous, as this has nothing to do with me, my profession, my personality and was just a ghastly 'buzz word' of the eighties. I was apoplectic with rage, but had already signed a contract, so had to bite the bullet.

The pantomime was a totally new experience and one I did not relish at first. I was playing 'Carabosse', the Black Fairy in *The Sleeping Beauty* and it was an eye-opener! We only had ten days' rehearsal. I made my first entrance in a wonderful winged chariot, pulled by my two henchmen. I had to 'fly' at the end of the first half. I also had to do a 'toy ballet' and I had a terrific 'vamp' number with the 'boys', followed by a sword-fight with the Prince. I learnt a hell of a lot! Firstly, to cope with the audiences booing, which was so vociferous that at one per-formance I came off in tears. I was assured that if they hated me that much, it was a personal triumph, as it meant that they believed me totally as a villainess! Well, I did my best to cope, but I found it quite distressing none the less.

Then there was the 'old lady' bit. The wicked fairy has to inveigle the Sleeping Beauty up to the turret room at the top of the palace and get her to prick her finger on the spindle. My disguise as the 'old lady' had to be minimal, as there was hardly any time to change. (They hadn't thought that through.) I changed my appearance as best as I was able, but the main thing was the performance. The biggest acting challenge I think I've ever had, was to convince 900 knowing children, who'd all read the story and knew exactly what was coming, that this 'old lady' was *not* the wicked fairy in disguise but another *real* old lady. It needed all of my histrionic powers to pull this feat off! And I've done several pantomimes since and my experience has been the same each time. One quite simply has to *believe absolutely* that one is an innocent crone, who possibly might be in the toils of 'Carabosse', or the 'Wicked Queen', or whoever. Children are so sophisticated these days and one must never patronise them.

It took every ounce of everything I had learnt in my 43 years in the theatre to do pantomime. It was, without exception, the most gruelling schedule I've ever had to undertake. Two shows every day and *three* on Saturday; hordes of screaming children plus teenagers and adults who are determined to spoil it for the little ones . . . The sheer energy and stamina required is monumental.

Most of our grandest actresses have never had to undertake anything like it, more's the pity. If they had, it would broaden their horizons and they would give performances that were more than just caricatures of themselves. I'd love to see *them* tackle pantomime. Unfortunately, they regard the genre as being beneath them, but pantomime is usually a child's first visit to a theatre and should be included in every actor's repertoire to ensure an audience for the future. Also, most of them don't tour. A week at Bath perhaps, or Richmond, before going straight into the West End, is the most they ever see of the provinces.

As the result of writing my book, I was commissioned to write two novels. They obviously thought I could write! Again, the titles were not of my choosing and had nothing to do with the content or story-line in any way whatsoever. I was disgusted, but there was nothing I could do but settle down to get them written. I set the first one, *When She Was Bad*, in the film business in the sixties and the second, *Good Time Girl*, in the TV industry in the seventies, both fields with which I am intimately familiar and both based on personal experiences. I am not sure that I would be capable of writing 'fiction' that was not based in reality, *my* reality.

Then word got out that I could sing! I was asked to take over from Nicola McCauliffe, an actress with a terrific voice. She had been starring in the RSC production of *Kiss Me Kate*, but presumably had had enough, or found another TV series to do. I had to go along to meet the musical director, Ian MacPherson. The production was by Adrian Noble and the new leg of the tour was to open at the Theatre Royal, Plymouth. My leading man was James Smillie, a musical star of many years' experience. I was terrified. Yes, I could sing, but acting is what I'm good at. Singing is an unknown quantity. I'm one of those people who goes around trilling to myself, snatches of arias from *The Magic Flute* or *Don Giovanni*, in an echoey passage. Not in the bath, because I seldom take baths. But this was to be a six-month tour and the role was Lilli Vanessi, a lyric soprano and the musical numbers are not easy.

When I met up with the musical director, I asked for the numbers to be put down by a tone or even a semi-tone, but he was adamant that it was not necessary. I was doubtful but allowed myself to be swayed by him. I went for singing coaching each week, for several weeks, before rehearsals began. It was all very frightening. When we finally opened in Plymouth, I was fine during the acting bits and the ensemble numbers, but when I got to my first solo, 'So in Love', I was utterly terrified. I had no previous experience to bolster me up. Richard, who was sitting out front on the first night, commented on this. So I was determined to look confident even if I didn't feel it. I wish I could say that I enjoyed that tour, but I didn't. I loathed every minute of it. I dreaded each performance. My understudy had a voice like Joan Sutherland and was openly contemptuous of me. My leading man, I know, thought my voice not up to it.

The critics were less harsh. They liked my voice and compared my performance to Katharine Hepburn at her best. Well, that was good enough for me. I was never off in the whole six months and I only lost my voice once. On my birthday, strangely enough. I went on and 'talked' the numbers. A hideous experience, but what else could I do? I swore I would never do another musical, but I did and it was even more frightening. The last leg of our tour was cancelled, as we were due to play the Grand Opera House, Belfast, where I had packed out as 'Cleopatra'. But the week before we were due to go, the theatre was bombed, so we all went home instead.

* * *

In the spring of 1992, I was suddenly summoned to the National Theatre to be in a promenade production of *The Provok'd Wife*, by Vanbrugh. It was part of the National's Studio activities and was extremely enjoyable. On the first day's rehearsal, we were all asked which of us could sing. I put my hand up and was asked to demonstrate. To my amazement, I found that 'Kiss Me Kate' had stretched my range, all because my vocal chords had had a rest for a few months and I found I could sing like a bird and terribly high! Everyone was surprised. So maybe Ian McPherson had been right all along.

It was a fascinating production, that featured, among others, Jerome Flynn. I had scenes opposite him, which was lovely as I'd played opposite his father in *Weavers Green*! We all had to bring vegetables and fruit to the Studio Space and leave it around everywhere, to get the authentic smell of the period. Horse manure was also imported! We had to rehearse in wigs and costumes. The ladies were not allowed to wear knickers as they didn't in the late seventeenth century! This authenticity was all very well, except that it was March and freezing! Several of the younger actresses came to me complaining of cystitis, which we believed was caused by the cold. What were they to do? 'Put on several pairs of knickers immediately,' I replied crisply, 'He's hardly likely to check, is he?,' I continued. By 'he,' I meant the director. Well, I mean, really! Peter Hall's daughter, Lucy, had designed a wonderful set out of rotting vegetables and altogether the whole experience was a very rewarding one!

* * *

Geraint Wyn Davies, who had been so wonderful as 'Hereward' in *The Last Englishman* was currently on tour in *Hamlet* playing the moody Dane himself. Richard and I decided we must try to see him somewhere. The nearest venue was Chichester at the Festival Theatre out of season. We went down and I found myself in the audience with my old chum, Alexandra Bastedo, with whom I had worked so often. She had married the Festival's then director, Patrick Garland, and they were living nearby. Geraint was being quite brilliant as 'Hamlet', and as a result of this visit, that Patrick Garland asked me if I'd ever done a season at Chichester. I said no, but I would absolutely adore to. I had played the theatre, I pointed out, and loved the space. The next day, my agent received an offer for me to join the '92 season to play 'Rosabel' in a revival of Christopher Fry's *Venus Observed*. Fine, great, I thought, but what else? 'They would see what else they could find me,' they replied. I knew that a play by Melvyn Bragg was due to be premiered there that season and I was determined to be in it!

Nothing happened for ages. The date for rehearsals to begin got nearer and nearer and still no offer of another part. It was when I was about to open at the National Theatre Studio, that I was asked to go along to Sadlers Wells Theatre for the Press launch of the Chichester season. I turned up and found lots of chums including Donald Sinden, Denis Quilley, Richard Briers, John Stride, Jean Boht and, of course, Alex Bastedo. Kenneth Branagh made a brief but startling appearance on a balcony above us all and gave a speech to the Press, the cameras and us! It transpired he was filming at Sadlers Wells, which is why we'd all been summoned there. I felt distinctly like a groundling as I gazed up at him, the golden-haired boy of the moment. His meteoric rise to fame had happened during my two years in the States, so that was something else I'd missed. He was gone in a trice and we all felt rather deflated after that. So I devoted myself to, what for me, was the business of the day.

I sought out Patrick Garland, the Festival's Director – and I doubt if there's ever been a better one – and paid my compliments. He was talking to two other members of the Festival Committee, Peter Stevens the managing director and Paul Rodgerson. They'd all availed themselves of the wine that was circulating the foyer where we were foregathered. Peter said, 'Ah, now, are you going to be in Melvyn's play?' I saw Patrick shoot him a warning look before he said, 'Er, Kate's in *Venus Observed*, and we're trying to find her something else in the Season.' Peter had missed Patrick's look and attempt at a cover-up. He went on blithely, 'There are a couple of marvellous parts for you, aren't there?' He turned to Patrick for confirmation. Patrick's smile was decidedly glassy. 'Are there?,' I asked, 'which one can I play then?' 'Well, er,' began Patrick nervously, 'Erm, what's your American accent like?' 'Excellent!' I countered. 'I've just been playing "Lilli Vanessi" in *Kiss Me Kate* and "Martha" in *Who's Afraid of Virginia Woolf?*, and I spent two years in the States doing *Dynasty*.'

'Of course you have, of course,' said Patrick, now realising he'd painted himself into a corner. 'Can I get my agent to ring you tomorrow?' I asked, determined to clinch the matter. 'By all means,' replied Patrick, who was always a paragon of politeness. I have to state here and now, Patrick Garland is one of the gentlemen of the theatrical profession and the literary world. He is the most charming, intelligent, multi-talented and affable of men and I had taken advantage of his good nature and impeccable manners, shamefully. But a girl's gotta do what a girl's gotta do!

So in the middle of rehearsals at the National Studio, I divested myself of my seventeenth-century garb and, in the cramped conditions of the loo, somehow managed to transform myself into my American glamorous girl image again. I had been sent a script the previous day with a charming note from Peter Stevens, asking me which of the two parts I would prefer to play. There was no doubt in my mind. Jacky, the American TV Chat Show hostess was the one. She was a combination of Ruby Wax, Joan Rivers and Barbara Walters; irrepressible, outrageous and lethal. I know a good part when I see one and this was one of the best I'd seen for a long time.

The rest of the cast at the National Studio gawped at me as I emerged from the loo, totally transformed into a super-bitch; glamour personified. I crept out of the rehearsal room. They all knew where I was going and various people gave me the thumbs up sign as I edged silently out of the studio door. I took a cab to the Vaudeville Theatre in the Strand, where they were seeing people. It was a bit of an extravagance but it was still only March and very cold and gusty and I intended to arrive looking immaculate.

I gave my name in at the Stage Door and was told to wait in a dressing room. There were other people being seen, I imagined for other parts. A stage manager appeared and made himself known to me. He asked me to look at two scenes from the play and rifled through his script to identify the page numbers. I stared at him horror-struck. 'I've come here to meet Melvyn Bragg,' I said in my best (or do I mean worst?) autocratic manner. 'I have *not* come here to audition!' I have always had a rather inflated opinion of my position in the profession, but after all, I had starred in the West End, on Shaftesbury Avenue, very recently and had enjoyed top billing a month before on tour. My high-handedness seemed to fluster him somewhat. 'Oh, er, I see, erm, well just a moment then.' He disappeared down a corridor, leaving me fuming. He seemed to be gone ages, but eventually reappeared, looking suitably chastened. 'Right,' he said firmly trying to re-establish his authority on the proceedings, 'you're to wait until everyone's been seen and then you can meet them.'

I calmed down and had another look at the script, which the stage manager was interested to see I was carrying and had secreted in my bag all the while. There was another lengthy pause, while he went to organise other hapless actors. Eventually, he came back. By this time I was feeling jittery. I had been awfully arrogant. 'I'll take you through now,' he announced grandly. I picked up my things and followed him through to the auditorium, via the foyer. I found myself in the stalls.

Patrick Garland was there and greeted me effusively and introduced me to Melvyn Bragg and Robert Fox, the producer, whom I had known way back in the sixties, long before he was a famous theatrical producer. (I have often thought that it's not a good thing to have known people before they've achieved their success. It doesn't seem to do one any good at all.) They all looked at me with a mixture of disbelief and apprehension. 'I've come dressed for the part!' I said by way of explanation for my slightly over the top outfit.

'What are you doing at the moment, Kate?' asked Patrick, giving me a heaven-sent cue, as he well knew. 'Oh, I'm working at the National,' I replied airily. My audience of two beamed their approval and started to look more relaxed. 'Which of the two parts do you feel you would prefer?' Patrick was certainly doing his stuff. Neither of the others had ventured a word. 'Oh, Jacky, without a doubt,' I said firmly. 'Oh, why is that?' I turned to the author, 'I know this woman,' I said authoritatively. 'I spent a couple of years in LA and I saw her prototype every day on TV. I think it's a wonderful play,' I added. Nobody had asked my opinion, but I never let things like that inhibit me. They smiled again and then Melvyn Bragg asked me how I would play her. I gave a short demonstration which seemed to satisfy all present and the part was mine. Patrick said, 'I don't think we could find better casting for Jacky than Kate, do you?' Having been railroaded into a decision, what could they do but agree? Patrick then murmured something about getting in touch with my agent and I left triumphant.

Part of my trouble in life is that I always assume that I'm going to get every job I go for. I'm the eternal optimist. To me, it's a foregone conclusion. This has its advantages in many ways, but it also sets one up for some nasty shocks and frightful disappointments in life. Anyway, this wonderful part was mine, another 'humdinger' if ever I saw one. I also happened to think the play a sensational piece of theatre.

It was loosely based on an occasion when Richard Burton had planned to do an off-Broadway 'Lear'. There were many parallels with the character in *King Lear* itself. 'Cordelia', the 'Fool', 'Goneril' and 'Regan' were all there. The play was called *King Lear in New York* and I have to say that untouched, which is the version I first read, it was terrific stuff. By the time we opened in Chichester, it had been savagely cut and, in my opinion, emasculated. I daresay it was too long, but I thought it a very fine play and it is sad that it never made it to the West End. I think the critics had it in for Bragg. I am not sure they like one of their own presuming to write plays!

Melvyn seemed very happy with my performance at the read-through, thankfully. Read-throughs are always nerve-wracking. One is, after all, only 'reading through' the play, but of course, it doesn't work as a piece of theatre, which is what it is, unless it is 'performed'. So I'm inclined to give it all I've got at 'read-throughs'. Anyway, it paid off on this occasion. It's inclined to make one look a bit of a show-off, but that can't be helped. Rehearsals went with a swing and I think everyone enjoyed themselves. It was quite an experience to be working with Johnnie Stride again! He actually is one of our great actors, but his own worst enemy. However, he has a dangerous presence on stage and is utterly charismatic and compelling.

Jenny Seagrove was playing his wife and she and I had some fantastic scenes together. *All* my scenes were fantastic. Although the play had been severely pruned, my part had remained virtually untouched, with the result that it now seemed much more prominent. 'Jacky' was a vastly entertaining character. She must have seemed completely over-the-top and outrageous to the Chichester audiences, but to any visiting Americans, she would have been instantly recognisable. I received a wealth of amazingly wonderful notices that only such a fabulous part can bring. One example, 'Kate O'Mara carries her own storm with her!'

My mother, an actress for over seventy years, used to say, 'Give me the part and I'll play it, but first give me the part!' Her greatest piece of advice to me was, 'Now don't forget dear, a nice clean performance and plenty of attack!' Well, I certainly took that advice for *King Lear in New York*. Attack? I went all out for it tooth and nail. Straight for the jugular. I often wonder now whether I went too far!

*   *   *

At Chichester, I met up again with Christopher Fry, as I was in the revival of his play *Venus Observed*. During rehearsals one day, I was watching a scene between Donald Sinden and a young actor. We were rehearsing in the Minerva Theatre, which is in the 'round'. Donald had the line 'equine equilibrium', which I thought wonderfully witty and clever, except that Donald was pronouncing it *eequine* equilibrium, thus for me destroying the point of Fry's choice of words. I murmured to Denis Quilley, who was sitting in front of me, 'Shouldn't it be *equine* equilibrium?' Denis asked me to repeat it. I did so, trying to keep my voice down so as not to disturb the actors. Denis nodded agreement. 'Yes, yes, I believe you're right.' As soon as there was a pause in the rehearsals on stage, Denis shouted out, 'Donald, Kate thinks it should be equine not *eequine*!' 'What? What's that?' Donald was immediately all ears. I groaned inwardly. I had no wish to correct the leading man on his pronunciation. Dennis yelled, 'Kate says you must say equine, not *eequine*!' 'Does she? Oh, *does* she! Equine, eh? Equine, equine, right, right.'

I wished the auditorium would open and swallow me up. Donald came to the edge of the stage and addressed his remark directly to me. 'You feel it should be *equine*?' 'Yes,' I said timorously, wishing with all my heart that I'd kept my mouth shut. 'EQUINE, EQUINE,' intoned Donald in that famous, fruity baritone of his. Then he turned away muttering to himself, 'Equine, equine, equine.' They went back to rehearsing the scene again. When he reached the famous line, he gave it my pronunciation, turned to look to me for approval, repeated it for good measure, then gave me the thumbs up sign and proceeded with the scene. I could have died with embarrassment!

Christopher Fry, Kit as he is known to his intimates, very sweetly wrote me some extra lines to get me off the huge open stage at Chichester. It is a 'thrust' stage and many of the entrances and exits are made through what are known as the 'vomitoria'. These are sloping passages that go through the auditorium. They are fine for Shakespeare because he always supplied actors with rhyming couplets to facilitate getting on and off stage, as there were no 'tabs' or curtains and, of course, no lights in the Elizabethan theatre. Kit also very much wanted me to play 'Jeanette Jourdemaine' in *The Lady's Not For Burning*, in a revival of his play and offered me the rights. Sadly I was not able to take up this wonderful offer and have much regretted it since.

Venus Observed was a huge box-office success. *King Lear in New York* was not. Chichester audiences, I feel, always go for the soft option, the 'known' quantity. We had a disaster halfway through the season. Donald had been in considerable pain for some time and it now transpired that he was going to require surgery on his hip. He was forced to leave the cast and went to a London hospital for an operation. Robert Portal, who was also in the play, went up to see him. We were all agog on his return and surrounded him in the Green Room. 'Well?' we said, more or less in unison, 'well, how was he?' Bertie 'milked' the moment. We became impatient. 'How *was* he? What did he *look* like.' Another pause. 'Well,' said Bertie casually, 'he looked like Donald Sinden in pyjamas really.' We all exploded.

Donald's hip was not the only mishap that season. Kenneth Branagh was starring as 'Coriolanus' in the opening production. Judi Dench was playing his mother 'Volumnia'. The play, one of Shakespeare's more fascinating observations on power and the abuse thereof, is famous for its battle scenes, fights and gore. I was a member of the first night audience. Prince Charles was the guest of honour. ('We're sitting on a time bomb,' an equerry was overheard to remark, referring to the rumours of an impending break-up between Charles and Diana.)

It was all going splendidly and then I suddenly became aware that Branagh was holding his left arm in a most peculiar manner. He's hurt his hand, I thought to myself. There's *something* wrong at any rate. He'd not only hurt it, he'd broken his arm fairly early on in the play and had to get through the rest of the evening with huge fight scenes and Royalty in the audience, in excruciating pain. God knows how he did it. 'Doctor Theatre', as he is known, obviously came to his aid! 'Doctor Theatre' or 'Doctor Greasepaint', is the name actors give to the buzz of adrenaline produced by the sheer, psychological survival instinct which enables an actor to go on stage and play, even when very ill or, as in this case, in extreme pain. It never fails.

One evening, security seemed to be even tighter than it had been for the visit of The Prince of Wales. We were performing *King Lear in New York* that evening. I was told there was to be a party after the show and that I was to go along to John Stride's dressing-room. 'Who let *you* in?' called out John in his usual, semi-joking manner. He loved to try to disarm people. I then found myself being introduced to Salman Rushdie, who was very complimentary about my performance. So *that's* what it's all about! I'm glad nobody told me that I was risking my life.

Act IV. Sc.I

In both the Fry and Bragg plays the assistant-director was Edward Hall, a most charming and talented young man and son of Sir Peter Hall. He was now being given the opportunity to direct a play of his choice at the Minerva. It was *Cain*, by Lord Byron. The eponymous role was to be played by Samuel West, who had just had an enormous success in the film *Howard's End*. It was a fascinating piece. I played 'Eve,' his mother, which seemed to me appropriate, as I had dandled Sam on my knee when he was a baby, when I was working with his father, Timothy West. His grandfather, Harry Lockwood West, had played *my* father in an episode of *Lord Peter Wimsey*, so this was all very nicely cyclicle. Sam later turned up to play my assistant in *Dr Who*, a special edition for 'Children in Need'. I was amazed when I saw his name on the cast list, but he explained that it had been his life-long ambition to be in *Dr Who* and here he was fulfilling his dream!

One gets asked to do some extraordinary things for Charity. On Red Nose Day, I was persuaded to be in a pretend episode of *Casualty*, having been run over by a steam roller! My legs, which had suffered most in the encounter, were stretched out all the way across the ward – about 12 feet! Sometimes, but not often, one gets paid for taking part in bizarre events. One such was the celebrations in 1987 for the 400th anniversary of the defeat of the Spanish Armada!

For this occasion, I was kitted out in an Elizabeth I dress and had to retrace her journey from Tower Bridge to Tilbury. This took two days. Again, I was fortunate with the weather. It was scorching hot for those two days, which as the event took place out of doors, was just as well. The only snag was my false nose! Because I bear absolutely no resemblance to Good Queen Bess, I decided to put on a putty nose with latex glue. I then gave myself a white make-up in imitation of the lead with which, it was rumoured, she caked her face. On top of all this I wore a curled, bright red wig. Obviously, I was clad in a farthingale hoop, countless petticoats, bum pads, hip pads, boned bodice, huge slashed sleeves, rebato (that's the amazing gauze and lace construction she wore around her neck and behind her shoulders that stood up miraculously, apparently unaided). I had to learn to ride side-saddle for the event and, I have to say, I earned the not inconsiderable sum I was paid.

We left Tower Bridge quite early in the morning of the first day in a shallop (a light boat). It was the same one used in the film *A Man For All Seasons*. The Queen's ferrymen were engaged to row us down the full stretch of the river almost to Tilbury. We would complete the journey on horseback, where I would review the troops and give the famous speech, 'I may have the body of a weak and feeble woman, but I have the heart and stomach of a Prince, ay and a Prince of England too!' All went wonderfully well, with the ferrymen perfectly in unison with their oars, until we tied-up at Greenwich for a sandwich and loo call. Unfortunately, there was alcohol on tap at this stop-off. The ferrymen got roaring drunk, and one nearly fell into the river as he was clambering aboard. The rowing was a shambles, with oars going in all directions and the ferrymen lurching all over the place.

To cap it all, as we approached Tilbury, although it's a miracle how we got there, the ferrymen broke into a rousing, raucous version of 'Viva España'. My screams of 'Treason! You'll all go to the Tower!' and 'Off with his head!' punctuated the drunken singing, all to no avail. 'Piss off yourself, your Maj!' was all I got in reply. I was very relieved to get off that shallop, which was in severe danger of capsizing. I then had a two-mile journey on horseback, accompanied by a sober retinue of actors clad likewise in Elizabethan garb. We improvised dialogue along the route in what we all hoped might pass for Elizabethan English; for example, 'The day looks set fair, your Grace.' 'Ay my Lord, 'tis passing well,' etc., etc. Unfortunately, my horse was terrified by the field ordinance which was fired to greet my arrival and became very skittish. Then there was a staged, attempted assassination by a man with a sword. He suddenly came out of the crowd and lunged at me. My horse reared, but I managed to keep my seat in spite of not being used to riding side-saddle.

The rest of that day and the following one was taken up with displays of archery, sword-play, tilting, hawking, Morris dancing, maypole plaiting and country dancing. I love all this sort of thing. I was particularly thrilled to be allowed to try the hawking and have a glorious bird swoop down towards me out of the sky and alight on my wrist. Just wonderful! But I fear my companions, after several hours of old English entertainment, had had enough and to my query, 'What falls out next my Lord?' I received the jaded reply 'Fuck knows, your Grace!'

* * *

The season at Chichester had, for me, been a wonderful experience, but neither of the plays transferred to London which was a bitter disappointment. At one point, Ken Branagh and I had discussed the possibility of our two companies joining forces to mount a production. At that time, he still had his company, Renaissance, but soon afterwards, he went into films in a big way and so that idea never got any further.

While I had been doing the season at Chichester, which lasted for five months all told, I had rented out the house in Sunbury. Unfortunately, the man to whom we rented it declined to pay us. This was a disaster. Then, two jobs I had done some time before, both for video companies, also back-fired. Both companies went to the wall and I never got paid. Financially, things went from bad to worse. I had been badly advised and over-committed myself.

I did another pantomime, this time *Snow White and the Seven Dwarfs*. Playing my henchman was Roger Lloyd-Pack, so brilliant as the gormless 'Trigger' in *Only Fools and Horses*. I enjoyed bullying him mercilessly! He was an absolute darling. The Prince was handsome and charming, with a look of Mel Gibson about him and was heard to remark 'Who needs Snow White, when one can have the Wicked Queen?' A lovely compliment! He was David Ian who, almost immediately after this, turned his full attention to producing and, with Paul Nicholas, was responsible for bringing back *Grease, Fame* and *The King and I* into the West End, among many others. Also in the cast was Warwick Davis, the star of *Willow*, the *Narnia Chronicles* on television, and *The Harry Potte*r movies. A most talented actor and a delightful man.

I was hard at it, trying my hand at being a novelist. I found it highly enjoyable. I loved writing the dialogue best of all and found, like many authors, that I became very proprietorial about my characters. But the recession had hit. Financially things were looking very bleak. The house had depreciated considerably in value, but we were forced to sell. Richard was sued for divorce and I was cited as co-respondent. I sold the house to David Essex's ex-wife, who turned out to be a most adorable woman. We got on famously and I felt I had left my house in very good hands.

I rented another property from the Duke of Northumberland, this time opposite his Syon Park estate. It was by the river. It overlooked the Park itself, where cows grazed on a regular basis. I had a huge garden and a beautiful little courtyard at the back which looked on to a churchyard. It was just gorgeous. The eleventh Duke was the most amenable of landlords. At that time, he shared his life with the extremely beautiful Brazilian actress Barbara Carreras, one of the very best of the Bond villainesses. It was a most congenial spot in which to live and, as I had my furniture around me, more than made up for the fact that it was not my own house.

One of the videos for which I never got paid was a presentation to the camera of Cliveden, infamous as being a rendezvous for the Profumo crowd in the sixties. This video was for British Airways and I had to interview various famous guests, among them were Prue Leith, Marcelle d'Argy Smith, Charlton (Chuck) Heston and

Will Carling. The England Captain had to be massaged while I interviewed him, which was extraordinary! He seemed very shy and tongue-tied and I had to do most of the talking. I met him again a few years later on *Noel's House Party*. He was a changed man, full of confidence, laid-back and in control. He greeted me with a kiss and an air of assurance. His friendship with Princess Diana had obviously done his ego a power of good!

I started to interview Chuck with genuine interest. He'd had such a varied career and done more than his fair share of theatre so, naturally, I was fascinated. At some point early in the interview I asked him the reason for his visit to London. He explained he was shooting a film about Sherlock Holmes, based on *The Sign of Four*. *The Sign of Four*? I asked, startled. 'Yes,' he affirmed. 'What's it called?' I asked. '*The Crucifer of Blood*,' he replied, 'it's based on a stage play of the same title.' 'I know,' I cried, 'I was in it!' 'What?' he exclaimed. 'I was in it at The Haymarket in London!' 'Good God!' he said, genuinely amazed, 'you mean you played Irene St. Clair?' 'Yes!' 'But what an extraordinary coincidence!' By this time, the director directing the video had given up. We'd ceased to be interviewer and interviewee and reverted to type and became a couple of actors having a good old gossip!

'Cut' called the director wearily as soon as we drew breath. 'We can't use any of that!' Chuck and I both stopped in our tracks and turned abruptly to face him. We'd completely forgotten we were being filmed. We had to do it all over again, this time without my interpolation. It seemed awfully tame by comparison. 'I preferred the real version,' observed Chuck dryly afterwards. Lots of my friends came back from trips abroad exclaiming, 'Guess what, Kate? I was sitting on the plane, half asleep and who should pop up on the screen but YOU!' They'd all seen it, but I never saw a penny for it. Oh, well, you win some, you lose some. Actually, I lost quite a lot, £160,000 to be exact, that year.

* * *

I was, therefore, very glad in 1993 to be offered a tour of Oscar Wilde's wonderful play *An Ideal Husband*. The role was the 'woman with a past,' 'Mrs Cheveley'. I had played the part years before at the Palace Theatre, Watford, 21 years before to be precise. I imagined that the lines would still be locked somewhere in my brain, but might need prising out again. So I asked to be sent a script and booked a week's holiday in Turkey, with my girl-friend Christine, who'd been my companion on previous trips abroad.

We had been to Jordan with *The Taming of the Shrew*, when my company had played a Roman Amphitheatre and Queen Noor of Jordan came to see the show with her shopping basket! On that visit we'd been to the 'Rose-Red city half as old as Time' – Petra – and gasped in awe at its roseate hue, which lived up so well to that quote. Chris had also been with me when I went with the *Howard's Way* unit to Malta. Richard was working away, so we shut up shop and betook ourselves to southern Turkey to an hotel which, one need hardly say, was not yet completed! We were the first people in there and we had the best holiday of our lives. They hadn't sent me a script of *An Ideal Husband*, so I took my *Complete Works of Oscar Wilde* with me and was as good as my word. I revised the whole thing on the beach.

On our return to England a mere five days later, I was word-perfect. Unfortunately, there, waiting for me, was a script of the play with my part cut to ribbons, with all my best lines gone. I couldn't believe it. I had one of my rages, phoned Michael Ladkin, my agent, and told him that in no circumstances would I perform this travesty. I heard a huge sigh at the other end of the phone – I daresay I can't be the easiest client to represent. He relayed my message to the Kenwright Office, who doubtless also sighed heavily. There was a stand-off. I absolutely refused to budge. A good third of my part had been cut, and some of my funniest lines. What on earth was Peter Hall thinking of? He who is renowned for his pedantic approach to a text. I stood my ground and eventually got my way. All of my cuts would be reinstated.

The director was my chum from Chichester, Edward Hall, on this occasion standing in for his father. The stars were the glorious Michael Denison and Dulcie Gray, just the best possible couple *ever*, Angharad Rees, whom I had not seen since

Hollywood days, Peter Brooke's daughter, Irena, one of the most beautiful girls ever and an old chum, David Robb, was playing opposite me. A lovely cast! And, indeed, we had a lovely tour. Richard, meantime, was touring in *The Invisible Man*. He was playing the Invisible one, so had to spend most of the show wrapped in bandages which seemed a bit of a waste. We met up occasionally at various points in the country, but really we hardly saw each other.

*　*　*

It was at the Theatre Royal, Newcastle, that I met with disaster. I was just about to make an entrance into the tea-party scene with Dulcie. I was at the top of a flight of concrete stairs backstage. I must have caught my heel in the hem of my petticoat, for as I turned to go down the stairs, I found myself flying through the air. I landed, crack, on my face, although I attempted to break my fall with an outstretched hand. It's a miracle I didn't break my wrist. Apparently they heard my scream on stage. I picked myself up and made my entrance with my wig looking like a bird's nest and my huge hat skew-whiff on top. The rest of the cast watched with alarm as my forehead grew visibly before their eyes, an enormous lump swelling up where I'd landed on the concrete. It was the Saturday matinee, so apart from getting ice to it at the interval, there was nothing I could do until I could get to the casualty department of the local hospital, after the evening performance. I was x-rayed and was decreed intact.

Over the weekend, my face went every colour of the rainbow and I had a completely blood-shot eye. I was not a pretty sight. By the time we opened at the King's Theatre, Edinburgh, on the Monday, I knew I had to do something drastic. I was, after all, playing an extremely glamorous part and had a reputation to maintain! I made myself a black velvet eye-patch on a very thin elastic, with a hole so that I could see where I was going. It worked a treat and there was absolutely no doubt that I was the villainess! I had to cake the make-up on to cover my many-hued face and I pulled curls down from my wig to cover the swelling.

She admittedly looked as though she'd just got out of bed, but I felt sure that Mrs Cheveley was a late-riser.

* * *

The week we were playing Guildford, Richard was playing Bromley, so as it was the only time we were likely to be within shouting distance of each other, we got married! We were not able to have a wedding night together though, nor were we able to have a honeymoon. Maybe these were, as I suspected, prescient auguries.

My mother was heard to observe grimly, 'I give it six months.' (I'm glad I didn't know that till afterwards). I was offered pantomime in Richmond, which was convenient as we were living in Isleworth – 'King Rat' in 'Dick Whittington'.

While I was in pantomime, I had been writing a show for Richard and me to perform at small venues at weekends. So at the beginning of 1994 we put it on. It was called *Kiss and Tell* and was, basically, a journey through sex, love and marriage in the late seventeenth century and an attempt on my part to show how life, or more particularly human beings, had altered little from the 1690s to the 1990s. It was an ambitious piece comprised of extracts from poems, plays, songs and writings of the period, each illustrating a stage in the road to perdition. From idealised, romantic love, to bored, loveless marriage, to disillusioned infidelity, to obsessive jealousy, debauchery and finally puri-fication and atonement. I spread my net wide in my choice of authors, encompassing the vigorous bawdiness of Vanbrugh and Etherege, the high-flown aestheticism of Donne and Marvell and the obsessive obscenity of the Earl of Rochester. There were eighteen items in the first half, all requiring costume changes and eighteen in the second. Thirty six different characters! Dozens of lighting, music and furniture changes and still the acting, the singing and the dancing. I painted the scenery and made or altered the costumes. Richard did the lighting and all the technical side. I ironed all the costumes, and set all the props. He rigged up the back-cloth and laid the carpet.

215

We began the show with a seventeenth-century Masque, in strange ethereal flowing robes and golden masks on sticks, which we held over our faces. We walked on from upstage on opposing sides to the strains of Monteverdi and I have a vivid memory of Richard in his exotic gear, but with 'cans' on his head, getting 'clearance' from the front of house staff, meaning that the audience were all in and we could start the show. I was waiting, apprehensively, in the wings upstage right. As soon as he got the 'all clear', he glanced across to my side and gave me the thumbs up sign, then hurriedly removed the cans from his head, gave instruction to the stage manager to start the show, then rushed to take his place on the opposite side of the stage and we were off.

It was a hectic show with endless, quick costume changes, very complicated dialogue and total changes of character. We were relying on a technical crew, who had never seen the show, to come in with lighting and sound cues at exactly the right moment. Plus the fact that we'd loaded up the van in Isleworth, driven to the venue, sometimes 300 miles away, unloaded, set-up, done a technical rehearsal, then had to do the show.

One particular venue, I think it was somewhere in East Anglia, we were unfortunate enough to have the wrong sound cue just before one of Richard's solo 'bits'. He was very upset afterwards, so much so that I felt obliged to give him a pep-talk when we got back to the hotel. He was lying exhausted, supine on the bed and I was pacing up and down haranguing him.

'It's like a tennis match,' I stated firmly, 'Acting is just like a game of tennis, one actor serves, the other receives it and returns it, skimming the net. The other one gives it a forehand smash, which is retrieved by the first actor who is gradually moving into the net.' I started warming to my theme. 'They have a rally, volleying to each other up at the net. Then one of them does a drop shot, the other rushes to it, manages to get it back right to the edge of the court, but it's called out, and it's match point! He thinks it was in, but has to accept the decision, has to put it behind him, has to play match point! Don't you see? It's just like a bad line call, you have to put it behind you. So, the cue was in the wrong place, but the audience didn't know that. They had no idea that anything was wrong. But you mustn't let it affect your performance. You have to go on and play match point!' I paused in my tirade and turned to him to see if he was taking it all in. He looked back at me. There was a pause then he said, 'New balls, please!'

It was certainly a nerve-racking show to do. We had one scene where we were seated back to back. The first half of the scene (it was the famous 'proviso scene' from *The Way of the World*) was 'my' bit and one night I 'went' in the middle of my big speech. I felt his back tense as he realised I'd dried. Then I remembered the next line and went on. Then we got to 'his' bit and he 'dried' in the middle of *his* big speech. I tensed, hoping to God he'd remember the next line, which he did, and he went on and I relaxed. The whole thing was very scary but we felt an enormous sense of achievement afterwards. We'd set ourselves a high mountain to climb and we'd got to the top.

*   *   *

One night at about eleven o'clock, we were clearing up in the kitchen in Isleworth, when the phone rang. It was Bill Kenwright. 'Are you doing anything, O'Mara?' My heart sank. This could only mean one thing, something frightful must have happened and he wanted me to take over at a moment's notice. I was right. It was a four-handed play called *On Approval* and Hannah Gordon had pulled out. Peter Hall was the director. The other actors were John Alderton, Belinda Lang and John Fortune. 'I can't,' I said immediately. 'Richard and I are doing a two-handed show and we're due to play St Albans. It clashes,' I added firmly. 'St Albans?' echoed Bill doubtfully, obviously not a venue on *his* list. 'What size is the house?' I looked at Richard for a figure.

The Abbey Theatre, St Albans was run by his father, an ex-actor. 'Two hundred and forty four' he mouthed. I passed this on to Bill. 'No problem,' he exclaimed. 'We'll buy the house out!' 'But, we're there for a week!' I protested. It was still not a problem. Bill was minus a leading lady in a Peter Hall production which was due to open in a week's time. What was a couple of thousand quid here or there? Richard mimed to me that I should accept, as it was an 'opportunity'. So I said yes and, as usual, there was a script on its way over by bike. Richard said his father, being an actor, would understand. I was very dubious and felt that I was letting his father down badly.

Anyway, the next day I presented myself at the Queen's Theatre on Shaftesbury Avenue, where I found a slightly bemused group of people, but they all seemed pleased to see me. I rehearsed for three days and at night tried frantically to learn the lines. After rehearsal on the Monday, as I came off stage, I was surprised to see Richard waiting backstage for me. He was due to go to the Leicester Haymarket to do *Hedda Gabler* and I deduced he had decided to go a day early and had come to say goodbye. Instead, he gave me the horrific news that my son Dickon had been involved in a dreadful accident and was on a life-support system in Kingston Hospital.

Act IV. Sc.II

We went in the car westwards, through the rush-hour traffic where, of course, we had countless hold-ups. I thought we would never get there. I hardly dared think or hope during that journey. When we finally reached the hospital, two doctors came to see me in a private waiting-room. They told me I had to brace myself for the worst, that it did not look good and that my son would very likely die during the night, or that if he lived, he was likely to be severely brain-damaged and on some sort of support system – that he might never come out of the coma. I turned to Richard and said 'He's going to live and he's going to be all right.' Richard took my hand and said, 'Kate, you must prepare yourself, he may die.' I repeated firmly, 'No, he's going to live and he's going to be all right.'

They then took me into intensive care to see him. He was lying there looking terrible, all wired up to machines that were monitoring his brain, his pulse, his heart. I didn't see a man in his thirties all bruised and battered; I saw a little golden-haired six-year-old boy, my baby. They told me I could stay with him for as long as I felt able, but that it might be a good idea if I got some sleep, as the crucial time would be the early hours of the morning, when I might be needed more. I was grateful for this as I was already exhausted, having had very little sleep the night before. I had been up learning lines and rehearsing literally every moment of the day, trying desperately to remember the lines that I'd learnt the night before and play them to Peter Hall's satisfaction.

The hospital authorities were kindness itself and offered me the use of a bed. I stayed with Dickon for several hours and then weariness overtook me and I went, thankfully, to the bed and lay down, fully dressed on top of it. Jeremy had rushed to the hospital on hearing the news and said he would do the first part of the vigil. As we know the show 'must go on', so Richard had by now left for Leicester. My dear friend Patricia had been the first to arrive at the hospital and, with her husband Alan, had given me strength for the ordeal. I fell asleep instantly asleep and slept for about two hours.

I suddenly awoke with a start. I glanced at my watch. It was 1 a.m. By some quirk of fate, the window of the room was on the inside of the building on an upper floor and looked straight down into the intensive care unit. I had noted that before I lay down. I rushed to the window, my heart pounding. It had been snowing earlier and now, in the early hours, had turned bitterly cold again. But it was as nothing to the icy fear that gripped my heart. I prayed as I'd never prayed before.

Suddenly, I saw a flurry of activity around the bed where my darling son lay. I ran from the room and tore down the stairs. I raced along the corridors looking for the signs to tell me the way. I got there finally. One of the nurses said, 'He moved his legs!' My heart fluttered with hope. I went to his side, he was still lying there, motionless. I took his hand and started to talk to him quietly. He half opened his eyes, seemed to take me in, then fell back into unconsciousness. They told me to continue to talk to him quietly and to watch the monitors constantly. I had to make sure that he wasn't over stimulated in case of a haemorrhage, but that the levels should not drop either, in case he sank beyond help.

I spent the hours until dawn willing him to live. I spoke to him of the countryside and all the things he loved and how we would see them again together. I was sure he could hear me, for at one point a tear slid out of the corner of his eye and trickled down his face. I continuously prayed, murmured quietly and stroked his hand all night, my eyes glancing every few seconds at the machines to ensure that the needles were steady in the centre of the monitor.

At dawn, I was relieved by a nurse who told me to go and get some tea. But I didn't want to go anywhere. I dared not leave Dickon. Eventually, two doctors arrived. I said 'There's hope, isn't there? He moved his legs and he opened his eyes briefly.' But they told me not to hope, that it was better not to hope. I felt despair start to surge up inside me and they told me to take a break for a while. I went to a washroom where I bathed my face and rinsed out my mouth. In the mirror, I saw my face was as white as a sheet, but that I looked very calm. I went to get a cup of tea. I put lots of sugar in it and, after a while, felt better.

I phoned Michael, my agent, and told him what had happened. He was very sympathetic and understanding and said he would get hold of Peter Hall and explain the situation. I said, 'Tell Peter I'll be back. I will open in this play, but that I have to get Dickon through this first. He'll understand. He's got children of his own.'

I went back to intensive care, to find that they were preparing to take Dickon elsewhere for a brain scan. There was no machine for this procedure at Kingston. The nearest one was a couple of miles away at the Atkinson Morley Hospital, on the outskirts of Wimbledon. An ambulance arrived and I was shooed out of the way while they got him on board. I heard the siren as it disappeared into the distance. There was nothing to do now except wait and hope. I hardly knew what to think. I was just clinging desperately to the fact that he had moved his legs, had opened his eyes briefly and looked at me and had shed a tear.

They brought him back to Kingston an hour or so later. They had rushed through the result of the scan. They said they could find no evidence of any brain damage. At last. Real hope. But still they advised caution. Then some time later that day he regained consciousness. I was allowed to see him. He just lay there, but he was awake and let me hold his hand. He mumbled something about being thirsty and I rang for a nurse. He became aware of the various tubes and wires and oxygen mask over his face and started trying to remove them. I explained, firmly, that they were essential to his well-being. The nursing staff then came in to attend to him and I was told to go home, as the crisis was past and they were going to clean him up, make him more comfortable and sedate him to make sure he got some rest. They suggested I did the same.

I phoned Michael again and told him the good news. He said that when I felt able, I should go straight to the Thorndike Theatre, Leatherhead, where rehearsals were in progress. I hadn't given the play a second thought for two days and wondered if I could remember anything of what I'd learnt before the recent happenings. I went home, had a bath and changed my clothes, much needed as I'd been wearing the same garments for two days.

* * *

I drove to Leatherhead and went into the darkened auditorium. On stage, they were lighting the set for Act I. I saw Peter Hall sitting on the end of a row in the stalls. I flung myself into his arms, apologised for my absence, thanked him brokenly for his compassion and apologised again. He hugged me and then gestured towards the stage where the lights were shining brightly. Out of the darkness he said, 'It's only a play.' I tried to laugh, but the strain of the last few days was beginning to tell and I could only cry.

I glanced to the stage and I saw an actor pacing up and down on the set, muttering lines to himself, as the lights were being focused. I recognised the portly frame of Jeremy Sinden, Donald's eldest son. I turned to Peter. 'What's Jeremy doing here?' Peter said casually, 'Oh, didn't anyone tell you. John Alderton left the show yesterday.' I rushed down the steps of the auditorium and leapt up onto the stage. 'Jeremy, how wonderful.

221

This is a totally unexpected pleasure!' Jeremy embraced me roundly and said he hoped he wasn't going to regret bravely stepping into the breach. It turned out he'd played the part a year ago and was hoping he might remember some of it. 'Well, I've only just learnt it,' I said, 'so we'll get through it somehow.' And we did. It was hairy, I admit.

When we opened on the Saturday afternoon, there was one point in Act II when I found myself alone on stage. I thought, 'What the hell happens now? Ah, the door's opening, good. Who's coming on, I wonder? Ah, it's Jeremy, good, now I know where we are.'

Peter was not there for the opening. He'd had to fly to Morocco to finish some filming he'd been directing. He turned up on the Wednesday and seemed reasonably pleased with the show. He said to me, 'You've made this part all your own.' I'm still not sure to this day whether that was approval or not! However, he instructed the designer to make me some new costumes, so I think I'd passed muster. Because of my late arrival in the cast and subsequent absence, they'd had to find me something out of the Kenwright wardrobe stock and I looked fairly ropey. The run at Leatherhead was to be followed by a lengthy tour and I was supposed to be playing a woman of considerable wealth.

I had managed to get through the play without 'drying', but there were a couple of lines in one scene I had with Jeremy which were identical and I came in with the wrong one, so that we found ourselves repeating the same page of dialogue again. Jeremy, being more familiar with the play than I, rescued us and got us back on track. I apologised afterwards. He said, 'Darling, I thought we were never going to get off the Circle Line. I kept trying to find a station, but we went on going past it!' I promised that I would look at the script and make sure that I didn't do the same thing again. But the next night, even though I'd gone over it again and again before the show, I made the same mistake. I was so sure that I'd got it right too, but seeing a glassy look come into Jeremy's eyes, I knew I hadn't and we were off on the Circle Line again! Sadly, two years later Jeremy died. He was a lovely man.

Dickon had been released from hospital and sent to Isleworth to stay with me, where I could keep an eye on his recuperation before I went on tour. It was an anxious time, as he seemed very vulnerable.

About ten days before we were due to finish at Leatherhead, I went into the theatre early. I was about to go on stage, as is my wont, when I became aware that rehearsals were taking place. I peered through and saw Simon Ward on stage, rehearsing Jeremy's part! I retreated hastily and went back to No. 1 dressing-room, which I was sharing with Belinda Lang, one of the most talented and adorable girls it has ever been my pleasure to work with. When she arrived, I told her what I'd seen. 'I say, Belinda,' I said conspiratorially, 'I've got something to tell you.' 'Oh my God!,' she exclaimed in her cut-glass accent, 'You're having an affair with my husband!' 'No, no, no, don't be silly,' I laughed. 'No, Simon Ward's on stage, rehearsing Jeremy's part!' 'Good Lord, not *another* change of cast!' she expostulated, 'it can't be!' But it was.

It seemed Jeremy Sinden, wonderful though he was in the part, was not considered a big enough 'name' to tour, so they'd come up with Simon. Three changes of cast in a four-hander isn't bad. But it wasn't to end there. We toured for about four months, ending up in Richmond. It was rumoured that we were going into London. Well, the play did, but not with us. After all that trauma and all that hard work, the only survivor was Simon! Belinda, John Fortune and myself were all replaced! I have to say, *en passant*, that John Fortune was one of the funniest men I've ever worked with and very droll off-stage as well. He used to tell me that I was the wisest woman he'd ever met. What could he have meant by that?

* * *

By now it was autumn and we were not transferring into town, so money had to be found from somewhere. I accepted another pantomime. *Dick Whittington* again, this time at High Wycombe. I was playing opposite a charming boy from one of the Australian soaps and 'Alice Fitzwarren' was Lucy Benjamin, who made such a hit in *EastEnders* recently. A most talented and delightful girl. Knight Mantell was also in the cast; so a very happy time was had by all.

Richard's mother and step-father spent Christmas with us at Isleworth and came to see the panto on Christmas Eve. The weather did one of those hoar-frost effects, when the countryside looks like an old-fashioned Christmas card. My cousin, the highly acclaimed business writer Carol Kennedy, was also spending the day with us, as she had recently lost her mother. We did our best to cheer her through the festivities. She was soon to repay this hospitality in kind and many times over.

Richard went to Stoke-on-Trent to play 'Rosencrantz' in *Hamlet*. On his way up north, he dropped in to the theatre at High Wycombe where I was in the middle of a matinee, to say goodbye. Little did I suspect that that would be the last time I saw him in happy circumstances. I finished the pantomime and was surprised that I had not heard from Richard since his departure.

It was barely three weeks after he left, on a bleak raw February morning that I opened a letter from him. Terse and to the point, it was requesting a divorce. I went completely to pieces, but did as I was asked. I went to a solicitor and filed for divorce. She advised me to reconsider. She told me that I was upset – that was the understatement of all time – I was distraught, that my emotions were in turmoil and I would change my mind several times over the next two years. Would to God I hadn't listened to her. I would have saved myself much pain, distress and anguish, not to say money, if I'd followed my instincts and 'amputated' instead. I endured two years of suffering and misery because of taking her advice. I learned after a few days that Richard had met someone else and fallen in love with her. Well, this happens to people. It's just unfortunate when it happens to be your husband and you are not the object of his affections.

* * *

I was asked to do a guest appearance in *Absolutely Fabulous*, to play a character based loosely on Jackie Onassis, who was in fact

'Patsy's' sister, an animal obsessive! They had wanted Charlotte Rampling for the part, but she had cried off. It was a wonderful role and it was lovely to see Joanna Lumley again. It was terribly difficult to put a brave face on things at rehearsals, but I don't think anyone suspected how deeply unhappy I was. I decided to play 'Jackie' as a cross between Ursula Andress and Brigitte Bardot, with my all-purpose 'continental' accent which is virtually unidentifiable, except that you know that the owner has learned her English through watching American TV and movies. Jennifer Saunders seemed very happy with my interpretation and rewrote the script for me each day. The episode went really well and I had high hopes of being asked back.

Sitting in the audience at the taping of 'Ab. Fab', was Sam Mendes, who was with Jane Horrocks at the time. She and Julia Sawalha were both enchanting girls and very welcoming and friendly towards me. As a result of this, Sam asked to see me for the Elaine Stritch part in the production of *Company*, which he was putting on at the Donmar Warehouse. I learned the song 'The Ladies who Lunch' and looked forward to meeting him.

I felt unable to stay in Isleworth and was invited by Irena Brook, who had become a good friend, to use some of the rooms in the large country house, built by Robert Adam, that she and her husband had bought in Sussex. These were on the ground floor and were charming. Irena was wonderfully sympathetic. At that time she was married to Neil Malarkey of the Comedy Store fame. She helped get me through the first nine months of my unhappiness. I went to meet Sam Mendes, whom I liked enormously. He was daunted by my lack of weight and later told my agent he hadn't realised I was so petite. I assured him that I had played 'Martha' in *Who's Afraid of Virginia Woolf*, which was a similar size of part! But he was not convinced. As I was leaving, he said, 'You're perfect casting for this part,' and then gave it to Sheila Gish! I wept bitterly when I heard.

* * *

Peter Woodward rang up one evening when I was in the depths of despair. He wanted me to resign as a director from BATCO.

This was the last straw. 'When sorrows come they come not single spies but in battalions.' I had lost my home, my husband, I had no work and no money. I couldn't lose the company as well. I refused point blank. The company was all I had left. Irena and Neil were both away, she in Paris, he working at the Comedy Store in London. Feeling very alone and utterly miserable, I took myself to bed and tried to forget my distress in sleep.

I woke suddenly in the middle of the night. I could hear someone trying to get in through the shutters of my bed-sitting room, which, of course, was on the ground floor. I became absolutely terrified. I was completely alone in the depths of the countryside in the pitch dark. My heart was in my mouth as I heard the handle turn. I thanked God that I had always taken the precaution of locking the door, even though the weather was still quite warm. I slid silently out of bed, grabbed a dressing-gown and crept out of the room without turning on a light. My mission was to get upstairs into Irena's quarters and phone the Police. I had no intention of calling them from my own phone in case the intruder heard me. I flew silently up the staircase and edged into Irena's sitting-room. There were huge French windows leading into an upstairs conservatory, which was propped up on several wooden pillars.

From my vantage point I could see a single lamp blazing out. So, it was a motor-cyclist. Which meant it wasn't a casual burglar. Unfortunately, the alternative was worse. A casual murderer! I had to get to the phone and get the Police out there as soon as possible. There was nothing to stop the intruder breaking a downstairs window and seeking me out. I didn't fancy a macabre game of cat and mouse and I knew the unbelievably loud beating of my heart would immediately give away my hiding place. I started to creep towards the desk, where I knew the phone usually was. It was then that I became aware that there were two lamps, one had been blocked out by the wall of the house. So, it was a car after all. I might be able to deal with just a burglar.

As I got nearer to the desk, the number plate of the car became visible. I couldn't believe it. It was Richard's car! But what the hell was he doing here in the middle of the night trying to make a surreptitious entry, when he was supposed to be with a girl-friend somewhere? With a huge sigh of relief, I went downstairs, switching on lights as I did. I unlocked the front door and saw him standing there in the porch-light, looking rather lost. It was a pointless visit and solved nothing, other than to strengthen my resolve to get a divorce. There were quite a few other visits before we finally went our separate ways. Why do men do this? This wretched to-ing and fro-ing?

* * *

At last I got a job! I went back to the Orange Tree in Richmond to do the London première of a Bernard Shaw play, *The Simpleton of the Unexpected Isles*, a rather risqué comedy for its time, all about 'free love'. I didn't want to know about free love, there'd been far too much of it in my life recently! I was playing an Anglo-Indian in 'The Simpleton', casting which caused the Asian section of Equity to protest volubly. I retaliated by pointing out that if Asian and black actors could play English parts, then English actors could play Asian or black parts and I stand by this argument and I look forward to the day when I am playing *Othello* (not blacked up, you understand). We are not supposed to notice colour so it *has* to cut *both* ways. There were also four Asian actors in the play with me and we all had a very jolly time. Obviously, it was impossible for me to commute from Sussex to Richmond each day for the run of the show, so I stayed with my cousin Carol in Wimbledon which helped me immeasurably in recovering from the break-up of my marriage.

* * *

I was approached in January 1996 about doing a stage version of Daphne du Maurier's famous novel, *My Cousin Rachel*. They – the Haymarket Theatre, Basingstoke – sent me a script which was truly dreadful. I said I would only contemplate it if I was allowed to alter the text. This apparently presented no problem, so I accepted. The production was to start at Basingstoke (and end in Vienna!) and would last until July. I left Irena and Neil's, put my furniture into store and went off on tour once more. I was now completely homeless, but at least I had a job. I would be able to earn enough money to buy a place of my own by the summer! The production broke box-office records.

The management was thrilled and asked me back for a production the following year, wanting me to do a Shakespeare and direct it myself with my own company but insisting 'You must be in it!' This is always the problem. I always have to be 'in' everything. It is all very flattering, but it means I am working virtually every night of my life, living out of a suitcase and longing to go home for just a *little* while. At that moment I didn't have a home to go to, but I was determined to get one. The newspapers had documented Richard's latest affair with an up-and-coming actress and written sympathetic articles describing me as 'sad Kate', who had been 'abandoned' by her husband, who had gone off with a younger woman. This image of myself did not marry up with my tough, independent, self-reliant view of myself and I decided to remedy it.

I pulled myself up by my bootstraps and spent my Sundays off house-hunting. It seemed that Richard was trying to effect a reconciliation. When I went to view a cottage in Suffolk, he turned up. Afterwards we went to the local pub for lunch. He admitted to me there that he was having another affair. We drove back across to Leicester, where he was playing. I stayed overnight in his digs, but slept hardly at all. I left very early the next morning to go to the next venue on the tour.

As I drove away without a backward glance, I suddenly realised that I had no idea where I was going. I had a feeling that it began with a 'C'. Was it Chelmsford, could it be Colchester? I had an idea that it was much further west than that. But where? I drove west, hoping that some signpost would give me a clue. It was only when I was within a few miles of Cheltenham that I realised that I was nearly at my destination. I had to do some publicity on my arrival and to get changed and made-up early. After I'd done the photo-shoot, I went back to my dressing-room and sat down and started to sob loudly. Various people came into the room and asked me what the matter was, but I was unable to tell them.

Then something very alarming happened. I went on for my first entrance and for a while everything was fine. Then the set and the theatre started to go out of focus and then to spin, quite slowly, but revolve none the less. I went hot and cold and felt sick. I was seized with the idea that I had no business to be there. I kept thinking, 'Where am I?' and then realising, 'Oh, I'm on stage, no, I shouldn't be here. I must leave.' As I thought all this, I quite slowly and deliberately left the stage and walked off into the 'wings'. I could see people looking alarmed. Someone asked me if I was ill. Someone else turned me around and pushed me back on stage again. I obeyed, went on and continued with the scene, but not for long. The same thing happened again. Again, I walked off. I suddenly came to and said off-stage, 'I don't know where I am.' Somebody produced a script and I looked at it with unseeing eyes. It meant nothing to me. I broke into a sweat and started shivering at the same time. I grabbed the script and searched it frantically for my next line. In a panic, I went back on and somehow got through to the end of the scene. Trembling with terror, I finished the play, not knowing what had happened.

The next day I got very good reviews. Nobody had noticed a thing. That night I treated myself to the most expensive hotel in Cheltenham. There was something wrong, such a thing had never happened to me before. Was I having a nervous break-down? I rang my mother and recounted the horrors of the previous night to her. She was very sympathetic and told me it was 'stress'. I daresay she was right. Various of my fellow actors suggested it was a combination of shock and tiredness. The next day, I arrived at the theatre early and went through the entire play, on stage, by myself. That night, I was scared but fine. I remained apprehensive for the rest of the week and have never forgotten the dreadful experience.

Richard turned up again while I was at Basingstoke, but I was in no mood to contemplate a reunion. I assumed, I think correctly, that his latest romance had broken up. I've never been able to understand why men seem to think that women will put up with endless infidelity and still be waiting, with arms ever open, for their return. I became more determined than ever to go ahead with the divorce.

My last port of call in England, before going to Vienna, was Taunton in Somerset. Richard and I had played the venue before, when we toured with *Kiss and Tell* and had found the technical standard of the girls who ran the show for us to be of the highest and by far and away, the best we had encountered in the country. At the time, an invitation had been extended from one of them, Paddy Stratton, to 'come and stay next time you're here.' I took her up on this offer, as the B&B we had stayed in previously had marshmallow beds and smelled of very damp dog.

I was invited out to supper after the two shows on Wednesday, to somewhere on Exmoor. Relations of Daphne du Maurier were among those present. I had been asked to stay the night in this superb house. At four o'clock in the morning I awoke, being violently ill. I vomited until nine o'clock, when someone came to find me wondering why I had not turned up for breakfast. A doctor was immediately summoned. He gave me some pills to stop me throwing up and somehow, later that day, I drove back to Taunton to do the evening show. I was as weak as a kitten and had to have a bucket placed in each wing. I availed myself of them after nearly every scene!

*   *   *

On the Sunday after the English leg of the tour had finished, I was due to go to Stevenage to publicise the pantomime I was doing there the following Christmas. On the Monday I was to fly to Vienna. I shall never know how I coped at Stevenage. I was still suffering from the effects of what had turned out to be severe food poisoning. It was a scorching hot day in June. I was dressed to the nines. There seemed to be thousands of people there. In a haze of heat and pain, I remember staggering across a playing field area, being handed a microphone by the Mayor and addressing this huge crowd. What I said or how I got through it, I shall never know. I remember a local disc jockey in a mobile radio station unit trying to interview me and my asking if he minded if I sat down. Eventually, it was over. I'd done my stuff, signed autographs, had photographs taken, been interviewed by the local Press. Then I was free to go to the hotel the panto management had kindly provided.

I collapsed, thankfully, onto the bed and lay in the darkened room for hours, trying to overcome the nausea which still assailed me. At ten o'clock, I roused myself, undressed and washed. I couldn't face a bath or shower. I could hardly stand. I slept soundly. The next morning, a sweet girl arrived to take me to Heathrow. It had been arranged that I would leave my car at the theatre while I was away for six weeks! They were kindness itself. The first thing I did on arriving at the airport was a final gesture. I posted the divorce petition.

I was still feeling queasy for the first two days after my arrival in Vienna. They were building a brand new set for our six-week season. Thankfully, by the time we opened on the Wednesday, my insides had more or less settled down, which was just as well as we received a tremendous reception afterwards. We were cheered, fêted, wined and dined. One never receives this sort of treatment in England, only abroad; 'a prophet is without honour in his own country,' I suppose.

The English-speaking theatre in Vienna is very beautiful. It was a couple of minutes' walk from my hotel, where I had a little flat which was delightful. We had no matinees, so my days were my own. I spent them exploring the beautiful city, as it was my first visit. At last I felt liberated, free. I had had the courage to post the divorce petition which, for some reason, I'd been putting off. Why I'm not sure, except that, for me, marriage was a serious step and I never give up lightly on any thing. I fight till the bitter end. I felt completely safe there in the loveliness of that historic city, the museums, the churches, the parks. Away from the pain and distress. I'd left those behind in England.

I'd been there about a week and was really beginning to enjoy my routine. I've always been an early riser and it's no different when I'm working in the theatre at night. So, every day I would get up and go for a walk, exploring various different parts of the city. I would breakfast on orange juice in the Volksgarten, take lunch in the Historische Museum, where I would go every day to gaze in awe at the Breugels, which I adored. Sadly, we'd never learned German at school, so it was a bit of a struggle for me, but I did my best.

One morning, I was just getting ready to go out, when the phone rang. I picked it up puzzled, no one ever rang me. The girl at reception was telling me that my husband was downstairs. I replied that that was not possible. She insisted it was so and the next moment there was a tap at the door and the concierge entered, followed by Richard! I was appalled. I was overwhelmed by a feeling of being trapped. There was no escape from the anguish, not even here, where a moment ago, I had felt free as a bird. He stayed a couple of days, saw the show again and criticised my performance. We had a reasonable time. I showed him the city, Beethoven's death mask, took him to the restaurant which dear Ludwig had frequented, but it was not the same. I supposed he'd received the divorce petition. Anyway, after a violent row, in which I reverted to type and started throwing things, he gave up and left.

I think it was having my sanctuary invaded that infuriated me most. Here I was, making a superhuman effort to recover from the emotional mayhem he'd wrought and I had been succeeding. I'd been immersing myself in the glories of Vienna, the beautiful old churches, the awesome paintings, the memories everywhere of the great eighteenth- and nineteenth-century composers. I felt that I'd been sent this job for just this purpose, to recover from the distress of my broken marriage and then he'd turned up to try to arrest that recovery.

Act V

I was able to enjoy the rest of my stay unmolested, uninterrupted and alone. While I was there, I started doing the preparation work for *Twelfth Night* for Basingstoke as I was to direct it. It was not due to rehearse for another nine months, but I had my days free while doing 'Rachel' and I knew I would have other work to do when I got home, so I got on with the 'blocking' while I had the opportunity. They had wanted *Macbeth*, but we'd just witnessed the horrors of the Dunblane massacre and I felt that the audience should not have to endure the evil that is rampant in the Scottish play, which includes a scene of the murder of two small children and their mother.

I left Vienna reluctantly. I'd been happy there for the first time for two years. I'd experienced an innate feeling of peace and I found the strength to put all the misery of the past two years behind me and forge a new life for myself alone. I went to stay with my newly acquired Somerset friends while I looked for my new abode. I found it within a couple of days, thanks to the tireless work on their part.

I then had an odd request from Kevin Wood, the management for whom I'd been doing pantomime each Christmas. Yes, he wanted me to do another one, but in the summer in Belfast! So, it wasn't *really* a panto, but a summer fairy story, but it was *Snow White*. I thought the idea completely off the wall but of course he was right. What else had the children of Belfast got to entertain them in the summer hols? It was only a short run, but it packed out and it was lovely to do the gruelling pantomime schedule knowing that one was not going to get the 'pantomime cold'!

* * *

When I got back, I was suddenly asked to go to Lithuania to film an episode of *The New Adventures of Robin Hood* for Warner Brothers. Michael Ladkin, my agent, had turned it down because the money was so paltry, but I felt it was important to work, particularly for the Americans, so I insisted that he retrieve the job. So, leaving the cottage I'd found in Somerset in the hands of the builders, I flew to Vilnius, the capital of Lithuania, a city which had suffered much in the Second World War and indeed an air of oppression and sadness still hung over it. The atmosphere was similar to that which I had experienced in much of the former Yugoslavia. Again, there seemed to be very few shops but many kiosks where a variety of inferior goods could be purchased. By contrast, there were quarters where it was possible to buy amber and gold and coins.

On my arrival in the hotel, I was greeted by John Forgeham, whom I had not seen for about thirty years! (He has recently had a personal success in *Footballers Wives*.) He'd had huge potential as a young actor and was obviously destined for a spectacular career. But he'd decided in favour of hell-raising and, like so many talented actors before and since, seemed to scupper his chances. But he hadn't.

He and I were playing the villains for the week and made the most of it. Although only late September, it was extremely cold, particularly on location. But I was not worried. We were supposed to be in the twelfth century, when people had covered themselves from head to toe with wool, fur and animal skins. Ah, but I'd reckoned without the Hollywood input! To my horror, authenticity had gone by the board and the wardrobe department had been instructed to dress me in black chiffon and gold lamé! And not much of it, at that. My only comfort was that they'd given me a lot of hair, which at least kept my back warm. The American producers, who were charming but plainly uninformed, insisted on plenty of cleavage and a ton of make-up. For the exterior scenes, *I* insisted that they provide me with a fur-lined cloak.

The wardrobe girl spoke no English and my Lithuanian was nonexistent but fortunately, we both spoke French, so I got my warm outer garb. The actors invariably come off better in these 'medieval' situations, since they're always clad in leather, suede, fur and armour, with wool cloaks, whereas we actresses, who are supplying the decorative element, are often practically naked, at least when the American influence holds sway. It's different on a British movie; then they're terribly keen to make everything as authentic as possible, which means one looks perfectly hideous in a wimple and no make-up at *all*. You can't win!

Then there were the props. When John and I arrived on set to do a scene in the banqueting hall, I was given a book of 'spells' to consult. (I was playing Maid Marion's sister-in-law who was a witch on the side). I gasped in horror. 'But printing hadn't been *invented*,' I protested. 'Kate,' said John quietly, 'just shut up and say the lines.' They had given me something that resembled a

Victorian bible, 'But, but . . .' Forgeham looked at me, *'Kate,'* he said warningly. I subsided and got on with the scene.

Two 'extras' playing guards suddenly appeared dressed in chain-mail, which was correct, but wearing helmets which were not worn for another five hundred years. Even the American producer drew the line at this. 'Oh, no,' she said doubtfully, 'I don't think *that's* right, no, I think we'll have to find them something else. They're, er, they're too, er too . . .' she paused for inspiration, 'Cromwellian!' I supplied the missing description in ringing tones from the other side of the set. 'Kate,' remonstrated Forgeham in a subdued aside, 'just shut up and say the lines.' The producer glanced in my direction. 'Yeah,' she agreed, 'they're er, that, find them something else!'

While the offending guards were removed, the unit shot the 'reverses' on the pretty little actress John and I were supposed to have kidnapped. Her lines to the guards on finding her way barred were, 'Move it or lose it!' I groaned out loud and sank my head into my hands. 'Kate,' warned Forgeham, *sotto voce*. The guards eventually returned. On their heads they were wearing modern firemen's helmets which had been sprayed silver! John's look dared me to speak. I kept my counsel. 'I guess that'll have to do,' said the producer dubiously, 'Yeah, okay, let's shoot it.' I gave up.

Well, not quite. When we went on location to shoot a scene of an encounter between Robin Hood and we villains, he was discovered lolling about nonchalantly on the greensward. By his side was not, as I had eagerly anticipated, a twelfth-century long bow made of yew, but a modern bow constructed of fibreglass, aluminium and some sort of composite wood. I pointed to the offending object unable to speak, which is just as well. 'I know, I know, don't tell me,' crowed John, nodding sagely, 'you're going to say that it's a modern bow, aren't you?' 'John,' I exploded, 'it's the *latest* model!' 'Yes, but, Kate, *who's* to *know*, apart from you? Now shut up, just shut up and say the lines!'

* * *

When Forgeham had found out that I was co-producing and directing *Twelfth Night*, he was insistent that *he* should play 'Malvolio'. I pointed out, gently, that I'd already cast it. In fact, one of the reasons I was doing the play was because Nicholas Day had asked me to put it on for him. He had brought his daughter, Becky, to see me in *Kiss me Kate* at Newcastle. We had had supper afterwards and he'd told me that I should get BATCO going again and that I should do *Twelfth Night*, as he wanted to play 'Malvolio'. I thought it a marvellous idea and so was doing just that. Forgeham was undeterred. 'Forget him, you need me. I understudied Donald Sinden at Stratford and *everyone* said I was better than he was.' 'John,' I explained patiently for the twentieth time, 'it's already cast. Nick's doing it. I've *promised* him.' I might as well have saved my breath to cool my porridge. John was insistent that *he* was going to play it. (And the odd thing is, he did.)

He was equally determined that I should meet an actor called Mark Noble, whom he said was perfect for the company. 'I've only got 'Valentine' and 'Curio' left,' I said, 'they're very small parts, although they will have to double.' 'He can do 'em,' was Forgeham's instant reply. 'Oh, and there's 'Sebastian' of course. I haven't cast him yet,' I added as an after-thought. 'Yes, he can do that as well,' he said immediately. I laughed and promised I would see him. Forgeham insisted on giving me the phone number and his agent's phone number. John said Mark was exactly the actor I needed in my show and the man I needed in my life. I was pleased about the former, but not about the latter. I was absolutely certain that I didn't need *any* man in my life!

6

'Who is Kate O'Mara?'

I got back from Vienna to find the first stages of renovation of my house completed. I had only had the essentials done. Cosmetic surgery would have to come later, after I'd earned some more money. The removal van containing all my furniture and personal effects arrived the day I was due to move in, 4 October. Unfortunately, I also had to do the panto launch at Stevenage on that very day. So I said to the removal men, 'Just bring everything into the main room. I'll sort it out when I get back later!' I instructed them to lock up and drop the keys through the door. I had a spare set with me. They stared as I left. I had, as usual, transformed myself in a short space of time and had done my glamour girl thing. I got to Stevenage, a drive of some three and a half hours, in record time.

I was tremendously excited at the prospect of moving into my own home at last. However, when I got to the Press Conference, somehow they'd got wind of my impending divorce. I had no desire to discuss this with them. I was there to publicise a family pantomime, *Sleeping Beauty*, again. I got myself into my glittering sequinned frock, put on several hair pieces and false eyelashes and presented myself for the cameras with my co-stars. But I'd already seen one of the photo-journalists sneak off to a telephone in the foyer. Someone had heard him on the phone to his editor, promising a 'story' about me. I feared the worst. By an unfortunate co-incidence,

4 October was also my wedding anniversary, so I knew they would have a 'hook' for their story.

However, help was at hand in the shape of my pantomime producer Kevin Wood's adorable wife, Helga. Together, we all plotted a ruse. After the press launch was over, I gave Kevin my car keys and I got into Helga's car with her. We all drove off towards the M1. A photographer with a telephoto lens camera had seen us and started to follow Helga and me. Kevin had gone off in my car in advance. We were all headed towards the South Mimms Service Station! Kevin got there first and hid my car, then got out and waited for us. Helga made sure the Press car had spotted us and was in pursuit and kept him in her sights until we neared our destination, when she put on a bit of a spurt. She and I got there ahead of the photographer and while Helga filled up with petrol, I grabbed my keys from Kevin and scurried off to my car. When Helga left a few moments later, with Kevin in the passenger seat, but crouched down low, so as not to be identifiable, they were followed for some considerable way by the Press. I would like to think that they followed the Woods all the way to Deal in Kent where they lived, but we can't be sure as it was, by now, pitch dark. All I know is that I travelled back to Somerset unaccompanied. But I kept checking my rear mirror just in case!

I got home, finally, to find that the removers had been as good as their word. Everything, but everything, was in the main room. It was chaos, but to me, a heavenly sight. I was in my own house at last! I started to put things to rights immediately. It was quite late, but I was full of energy. I unpacked the essentials, making sure I had the necessities of life available. I made up the bed and emptied a few packing cases to make sure my treasured possessions were safe. As I finished with each packing case, I took it outside to the porch to make more room inside. With hindsight, it would have been sensible to have locked the door each time, but I was confident I could get quite a lot done that night.

I was upstairs putting pillow cases on the pillows, when I heard a noise outside. I froze. My heart stood still as I heard the front door open. I decided to be brave and confront the intruder.

As I reached the head of the stairs, Richard came through the door. 'Happy anniversary, darling,' he called up and, glancing at his watch, he added, 'I just made it. It's not quite midnight!' I stood transfixed at the top of the stairs, not able to believe my eyes. He'd ruined my day again. But then I remembered. We were divorced. The decree absolute had not come through yet but it would any day. I tried not to let his presence affect me too much. I was feeling much stronger, although, plainly, Richard was trying to effect a reconciliation. But I knew that that way madness lay. Fortunately, he only stayed for a day, so I was able to get on with enjoying my new abode.

* * *

When I got myself straight, I turned my attentions once more to *Twelfth Night*. Rehearsals were due to start the last week of my pantomime but, fortunately, during that week I had only one performance a night (plus matinees), so it was just possible. Of course, I was going to be in the show as well. I cast myself as 'Olivia', as there was really nothing else I could possibly play. I took myself up to London a couple of weeks later and arranged to see some actors for the parts not yet cast. I was using an office in New Row as a temporary home for BATCO. They belonged to Bill Freedman, whom I'd worked for in *Suddenly At Home*.

The first person I was due to see was Mark Noble, whom John Forgeham had recommended so highly. For some reason, I had neither a photograph nor a CV of him; possibly his agent hadn't sent one or it had ended up in one of the other offices. At any rate, I had no idea what to expect. I needed to cast 'Sebastian' with care. He is supposed to fall in love with 'Olivia' at first sight. I was far too old to be playing 'Olivia', but thought as she was a rich countess, that with Jenny Cane's lighting and some flattering costumes, I might just get away with it. So the actor playing 'Sebastian' would not have to look too young! But he was also supposed to be 'Viola's' twin. She was being played by Constance Barrie, who was all of 27!

Then, of course, he couldn't be too tall; otherwise he'd never pass for her twin. Constance was 5ft 8in and blonde, so an inch or so either way was the most the actor could get away. He would need to be blond, or I'd have to get him a wig! It was a tall order! Anyway, Mark Noble arrived. He was about 5ft 9in, a natural blond and in his late thirties. He was perfect. I asked him to read with me. I had no qualms. I offered him the part there and then. He accepted immediately and I heaved a sigh of relief. One down, two to go. As he left, he gave me what can only be described as an old-fashioned look.

The phone rang a couple of minutes after he left. 'Yes, who's next?' I asked. 'Your husband to see you, Miss O'Mara' came the reply. 'What?' I exclaimed. 'I don't have a husband!' 'Well, whoever he is he wants to see you. Shall I send him up?' 'Yes' I sighed heavily, 'send him up.' A few seconds later, Richard appeared. How the hell he'd known where I was, I simply couldn't fathom. He wanted, it seemed, to take me out to lunch. I told him I had two other actors to see. He said he'd wait for me at a café across the passage. I agreed to meet him there. Now what?, I thought. After lunch, I was none the wiser.

* * *

A month later, the decree absolute came through and I left home to go to do pantomime in Stevenage. On the wall of my dressing-room, I stuck two photographs; one was the stunning panoramic view from the top of my hill in Somerset, the other was a snapshot I'd taken of Tesco's in Stevenage in the rain, the remains of snowy sludge on the ground. The contrast was startling, but I had them there for a reason. It was to remind myself that I was enduring the one, so that I could enjoy the other! It worked. It kept me going.

We always say that when we are doing the hideous pantomime schedule, that 'Christmas is Cancelled' because, invariably, Christmas Day is the only day in the year when there are no performances. That year, I managed to get home late on Christmas Eve and had Christmas Day off but then had to get to Stevenage for the Boxing Day matinee. Needless to say, Richard turned up, but I didn't let it faze me as we were now completely divorced. But I used to dread seeing his car when I returned home at the weekends. Eventually, I had to throw him out with the help of various girl-friends as the situation was beginning to get on my nerves. I was seeing more of him since we'd been divorced than when we were married!

* * *

At last, the first day of rehearsals for *Twelfth Night* arrived. First days are always nerve-wracking. True to his word, John Forgeham *was* playing 'Malvolio'. About a month or so before, Nick Day had sent me an apologetic note saying that he'd been asked to do a play on Broadway and I did understand, didn't I? Of course I did, but it seemed ironic, as I'd only put the play on because he'd wanted to do it! As soon as I'd received Nick's brief missive, I rang John and told him what had happened. 'You want me to do it?' he queried in his usual blunt way. 'If you really want to,' I replied. 'You know the money's terrible and we only have three weeks' rehearsal.' 'I'll do it,' he'd said immediately.

So there he was and there was everyone else. The most onerous task on a first day is that one has to introduce everyone to each other and hope to God one can remember everyone's name! At least that's what used to happen. Recently, there has been the introduction of an American idea called 'Meet and Greet' – ugh! This lets the director off the hook, as each member of the cast introduces him or herself to the other members, along with the name of the character they're playing or the task they're ful- filling. However, I was still employing the old-fashioned method and I came through the ordeal unscathed. We then all looked at the designs and model of the set, which was delightful. As I would have to leave to go to Stevenage each day, we started 'blocking' at once without doing a 'read-through'.

The trouble with directing something and being in it as well, means that you have to have a split personality in order to observe what is happening on stage, as well as being a part of it all. I've done it a few times now and I have to say it's very tricky and I prefer to do one or the other – not both. In spite of the fact that I was commuting to Stevenage each day for the first four days, we got a considerable amount of work done, but I was glad when I could concentrate solely on the Shakespeare.

* * *

My stage manager, Pauline Goldsworthy, whom I'd brought with me from Taunton, was in charge. She'd been part of the team of two who'd produced such technical excellence when Richard and I had performed *Kiss and Tell* at the Brewhouse. Mark Noble offered to help me with my scenes and read in the other parts for me. I was suitably grateful and in return, offered to rehearse his sword fights with him. I absolutely adored fencing and said if he would teach me his fights, I would pick them up and then he could practice with me. He agreed and went off to retrieve the swords from where they were locked up. On his return, as he handed me a sword he quipped, 'Be gentle with me!' I roared with laughter. There's nothing I like better than a good fight, especially with a man, whether verbal or physical. They are my natural enemy and I relish an opportunity to cross swords with them. In this case quite literally! It didn't take me long to learn the fight and we were soon fencing for 'real'. Pauline later declared she felt as though she was playing 'gooseberry' during the proceedings! Romantically enough, we were opening on St Valentine's Day. Although I had been strongly attracted to Mark, I had been far too busy to think about such things. All I cared about at that moment was the show.

My 'Sir Andrew Aguecheek' was Arthur Bostrom of *Allo, Allo* fame. His casting came about in an extraordinary manner. I had been appearing as a guest on *Noel's House Party*. Arthur was also a guest. We had never met before. In the Green Room at the BBC we introduced ourselves. I mentioned that I was relaunching my company. He said that what he really wanted to do more than anything else was some classical theatre. So when I came to casting 'Sir Andrew', I offered it to him. He accepted at once. I do so like actors who don't mess me around, but say yes or no at once. So I had Noel Edmonds to thank for Arthur, whose performance as 'Sir Andrew' was described as 'definitive'.

242

The production went down a storm. The reviews were ecstatic. We received dozens of letters extolling its virtues. We had a triumph on our hands. Forgeham was a hit! He had insisted on playing 'Malvolio' with an Italian accent. I was very unsure to start with, but he is such a brilliant actor, so full of invention and so technically accomplished that he pulled it off and the audience loved him! Mark and I were in the same digs together with Pauline. She was only there for the pre-production so she left after the first night. Mark and I celebrated the triumphant first night by having our very own first night. On St. Valentine's Day!

People raised their eyebrows. He was twenty years younger than I was and to be honest, I gave it a short shelf-life. However, we have now been an item for six years and the age difference really doesn't seem to matter. Then a letter arrived from Richard's solicitor informing me that his client was going to ask the courts to have the divorce 'set aside'. I didn't think that such a thing was possible. I thought once the decree absolute had come through, that was it. In any case, it was he who'd first asked for a divorce. I still had the ghastly letter he'd written and it was dated. I mentioned this to my solicitor who said that the request was risible and she'd said as much to his solicitor. Really, one is in the wrong profession. Law is where the money is!

* * *

Bill Kenwright resurfaced again and asked me to recreate my old part in *An Ideal Husband*, with an entirely different cast, a short tour of England and then off to the Israel Festival. I was playing opposite Simon Ward once more and my chum Barbara Murray was in the cast, so was Richard Todd and another dear friend, Deborah Grant. I found that quite a few of my cuts had been reinstated including most of my big speech, so I was able to enjoy myself. Jerusalem was a severe disappointment to me, with three religions claiming it for their own; the atmosphere was anything but religious. I was bitterly disillusioned with the Mount of Olives, the Temple of the Holy Sepulchre and most particularly, with the Garden of Gethsemane. When I had visited Jordan I had seen the land Moses had looked out over and I had felt a sense of history, but I was only aware of the commercialism in Jerusalem.

Most of my friends and all of my family were appalled when I moved to Somerset. 'But it's miles away. We'll never see you and anyway, actors should live in London, that's where the work is.' 'Not for me,' I replied briskly. 'I spend my life on tour, or filming on location. It's twelve years since I was in the West End, so I don't need to be in or even near London.' I'd hardly got the words out of my mouth when Kenwright announced that he was taking *An Ideal Husband* back in to the West End, to the Haymarket, with the divine Martin Shaw playing 'Lord Goring', for which he'd won awards. Simon Ward was now playing 'Sir Robert Chiltern', so I was extremely fortunate in having two absolutely brilliant leading men.

Sir Peter Hall was again directing and I was anxious to get back one of my funnier lines, which he'd cut for the earlier production. Sir Peter is notorious for his inflexibility, so I prepared my argument carefully and plucked up courage. As it affected Martin, he had to be consulted as well. I tackled them both when there were just the three of us rehearsing in the rehearsal room at the top of the Old Vic. I put forward my point of view. I was heard in silence. I waxed eloquent, pressing home my reasoning for what seemed like an eternity. There was silence, then Peter agreed that I could have the line back in. Martin raised no objection and I was a much happier woman.

My darling Dulcie Gray and her beloved husband, Michael Denison, were with me once more. I was back at the Haymarket, the oldest and most beautiful theatre in London. I was the leading lady in a highly successful production of a wonderful play. I had the most stunning part, and the set and the costumes by Carl Toms were sensational. I was working for the top director in the country – what more could a girl want? Occasionally, just occasionally, things do go right and one has to remember this when the bad times hit one.

My notices were excellent, but I only know that because they were quoted and blown up and put outside the theatre. I never read reviews until the play is over and not always then. My reasoning is that if you're going to believe the good ones, then you've got to accept the bad ones as well. And that can destroy your confidence. I have seen a mediocre, never mind a bad notice diminish an actor's performance. I like the funny ones best. But I couldn't miss the ones for *An Ideal Husband* as they were writ large.

It was a boiling hot summer and there was no air-conditioning in the theatre. The set was all gold. The floor was gold and reflected the lights which were blinding and numerous. At one performance, I was so hot I thought I was going to faint. The theatre began to revolve slowly round me in the middle of my big scene with Simon and I started to talk gibberish. He looked at me with polite, but slightly pained, surprise which brought me to my senses with a jolt and I got back on text again.

Diana, Princess of Wales, was killed that summer. We were all profoundly shocked and found the performance that we had to give the day after the news broke, very difficult. I particularly had some apposite lines to speak.

> Suppose if when I leave this house, I drive down to some newspaper office and give them this story and the proofs of it. Think of their loathsome joy, think of the delight they would have in dragging you down, of the mud and the mire they would plunge you in, think of the hypocrite with his greasy smile, penning his leading article and arranging the foulness of the public placards!

My voice shook with emotion when I had to say these words and I only just managed to control myself. The Haymarket Theatre is just around the corner from The Mall, so we were very aware of the public feeling and witnessed every day the tide of popular emotion.

I was very glad that my mother was able to see me in that production. It was the sort of theatre she loved. She was a marvellous member of an audience, being possessed of a wonderful sense of humour; she was always the first person to laugh in the stalls. She had to sit very near the front, as she was so blind, not to mention deaf. She came to a matinee performance of *An Ideal Husband* and, happily, it was one of the best. We had cheers at the curtain call. She couldn't have wished for more. Six months later she was dead. She was just a few days short of her 90th birthday – I don't think she really wanted to be 90!

We had transferred to the Gielgud Theatre, formerly the Globe, on Shaftesbury Avenue. It was January 1998. I was on my way to a matinee and decided to call in to see my mother. I had seen her the night before and had promised to return the next morning. She had been very unwell and we had more or less railroaded her into Denville Hall, which is a home for retired actors. She was furious and checked herself out. But although she was happy to be back in her flat in Wimbledon, she kept saying that she'd 'outstayed her welcome in this world.'

I always like to be at the theatre early, at least two hours, if not more, before a show. I like to get into the atmosphere of the place, the play and the part, to centre myself. That day was no exception. I had keys to my mother's flat, but I rang the bell anyway. There was no response. I rang again and peered through the letter-box. Some of the lights were on, which was unusual. I let myself in and called out. No reply. I went into the living-room. She was sitting up in the chair by the fire. Her cheek was resting on her hand. Her elbow was propped up on the arm rest. She was smiling and looked incredibly happy. I didn't go any nearer. I knew she was dead. I didn't touch her. I just looked at her then turned on my heel and let myself out. I should have called my sister, the doctor, anybody. But I didn't. I just left and made my way to central London. I walked down the hill and, inexplicably, bought an orthopaedic pillow at the first shop I came to. I had no need of it, but I carted it off to the train and went to Piccadilly Circus.

I went to my dressing-room and called my agent to tell her what had happened. She was very sympathetic and asked me if she should ask the management if I could have the two shows 'off'. 'Don't be silly,' I replied with a chuckle, 'my mother would never forgive me!' Everyone was extremely kind and sympathetic, especially dear Dulcie. She and Michael (and Brett their corgi) had the interconnecting dressing-room next door. I received a regular visit from Brett most days, gazing up at me patiently, his feet in third position, while I ate my between-the-show sandwich, hoping for a crust – which he invariably had.

I got on with the show as my mother would have wished and everything was going fine until my big scene with Martin, at the end of the first act. I had to say, 'I loved you, Arthur.' 'Yes,' he replied, 'And you loved me,' I continued. 'You know you loved me, and love is a very wonderful thing.' As I started to say these words, I began to cry and the tears ran down my cheeks. As Martin replied, he too began to cry. I thought to myself, I must pull myself together, this is *not* what this scene is about! This is a scene between two ex-lovers who are both sophisticated, cynical, world-weary members of a rich elite, who for a split second, show a moment of vulnerability and face the truth. But only for a second and they certainly wouldn't cry. I forced myself back to the brittle, manipulative woman I was playing.

Afterwards, I apologised profusely to Martin. He was very sweet about it and said, 'It was a different scene we played this afternoon. Perhaps they *had* loved each other more than either of them dared to acknowledge.' I accepted that explanation, although I fear it was not what Oscar Wilde had intended. Then I remembered the more sentimental attitudes of the late nineteenth century and decided that the playing was, after all, acceptable. But I was mortified at not being able to keep my feelings under control. What was even more puzzling, was my reaction to finding my mother dead.

My sister had rung me at the theatre and said 'Well, I'm afraid she's gone,' in a subdued voice. 'Yes, I know,' I replied. She was amazed. 'You know? How do you know?' 'Because, she was dead when I called in the morning.' My sister was at once disbelieving and furious. She couldn't understand why I hadn't phoned her at once. And, frankly, neither could I. 'Well, I knew you'd be getting there soon after,' I said lamely. It was no explanation and I knew it, but I had none other to offer. My behaviour had been irresponsible and inexplicable and to this day, I cannot fathom it. I suppose I was in some sort of denial.

Soon after this trauma, Martin Shaw left the cast, as did Michael and Dulcie, so we were in the thick of rehearsals again. In their place came Christopher Cazenove, Barbara Murray and Richard Todd. It was wonderful to have Barbara with me again. We shared a dressing-room when we transferred to the Albery Theatre. Her two dogs, Benjie and Percy, were also in situ. They were tiny creatures and Percy used to sit on my knee while I got made-up, which was sweet but rather inhibiting as one was rooted to the spot.

My mother and grandmother had both had dogs with them in the theatre. Two were called 'Progs' and 'Chocs', short for 'Programmes and Chocolates', which was what the usherettes called out from time to time in the auditorium to advertise their wares. These particular dogs were well-trained in the ways of the theatre. In those days, the National Anthem was always played at the end of a theatre performance and as soon as 'Progs' and 'Chocs' heard the first strains of 'God Save the King', as it was then, they would rouse themselves, yawn, stretch their limbs and sit up looking expectant, as they knew it was time to go home!

Richard Todd had recently suffered a most terrible tragedy: the loss of his beloved youngest son in a shooting incident at home. This crushing blow would have defeated a lesser man, but Toddie was made of sterner stuff. He'd been a hero in the Second World War, being among the first officers to land on the Normandy beaches on D-Day. It seemed so cruel that, having risked his life for his country, he had been called upon to make this huge personal sacrifice in his eighties. His pain was almost tangible and although incredibly brave, there were occasions when he would come into our dressing-room with tears pouring down his cheeks and I could do nothing but put my arms around him to try to bring him some comfort. It was usually a sympathetic letter from a member of the public, who had suffered similarly, which prompted his emotion. He was normally so self-controlled, although there were times when I had to practically lift him onto the stage to take his curtain call beside me. A man of unbelievable courage.

By some ghastly quirk of fate, Chris Cazenove, one of the sweetest men in the world, had to endure a like tragedy a couple of years later. His eldest son was killed in a car crash, having just come down from Cambridge with an MA at the tender age of 25. I had known the boy, Lindford, since he was a baby and watched him grow up. He'd been out in LA and had gone to a local school there as a teenager. His mother, Angharad Rees, had been in the previous production of the Wilde on tour with me and had proudly presented her son, Lindford, to me. He was a charming teenager. How those dear people coped with their loss I cannot imagine. Having so nearly lost my own precious son, I can only wonder at their fortitude in the face of over-whelming adversity and admire their courage.

'Standby for the Curtain'

Over the extended run of *An Ideal Husband*, I had sustained a torn cartilage in my right knee. It had been strapped up for months and I was only able to get on the stage, which was severely 'raked', with the aid of painkillers. When my contract came to an end, I was obliged to leave the show, in spite of exhortations from the management for me to stay, to take myself off into hospital for keyhole surgery. Suzannah York replaced me, a dear girl. Our paths have crossed on more than one occasion, although the only time we were ever together on the same stage was at a charity performance of *Cinderella* at St James's Church in Piccadilly. Believe it or not, I was playing 'Cinders', Suzannah was 'Prince Charming', and Simon Callow and Liz Smith were the 'Ugly Sisters'!

I recovered from my knee operation remarkably quickly, although at first Mark had to carry me everywhere! I was then asked to go to Cyprus to make a film about the confrontation between the Turks and the Greek Cypriots in 1974. The adventures which we had off-set, were far more entertaining than those on, since John Forgeham was also in the movie! His involvement with a very beautiful young girl, whom he suspected (and I was convinced) was in the toils of the local

Mafia, meant that every time we left the hotel (and he always insisted that I accompany him) we were forever looking over our shoulders, waiting for hoodlums to gun us down. It was fairly nerve-racking! When I did manage to get out on my own, I found I was continually pestered by men, who either thought I was an elderly prostitute, or wanted me to go to work for them in their brothels! This got very tedious and inhibited me severely, as one of the joys of going to foreign climes, for me, is to explore the place on foot. But it was not to be.

There was a scene in the movie, which was called *The Road to Ithaca*, in which I had to join in some Greek dancing at a Greek wedding. I protested and told the Greek Cypriot director I'd just undergone surgery on my knee. He shrugged his shoulders, which I took to mean 'Tough!' So I had to do it, but seemed none the worse for the experience.

* * *

The Salisbury Playhouse, a theatre where I'd always wanted to work, then got in touch. Jonathan Church offered me another 'humdinger' of a part in an adaptation of a play by Anouilh, *Colombe*. It had been 'freely' translated by Jeremy Samms. It was witty, hilarious, moving and utterly brilliant. I was playing a French actress, a rival of Sarah Bernhardt – an outrageous monster of a woman. The dialogue was blistering, but it required comedy timing of a high order. I would have my work cut out to pull it off.

On the whole, people not in the profession have absolutely no idea how difficult comedy is. They think that the 'tragic' actors are the great performers, not realising that it is the 'clowns' who have the real talent. To make an audience laugh is the most rewarding, yet the most difficult, thing in the world. Ask any stand-up comic who's 'died' on stage in a working man's club, or worse still, who's been given 'the bird'. Well, I pulled this one off. Again, the notices were great, my favourite of which was, 'There are many good reasons for seeing this production, most of them are Kate O'Mara!' To publicise this production, I went on the *Graham Norton Show*, unnerving to say the least. I found him utterly charming, but knew that I was fair game.

* * *

I had only just recovered from doing *Colombe* (another production which was supposed to transfer to London but never did), when I was asked to play 'Gertrude Lawrence' in *Noël and Gertie*, Sheridan Morley's charming play about the relationship between Gertrude Lawrence and Noël Coward, illustrated by excerpts from his plays and musicals. There were no less than nineteen numbers to learn. 'Oh you know them, don't you, darling?' said Chris Wren, the director, blithely. But I didn't know *any* of them at all. Being a classical music buff to the exclusion of all else, shuts one off to a whole other world! I had to learn them and pretty damn fast.

Noël was played brilliantly by Ian Lavender who, with his wonderful comedic talent, had endeared himself to generations of television audiences as the 'stupid boy' of everybody's favourite comedy series, *Dad's Army*. Not obvious casting, some might have said, for the smooth, svelte, acerbically camp Noël Coward. How wrong they would have been. He gave a performance that was pure enchantment. It was light, witty, debonair and at times unbearably moving. He sang like a dream. True, his dancing was less than magical, but we managed!

We were frightened witless when we opened and I have a potent memory of the two of us, standing rigid with nerves behind the set, clutching each other's hands in terror as we waited to go on. We promised faithfully that we would rescue each other if anything went wrong. There were, after all, just the two of us and the pianist. We were on our own. Then our musical cue came and we had to separate, he to go on stage left, I stage right. I stood, poised by the piano, giving Greg, the pianist, a gracious smile of reassurance, which belied my innermost feelings, convinced that the audience could hear the immense noise which was emanating from my ribcage, namely the beating of my heart. It was a wonderful experience, that production, it was lovely being able to revive so many memories for an older generation.

Then, yet another pantomime. This time, *Aladdin* with Robert Powell. For the first time, I was playing a 'goodie', the 'Genie of the Lamp'. It was my first and only panto not under the aegis of Kevin Wood. The Genie was a very small part and didn't come on until just before the interval. I have never been good at playing small parts and lost my confidence badly. I was literally shaking with nerves just before my first entrance. I was very relieved when it was all over.

I had to regain my confidence in a hurry because, while on tour with *Noël and Gertie*, Ian Lavender and I had been asked to do a stage version of the Ealing Film comedy *Passport to Pimlico*, at the start of the year 2000. There were 46 parts but only eight actors and Ian's character didn't double with any other part! Charles Vance was the producer, an adorable rascal! The idea appealed to me enormously, as I love ensemble acting, but seldom get the chance to do it. Ian was playing the Stanley Holloway part, but Charles had asked me to play the Hermione Baddeley part, which was not very big. I had my eye on the Margaret Rutherford role; admittedly I didn't have the girth or the dewlaps, but I was sure I could play it in a different way.

I had studied the script closely and found I could just about make the quick changes without meeting myself coming off! Charles was thrilled. I organised my own changes and the wardrobe people were very helpful. They made me a very slim-fitting, red silk, forties dress which I kept on all the time, as I did the seamed stockings, with the addition of red, high-heeled, sling-backs and red lipstick. This formed the basis of 'Edie', the glamorous dress-shop owner played in the film by Hermione Baddeley. I pinned my hair up under a stocking-top in time-honoured fashion. On top of this for 'Edie', went a dark brown, pageboy bob wig, kept in place by a matching red silk scarf. That was 'Edie'.

To change to Professor Hatton-Jones – the Margaret Rutherford part – I came off stage, pulled off my wig and shoes and donned a pair of thick, lisle stockings which were elasticated at the thigh. A pair of tan leather bootees were then shoved onto my feet. The laces had been removed and replaced by thin elastic so I could force my feet into them quickly. I mutilated a shirt so that it only had a front, with a collar that Velcroed at the back and a tie permanently sewn in. A long tweed skirt with a single big fastening, which I could step into, came next. Then, a matching tweed jacket with a tie belt to hold it in place. A pale red, very short wig went on my head, with a little trilby on top. I removed 'Edie's' lipstick with stick concealer and a pair of round, thirties glasses completed the transformation. As soon as I had finished a scene as 'Professor Hatton-Jones', I had to come off and reverse the procedure for 'Edie' and back again! There were several nights when I only just made it, but the gratifying thing is that at the curtain call, which I took as 'Edie', people were looking along the line-up for the Professor!

*　　*　　*

When I got back to Somerset, I was approached by my local theatre to run a Youth Theatre Group. I was to have a class of twenty young people between the ages of sixteen and twenty-five. My directive was to coach them for two and a half weeks, by the end of which time we had to mount a show, which would be played before a paying audience at the theatre for four performances. Quite an undertaking.

I decided, as we were in Somerset, to go for the local hero 'King Arthur'. So I wrote my own version of the legends and called it *The Quest for Arthur*. I found that I had some talented young people, all full of enthusiasm for the project. They responded well to the many acting exercises I set them and learned their parts quickly. Would that all professional young actors were as thorough!

I had invaluable help: A brilliant musician, a truly gifted Welshman, Steve Allan Jones, who composed the music especially for the show, and a young actor, Al Duncan, who, apart from being talented in his own right, had a natural gift for teaching others. My son Dickon and I painted a huge backcloth depicting Camelot, Glastonbury, Tintagel and Shallot. He also created the most marvellous Round Table, made up of twelve shields, one for each Knight. He designed the lighting, which included a wonderful strobe effect for the appearance of the Holy Grail. He made a barge, which traversed the stage amid the mist as if by magic. Between us, we achieved a production that was quite special. The local reviewer said it was the most imaginative production he had ever seen at the Brewhouse, but the real reward was to see the shining faces of the youngsters after each performance when they experienced the joy of achievement.

* * *

After this minor triumph, I was asked in 2001 by the Brewhouse to bring my company and mount some shows, to satisfy popular demand. My mother had banged on for years about a play she had starred in, in the thirties. It was called *The Crime at Blossoms* and she kept suggesting it as a vehicle for the company to revive, specialising as it did in classics of all periods. She reckoned this one was a classic of its type and way ahead of its day. For years I had ignored her. Then, coming upon it on my shelves one day, I started to read it and realised she was right. She had always said, 'And there's a marvellous part for you in it, darling. You come on in this red dress and say in a low, dramatic voice, 'Will you all be very quiet please,' and she suited the action to the word. As I read, I could see the dramatic possibilities.

The Crime at Blossoms sounds like a cosy thriller and, indeed, a murder has taken place, but the 'Crime' of the title is, in fact, the exploitation of which the heroine is guilty – of pandering to people's morbid obsession with murder, which is still prevalent today. Written in 1929, it was way ahead of its time. So I put it on and the theatre was packed to the gills. There was literally not a seat to be had at any performance; I even wore the original red dress my mother had worn in 1934!

* * *

I was becoming very aware that there was a younger audience growing up to whom I was totally unknown. They were all too young to know of my television appearances, unless of course they were glued to the satellite channels, when they might have seen me in repeats of everything I'd ever done! I was delighted, therefore, to be cast in *Bad Girls*, a series which had achieved cult

254

status with the young and, indeed, very young! As a result of doing only five episodes, I found myself with a whole new audience of nine-year-olds!

Filming *Bad Girls* was a very mixed experience. The cast and crew were a joy, the conditions fairly horrendous, mainly because it was extremely cold. We were on location in the East End of London, where they had built an exact replica of the inside of Oxford Prison. It was a brilliant set and rather too realistic for comfort! I have found myself incarcerated before now, notably in *Dynasty*, when I was continually being sent back to gaol by Joan Collins' character, 'Alexis'. But then we were on an indoor film set and we were warm! It was supposed to be in South America and I was rescued by two of the most glamorous actors, in jungle fatigues carrying sten-guns, whom I have ever seen in my life! They were Michael Nader and Ted McGinley.

Nothing like that at Bromley-by-Bow! Conditions were Spartan and in keeping with the subject matter. The dressing-rooms were virtually cubicles, no more, and it was freezing on set. I feel the cold terribly for some reason, so the wardrobe very sweetly found me one of those puffy coats which are like duvets. As I was confined to a wheelchair for a great deal of my contri-bution to the series, this was very necessary, as I was not able to move around to keep warm. They finished me off in the bath after five episodes, an unpleasant morning's shooting. Being drowned is one thing, but in *soapy* water – most unpleasant!

The cast of *Bad Girls* were delightful and welcomed me with open arms. It was lovely working with so many young people, for some of whom this was their first job. I was staying in Arthur Bostrom's house while filming, which was just around the corner from Linda Henry, the actress playing Yvonne. This was highly convenient, as we were occasionally able to share a car to and from the studio. You were allowed a car to pick you up if you were called before six in the morning and finished after seven at night. This was just as well, as that part of London is a closed book to me. Yvonne and her husband were kindness itself to me. I also made chums with Victoria Alcock, who played one of the two 'Julies' and who still keeps in touch.

* * *

My next production at the Brewhouse was *The Rape of the Belt*, a very funny anti-war play written in the fifties. One joy of being a producer and a director is that one is able to cast one's friends! I hasten to add that I give a whole lot of strangers jobs as well! I have, in fact, given many students just leaving drama school their start in the profession. In this instance, the main protagonists in the play were supposed to be a little more mature, so I was able to use my great friend Patricia Shakesby, Sabina Franklyn, who had been with us on *The Relapse* and Giles Watling, one of Mark's mates, whom I also knew. Mark also was in the show. Dickon designed the set and lighting, so it was one big happy family.

I had trouble casting one of the parts. I needed a mountain of a woman. She was supposed to be a blacksmith and big with it. I suddenly remembered a friend of mine from way back, Miranda Forbes. She'd been one of the two girls with whom I'd shared my basement flat, in the bleak days of the early sixties. I'd seen her on television from time to time, playing assorted Junoesque ladies, most particularly in *Within these Walls*, in which she was a regular, and most recently in *The Prince and the Pauper*. I rang her saying, 'Here's a blast from the past. What are you up to and if it's nothing, then get your arse down here, because you're needed!' She roared with laughter. I was delighted when she said she was out of work and would love to do it. But there was a problem, she said, there was something wrong with her stomach. It had always been large, but it was now hard as well. No, she hadn't been to see a doctor, she supposed she ought, but she was hoping it would get better. In hindsight, I should have taken more notice of those fateful words.

The divine actor Michael Stroud joined us to play, appropriately, the God 'Zeus' – a joy! It was all perfect. I had the ideal cast, the set looked divine, the lighting was magical, the music sublime and it was a very funny play. What could possibly go wrong? Two extraordinary things happened. Giles's father, the wonderful actor Jack Watling, whom I had worked with in

Pathfinders years ago, had been ill for some time. During rehearsals, he got much much worse; in fact, he was dying. Giles had to leave us, but promised that he would be back. He was as good as his word. His dear father died, but Giles came back, knowing his lines and being brilliant – in a comedy! Like me, he was a chip off the old block and he knew it's what his father would have wanted. He was superb in the part and we dedicated the production to Jack, his father.

We opened to ecstatic reviews and then Miranda was taken ill after the second performance. She was in such pain that she was unable to go on. I learnt the part the next morning and went on that night. I couldn't have been more wrong for it, but I tried to make up for my lack of weight by making a lot of noise. Miranda came back for the Friday night performance but by Saturday, she was desperately ill and was taken to hospital. The doctors discovered that she had had leukaemia for some time without knowing it and had contracted the awful, flesh-eating disease, necrotising fasceiitis. The leukaemia, which she'd had for some time, but had no idea of its presence, meant that she had no resistance to the bug. She had been a keen gardener and we are given to understand that gardening is how the disease takes hold. A week later, Miranda was dead. It was profoundly shocking. The only thing we could console ourselves with, was that she'd had a wonderful time at rehearsals and had died while doing what she loved doing most: Acting.

* * *

I had been contracted to do another Youth Theatre Project and *The Railway Children* was suggested. I had spent the last few months adapting E Nesbit's book myself. Not easy. We had a chorus, who told the story as a music-hall number of the period and a cast of twenty odd to play all the parts. There were a couple of young people from the previous year, but on the whole, they were new and, again, I was astounded at the talent, but not just that, it was the commitment, the energy and the enthusiasm that they put into the project. One, however, dropped out after the first day. She thought the whole thing beneath her, such is the arrogance of youth. She'll learn! But never in *my* company. The production was a huge commercial and artistic success. We even had a full-sized steam-engine on stage built by Dickon, who also did wonders with the lighting. Rave reviews again.

*   *   *

My next production was Ronald Harwood's wonderful play *The Dresser*. At first, I couldn't get the rights as the National Theatre was sitting on them, but through the intervention of the redoubtable Patrick Garland, Ronald Harwood very generously and sweetly gave me a special dispensation so I was able to produce the play.

I could not have been more fortunate in my cast. My old mucker mate, Ian Lavender, gave the most charismatic performance as 'Norman', the 'dresser' of the title. Again, he was unbearably moving and funny by turns. Michael Stroud, who had, incidentally, been with me in *Colombe* at Salisbury, played 'Sir' as only an actor of his experience and accomplishment could. He had understudied Sir Laurence Olivier in earlier days and been on for him and we could all see why. My dear friend, Vivien Heilbron, came down to play 'Her Ladyship'. She was wonderful and I had the joy of her staying with me the whiles. Knight Mantell, whose direction one cannot fault, directed and my son Dickon produced another atmospheric set, beautifully lit. Again, marvellous reviews.

Then it was off to do yet *another* pantomime, this time with the hilarious Gordon Kaye as my henchman in *Snow White*. I renewed my acquaintance with Warwick Davis, whom I am still determined to use in a production as soon as I get the opportunity.

*   *   *

In 2002 I was asked by Bill (Kenwright) to do *A Woman of No Importance*, quite a tricky play by Oscar Wilde. It has a very strong storyline but is a touch on the melodramatic side, which sits uneasily by the side of the brilliant, Wildean epigrams. It was a play about the relationship between a mother and a son, so caused me a great deal of anguish each night. Also, as a melodrama, it took all my skills as an actress *not* to get laughs in the wrong places. Very good practice. I was playing the eponymous role, not my usual vamp. She was a woman with a past, but she was one of life's victims. I am not used to playing victims, so I reckoned it would be a tough challenge and would 'stretch' me. My co-stars were Oliver Tobias, Debbie Grant (hurrah!) and the glorious Josephine Tewson. The director was Elijah Moshinsky, for whom I had worked before.

While we were opening at Windsor, we asked the management if they would consider a co-production with BATCO. They said they would. We decided on *The Rivals*, by Sheridan, a glorious comedy which features the inimitable 'Mrs Malaprop' and her exuberant misappropriation of the English language. We had Jean Marsh in this role and the scrumptious Michael Jayston as 'Sir Anthony Absolute'. Arthur Bostrom was a fey, but deliciously funny 'Sir Lucius O'Trigger' and I opted for the minor role of 'Lucy' the maid. There was a brilliant supporting cast and I spent my weekends dashing home from the Wilde play to paint a backcloth that was 30ft × 20ft and to help my son paint the scenery. He made the most glorious set for the production but, sadly, it was too large for us to store afterwards.

A week before we were due to start rehearsals, Jean Marsh, who had been suffering with an acute back problem, had to have hospital treatment and was forced to resign from the show. This was a bitter blow, especially as we'd just had the posters printed. Life is never simple. Rescue was at hand in the shape of the delightful Gabrielle Drake. She and I had been in the same season at Regent's Park together, but not in the same play. But we had had to do the publicity for the two-week season at Arundel Castle together and I well remember sitting a-top a stone lion, outside the gates of the castle being exhorted by the photographer to 'show a leg'. Alexandra Bastedo was also present. There we were, a blonde, a brunette and a redhead, all somewhere in our forties, all still having to do our 'glamour girl' bit, even though we were appearing in a Shakespeare Season! Some things never change!

However (and we knew this from the start), Gaby was *not* going to be able to do the last week of our tour, which was in Norwich. Needless to say, I was commandeered to take over from her. With only two rehearsals, I find myself waiting in the wings, in Gaby's costume and wearing Gaby's wig, listening for my cue, before bustling on ahead of Michael Jayston. I heard my voice speaking the opening lines, 'There, Sir Anthony, there sits the deliberate simpleton . . .' 'Is it me saying these lines? I mustn't think, just say them!' I am consumed with nerves and first night terror. Oh, well, the show must go on!

7

Encores/Outtakes

Men Behaving Badly

It's an extraordinary thing about this profession, but the women seem to be able to cope much better than the men (as in life). Yet there are so few parts for us girls. Even in Shakespeare the ratio is about one to thirty! Perhaps that's it, we have such a thin time of it that we don't want to jeopardise our chances of work by behaving badly. After all, it's difficult enough to get jobs in the first place, and perhaps, it's a more natural occupation for a woman. Getting dressed up, putting on make-up and pretending to be someone else!

The stresses of the profession seem to affect the male of the species in differing ways, although in the following examples, drink seems to be the common denominator. These anecdotes have been included because I couldn't resist them, but the names of the Dramatis Personae have been excised to protect the Guilty.

I worked once with an extremely talented actor, who, it transpired, was unable to get on the stage unless well-oiled with alcohol in advance. He had the reputation of being difficult and charges of sexual harassment had been levelled against him. It was with some trepidation that I embarked on this particular job! I was not disappointed.

Each evening before the show, he turned up, as required by Equity and theatre rules, 35 minutes before the performance and signed in at the Stage Door. This procedure enables the stage management to be certain that all the actors are in the theatre in good time before the show and that no understudies will be required. I prefer to be in at least two hours before curtain up. I don't think 35 minutes is nearly long enough to get one acclimatised and settled and ready for a performance. However, that's me and other actors are less thorough.

Well, this particular actor would arrive, sign in, and then, unbeknown to the rest of us, slip out again and head straight for the nearest pub. This is absolutely against all the rules. Alcohol is not permitted backstage for obvious reasons, so this was the only way he could get an apparently very necessary drink before the show. This ruse was discovered quite quickly by an unfortunate ASM checking his dressing-room. We never suspected anything.

Some actors like to do a vocal warm-up in their dressing-room. Although this is commendable, it can be intensely irritating to those within earshot! Others prefer to meditate and hum quietly to themselves. This is infinitely preferable. Some chatter, some remain silent. Some go through their lines and check their props, others don't bother. However, it is generally accepted that actors are sensitive and artistic creatures and therefore to be indulged in their own methods of preparation. (Stanislavsky would have a fit if he were granted a peep into most dressing-rooms these days. His famous tome *An Actor Prepares* is abandoned by most on leaving drama school.) So we were in ignorance of this actor's particular brand of 'preparation'.

It was not until I got on stage with him that I would realise that he was pissed. Some nights it was worse than others. At some performances I would be given a 'thumbs down' sign in the wings by one of my fellow-actors who had already been on and was warning me what to expect. The trouble was, *one didn't know* what to expect. Would he remember all his lines? Would he inadvertently 'cut' some? Would his speech be slurred and unintelligible? It was all extremely nerve-racking.

Soon after the discovery of his truancy, the company manager was informed and went to confront him in the pub, where he was caught red-handed and roundly admonished. This telling-off was not well received by the actor who stormed back to his dressing-room, which he proceeded to demolish! I was in the room next door and the noise of tables and chairs being thrown around was cataclysmic. This was accompanied by bellows of rage. The ASM was summoned, slammed up against the wall and verbally abused. She eventually ran out in tears.

The call came for his first entrance and he departed for the stage and an unsuspecting audience. There was a brief silence before all the other dressing-room doors opened and we all peered out wonderingly as we speculated as to what on earth had happened. The tragedy was that this actor was one of the most exciting I have ever appeared with on stage. A terrible waste of talent.

That endearing old hell-raiser, Oliver Reed, comes into this category, although to his credit I believe he was always on set on time and always knew his lines. But he obviously didn't trust himself enough to make a career in the theatre. I remember running into him in a pub (needless to say) when I was rehearsing. He was fascinated by the fact that I had my own theatre company and was talking to me about it. I asked him to come and join us. A strange light came into his eyes and I could see he relished the prospect.

'How about *Macbeth*?' I suggested, 'you'd be wonderful.' There was a long pause, his eyes never left my face. 'I'd love it,' he said eventually, but very quietly. For one brief glorious moment I could see an electrifying Scottish King and 'House Full' boards outside the theatres. He turned away and took a long look at the bottom of his glass before knocking back the contents. 'Well,' I persisted, 'how about it? When are you free?' There was another long pause, then he turned to me with a look of unutterable sadness. Finally he said, 'I haven't got the bottle.' And we both knew that he hadn't.

The last time I saw Ollie was at one of Noel Edmond's *Noel's House Party* shows. Noel had invited 40 guest stars who had appeared on his show to go along for a 'special'. Ollie and I were both among those present. At the BBC we were all put in a sort of conference room that was doubling as a hospitality suite. I noted, with interest, that there were 38 guests on one side of the room and Ollie and I on the other! He was already extremely drunk and the show was not due to be recorded for a couple of hours.

We were called to rehearse a big musical number which was to be the highlight of the show. On arriving on the studio floor, I found I was partnered by Ollie. We went through the number countless times, before we were sent back to our dressing-rooms to get changed for the show. We then went to make-up. But there was no sigh of Ollie anywhere. He'd gone home. Thinking he'd done the show, he'd poured himself into a taxi and departed. I was partnered instead by a very sober Frank Bruno!

The other thing that happens to some men as they become famous is a compulsion to seduce anything that moves. I suppose it's because women are inclined to fling themselves at film stars so there is a plentiful supply of females and endless opportunity.

Two extremely famous film stars both made a play for me – one by prostrating himself at my feet as I was passing. I ignored him and did not succumb. And as a girl, I had idolised him! The other, when I found myself in a compromising situation with him, attempted to seduce me. I was not even remotely interested, but realised I'd been gullible and painted myself into a corner and could see no way out. Fortunately, also due to the effects of alcohol, he was not able to 'perform' and attempted to replace his 'manhood' with the handle of a hair-brush! I declined to accommodate him and he finally fell asleep and I escaped.

My last example of an actor behaving badly is not a display of overindulgence in alcohol, but of megalomania. This is another disease that can affect actors when they become successful. It goes to their heads. This particular actor, who has had some success on television, had no need of alcohol to boost his self-confidence. He had a rabid self-belief. He was not uncharming, in fact, quite the contrary. He was not untalented, but he displayed his ability in such an arrogant self-indulgent manner, that it was impossible to do anything other than despise him. I have known him turn up in scenes he was not in because he imagined the audience to be bored when he was not on-stage. He ruins other actors big 'moments' by upstaging them. He destroys scenes by deliberately making a mistake and then admitting it in dumb-show to the audience, the more gullible of whom lap it up.

He insists on top billing and dressing-room No.1, even when acting with people far better known and far more experienced than he. He will not relinquish this privilege even when there is a lady in the cast who, by virtue of seniority, should be accorded the honour. It is not pleasant to see females of advanced years staggering up and down stairs backstage, exhausted and out of breath, while this extremely selfish and self-deluded man disports himself on a chaise-longue on stage level. I witnessed him actually physically attack one of this country's best-loved comic actors as he was about to make his first entrance on stage. The two of them had to be parted by the stage manager. I have been known to turn down jobs and refuse parts when I learnt he was to be a member of the cast. He is universally loathed by actors and actresses, and yet he still gets employment. It's an unfair profession but I wouldn't be in any other and the show must go on!

Oh, and one woman!

On the first day's rehearsal of a new production, one of the first things to happen is that everyone grabs a cup of coffee and jostles around a table to look at the set and costume designs. The play had been written and produced on Broadway in 1947, but had never been seen in London. It was going to be played as if in that year and Michael Levine, who had designed the set, had got it exactly right, a classy American hotel just reeking of the period.

Sally Gardiner's costumes were also perfect. I was delighted to see that she had designed for me a gorgeous silver panne velvet evening dress, topped with an unswept platinum blonde wig, which exactly echoed the fact that the character was an ice-skating star. I was over the moon! I then took in all the other costume designs and noted that Sally had envisaged the Broadway star in midnight blue velvet, with a brunette wig.

Perfect. What a clever girl this designer is, I thought, she knows her stuff. Sadly for me, the actress playing the part had other ideas! She suddenly appeared at my side and said, 'Excuse me Kate, I'm sorry, but I'm having this,' leaned across me and took my design away. I gasped and followed her with my eyes as she walked determinedly over to the designer.

One of the other actresses, one of the great ladies of the theatre, overheard this and muttered, 'She can't do that. That's *your* design.' I went up to the designer who was looking thunderous. 'Erm, er, what's happened to my design?' I asked as tactfully as I could. She glared balefully across the room at the actress's retreating figure. 'Talk to the producer,' she spat out between clenched teeth. I looked around but there was no sign of him anywhere. He'd obviously sensed trouble and decided to remove himself from the scene until it had blown over. As a putative producer myself, this was a valuable lesson to learn. Bitterly disappointed, I accepted my lot, reminded myself that I'd got a wonderful part and told myself to get on with it.

The designer subsequently created a 'shocking pink' dress and a strawberry blonde wig for me and I made the best of it. I arrived early for the first Saturday matinee only to find that I was unable to get into the dressing room. The 'Broadway star' and I were sharing dressing-room No. 1. I had come off well here, as she had scores of admirers and the place was like a florists' shop and smelled divine. However, it was full to bursting with people, wig makers, dressmakers, fitters and their assistants. It was a tiny room with only just enough room for the two of us. So plainly, at the moment, I was not required on voyage. 'It's all right, I'll come back later,' I called out and went off to do some weekend food shopping.

As my friend Patricia had once remarked, 'What every actress needs at home, is a wife!' One certainly needs to be some sort of super-woman to combine the roles of career-woman, housewife, mother and general factotum. Another chum, Stephanie Beacham, has also been heard to make a few well-chosen and pointed remarks about 'the loo fairy'. All men have a fervent belief in the little sprite that skips in every evening, cleans the loo-pan, replaces the loo-roll, replenishes the freshener in the cistern and keeps the place smelling fragrant. Ahh!

On my return to the theatre, I left my Sainsbury's shopping in the car as plainly there would be no space for it in No.1 – fittings were still in progress and the actress was being pinned into a silk dress of one of the most hideous shades of green that I'd ever seen. My beloved silver panne velvet lay abandoned, cast aside, unwanted on the floor. The platinum wig, too, was being replaced by a honey-coloured effort, which, in my view, was totally wrong for the character, but I deemed it prudent to hold my tongue. Even before we opened yet *another* dress had been added to the array now adorning the hangers in No. 1. An amazing sheath-like garment made entirely of multi-coloured sequins. She looked absolutely stunning in it, but it was a 'film star's' dress *not* a 'Broadway actress's gown', and there is a huge difference. She looked as Rita Hayworth or Lana Turner might have done, whereas she should have been looking like Katharine Hepburn or Constance Bennett. A class act was required.

When the show was revived two years later, the actress was no longer in the cast, so I was able to have my lovely silver dress and wig after all! I was extremely happy!

8

Epilogue

And on . . . and on . . .

Dickon now has his own gorgeous little Gothic house with a wonderful woodland garden. Being an accomplished carpenter, as well as designer, he is able to effect his own improvements and build his own furniture. He is also a marvellous cook, probably due to the number of times he has had to get his own supper when I have been working! I always used to read to him when he was a small boy and he couldn't wait to read for himself. He has been reading nonstop ever since. He is a crossword freak and we share a total delight in P G Wodehouse. He is very talented, highly intelligent and very artistic. He is also tall and handsome and I am inordinately proud of him.

I am fortunate to have found Mark, the man with whom I share my life. He is good and honourable and extremely supportive. Although he is twenty years younger than I, we seem to get along quite well, possibly because he has an older sister. He is eternally affable and optimistic, which is an asset in our profession! The one dissenting fact in our relationship is our disparate sleeping arrangements. I awake at dawn and am up and raring to start the day at 5 a.m. He would prefer to sleep until midday if he were able to do so, so I have to endure hours on my own waiting for him to wake up! Once awake he makes up for it by being extremely jolly! We are both perfectionists in our own way and we both love to be surrounded by wood. He is very witty and an extremely good dancer. I like to think that I too excel in both these accomplishments! So we have quite a lot in common.

I am currently rehearsing for a two-hander I wrote myself about Mary Queen of Scots and Elizabeth I with my dear chum Patricia playing Elizabeth and me playing Mary and, as I wrote the lines myself, hopefully I'll remember them! Another guest appearance in 'Ab Fab', then another huge tour in the theatre, *The Marquise*, by Noël Coward – for twenty weeks. The show goes on . . . and on . . . and on . . . and on.

My mother, I hope, would be proud of me!